# The Non-Violent
# Militant

# WOMEN'S SOURCE LIBRARY

*Series Editors*:
Dale Spender and Candida Ann Lacey

This new series brings together the most important, but still too little known, written sources which document the history of women's struggles for liberation. Taken from the principal women's archive in Britain, The Fawcett Library at the City of London Polytechnic, and reprinted in full wherever possible, the pamphlets and papers included in this series illustrate major debates on a range of issues including suffrage, education, work, science and medicine, as well as making the words of individual women available for the first time.

The books in this series are designed to provide scholars and teachers in History and Women's Studies with a developing and easily accessible resource of primary documents from women's history. Each volume contains a historical Introduction to the material and biographical details of those campaigners who sought to improve the social, economic and legal status of women.

The series was devised in collaboration with Catherine Ireland and David Doughan of The Fawcett Library, both of whom greatly assisted in the selection and compilation of material.

*Other titles in this series are*:

*Barbara Leigh Smith Bodichon and the Langham Place Group* edited by
   Candida Ann Lacey
*The Sexuality Debates* edited by Sheila Jeffries
*The Education Papers: Women's Quest for Equality in Britain, 1850–
   1912* edited by Dale Spender
*Before the Vote was Won: Arguments For and Against Women's Suffrage,
   1864–1896* edited by Jane Lewis

*Forthcoming titles include*:

*Women's Fabian Tracts* edited by Sally Alexander
*Suffrage and the Pankhursts* edited by Jane Marcus
*The Lily* edited by Cheris Kramarae and Ann Russo
*The Revolution* edited by Cheris Kramarae and Lana Rakow
*Sex and Social Order in Britain, 1630–1730* edited by Carol Barash
   and Rachel Weil

# The Non-Violent Militant

*Selected Writings of
Teresa Billington-Greig*

Edited by
## Carol McPhee
and
## Ann FitzGerald

## Routledge & Kegan Paul
London and New York

To Linna Thomas, Liz Apfelberg, Sandy Silver,
Raye Fleming and Anne Cruikshanks,
who have lived by the words of
Teresa Billington-Greig:
'If we do our work as well as we can, what else matters?'

First published in 1987 by
Routledge & Kegan Paul Ltd
11 New Fetter Lane, London EC4P 4EE

Published in the USA by
Routledge & Kegan Paul Inc.
in association with Methuen Inc.
29 West 35th Street, New York, NY 10001

Set in Bembo 10 on 11pt.
by Typesetting Ltd Inforum
and printed in Great Britain
by T.J. Press Ltd.
Padstow, Cornwall

Library of Congress Cataloging in Publication Data and
British Library CIP Data available
ISBN 0-7102-1232-1 (c)

# Contents

Acknowledgments     vii

Introduction: An Appreciation     1


*Part I The Genesis of a Feminist: Autobiographical Fragments*     25

My Mother     27
My Childhood and Education     34
My Loss of Religious Belief     51
Running away from Home     56
Study and Work in Manchester     65
Mrs Pankhurst and the WSPU     88
The Birth of the Women's Freedom League     102


*Part II Theory in the Midst of Battle: Essays of a Suffragette*     109

'The Militant Policy of Women Suffragists'     111
'Woman's Liberty and Man's Fear'     120
'The Woman with the Whip'     125
'Socialism and Sex-Equality'     131


*Part III The Militant Suffrage Movement: Emancipation in a Hurry*     135

Chapter I:     Personal Foreword     137
Chapter II:     The Genesis of the Movement     143
Chapter III:     The Chosen Gateway     149
Chapter IV:     Against the Government     155
Chapter V:     Success That Brought Defeat     161

# Contents

Chapter VI:     The Freedom League Failure          171
Chapter VII:    The Domination Established           179
Chapter VIII:   A Criticism of Militancy             185
Chapter IX:     Hostages to Hurry                    194
Chapter X:      Claims Examined                      202
Chapter XI:     The Broken Truce                     207
Chapter XII:    Parnell the Prototype                213
Chapter XIII:   Looking Forward                      219

Part IV  Against the State                           223

'Feminism and Politics'                              225
'Women and Government'                               236
'The Feminist Revolt: An Alternate Policy'           240

Part V  The Consumer in Revolt: Selections           249

Chapter I:      An Economic Divorce                  251
Chapter II:     The Victimisation of the Consumer    263
Chapter III:    Woman, the Consumer                  268
Chapter IV:     The Failure of the Labour Revolt     274
Chapter V:      Past Efforts to Secure Union         280
Chapter VI:     The Work to be Done                  286

Notes                                                295

Index                                                306

# Acknowledgments

Our sincere thanks to all those who have assisted us, formally and informally, in presenting Teresa Billington-Greig to the public once more. We are especially grateful to Fiona Billington-Greig, who has not only given permission to reprint her mother's works, but has spent hours of time with us recounting all she knows of her mother's history; to Catherine Ireland, Fawcett Librarian, who introduced us to Miss Billington-Greig and brought our work to the attention of the editors of this series, as well as smoothing our path as researchers both in and out of the Fawcett's precincts; to David Doughan, Assistant Librarian, who seems to have committed the entire catalogue of the Fawcett to memory; to Margaret Sweet, Fawcett Archivist and cataloguer of a great part of the Billington-Greig papers, who gave us access to her precious hoard and has been responding to queries ever since; to Diane Atkinson of the Museum of the City of London, who provided invaluable assistance with the Women's Freedom League and Suffragette Fellowship papers; to Jean Gordon of the California Polytechnic State University, who searched libraries from Maine to Hawaii for us; to the University of California, Berkeley, Library for keeping a copy of *The Militant Suffrage Movement*, and to Dan Krieger for helping us to obtain it and for sharing with us the benefits of his scholarship in British history; to the University of California, Santa Barbara, Library for *Towards Woman's Liberty* and for maintaining collections of early twentieth-century British newspapers and periodicals; to David Grant, Ellen Somers Horgan, and Louise Lubbe who generously gave of their time to read and comment; and to Dale Spender and Candida Lacey, series editors of the Women's Source Library, who share our enthusiasm for Teresa Billington-Greig.

# Introduction:
# An Appreciation

Looking back from the perspective of more than eighty years, Teresa Billington-Greig, suffragette, activist, and political theorist, saw herself as a rebel, a woman of conscience, a feminist, a critic – and a failure.

One of the few militants who had concentrated in her writing on the political methods of the movement, she had developed between 1905 and 1914 a concept of how women could use non-violent direct action to achieve a social revolution that would take them farther toward liberation than the vote. But she had lived to see her works forgotten, the organizations she had founded abandoned, a new generation indifferent, and the feminist revolution she had devoted her life to still in the future.

This book of her selected writings is an attempt to deny her claim to personal failure and to make the ideas of this remarkable woman once again available to everyone interested in the people's movements of this century. In addition to several essays and two books, long out of print, which present her political analyses, it includes a few of her unpublished autobiographical fragments showing how she developed the sensitive conscience that led her to examine the ethics of direct action.[1]

## TBG*: The Genesis of a Feminist Rebel, 1877–1903

The second daughter of Helen Orrell Wilson and William Billington, TBG was born above her parents' shop in Preston, England, in the year 1877.[2] Her mother, a Roman Catholic, had been educated in

* For most of her public life Teresa Billington-Greig signed herself and was often addressed as 'TBG'. Rather than call her 'Teresa' or 'Tess' or 'Billington-Greig', we have used 'TBG' throughout the Introduction.

1

a convent and had hoped to become a nun. Her father, eldest of a large family, had been put to work at the age of nine. From her mother, TBG learned a will to succeed in spite of obstacles, a sensitivity of conscience, and the need for women to be independent both economically and sexually. From her father, she learned not only how to charm people, but also to despise those men who take advantage of women's disabilities.

Helen Wilson had been a reluctant bride. Her father had buried three wives before Helen was sixteen, and the nuns had sent her from the convent in France to keep house for him. When she arrived in Preston, she discovered that her father had taken a fourth wife, this time a former servant in the household.

To escape from home, Helen persuaded her father to subsidize a small shop in partnership with two women friends. Although Helen enjoyed her independent life, her father began to press her to marry the tall, handsome William Billington. As a successful founder of Preston's first department store, John Wilson probably felt his daughter needed a man's help to make her business a success, especially after one of her partners had left to marry. But Wilson misjudged his man. The marriage was not a success. Helen's health and independence were sacrificed to child-bearing; she had three children in four years succeeded by a series of miscarriages. William tyrannized his children, beating his son, though the girls were protected by their mother. Because he failed to make a success of the business, the family were eventually forced to move to the industrial town of Blackburn where he was able to find a job with a boiler-making firm.

By the time of the move to Blackburn, the Billingtons were poor, depending for assistance in the children's education on the occasional generosity of relatives. Until they were in their early teens, TBG and her elder sister attended the Convent of Notre Dame, where the curriculum was limited and instruction inadequate. Thereafter, Helen tried to ensure that TBG would be able to support herself. She appealed to a relative for financial assistance so her daughter could become a pupil-teacher. That failing, she tried apprenticing her to a milliner, and searched out other possibilities to thwart William's frequent suggestions that the girl become a mill-worker. When TBG sold a few stories to a Roman Catholic magazine before she was fifteen, Helen engaged a tutor in English literature for her, but when subsequent stories failed to sell, the tutor had to be dismissed.

In spite of the lack of opportunity, TBG was determined to get an education. She read voraciously but without direction; she wrote constantly – poetry, essays, stories; and, much to the distress of her deeply religious mother, she questioned everything, including the teachings of the Roman Catholic Church. Seeing her thirteen-year-old as a possible apostate, Helen sent her to weekly sessions with a priest where TBG learned to turn her questions into arguments. But verbal sparring with Canon Lonsdale was hardly the education TBG knew she needed. And time for home study diminished as her mother's religious fanaticism took her away from home for long sessions of prayer, meditation, and attendance at several church services every day. When TBG realized that she was going to be required to do all the work of the household and work outside the home, she decided that her only option was to run away. She was seventeen.

Her first thought was that her Wilson grandfather might hire her in his Preston department store and that she could continue her studies at night. Although he angered her at first by turning her away with instructions to return home, he and the rest of the family finally arranged for her to live in Manchester with her widowed uncle George Wilson and his family.

In Manchester, TBG was able to make use of her energy and intelligence to resolve some of the conflicts with which she had struggled. She became an assistant teacher by passing the Queen's Scholarship Examination, obtained her teaching certificates through night-school classes, and began a course of study leading to the B. Sc. degree from the University of London. Once she was financially independent enough to live separately from her Roman Catholic relatives and freed for a time from intensive study, she began again to examine her religious doubts and to read widely in ethical, social, and natural philosophy. Finally, she decided to renounce the Church, and thereafter characterized herself as an agnostic.

During this same period, TBG was finding her place in a new society, the Ancoats University Settlement, which drew young intellectuals with progressive ideas and social consciences to its variety of activities, ranging from debates to excursions in the country with the children of Manchester's slums. An attractive young woman, a little over average height, with an abundant head of chestnut hair, green eyes,[3] and a habit of speaking out in an unconventional and forthright manner, she drew people to her, making friendships which lasted a lifetime. As Honorary Secretary of the Associates, she began to learn the organizing skills she used in feminist causes all her life. Through the Settlement debates, she also perfected her oratorical style with its carefully measured phrasing, delivered in a pleasant contralto voice, and the argumentative techniques that made her a renowned debater in just a few years. At Ancoats, too, she heard a variety of political opinions and was drawn to a number of causes which she listed in the notes for her autobiography. Determined to devote her life to one, she considered the Ethical Society and its program of inculcating logical and moral attitudes for bringing about world change; she considered health and humanitarian social services; and Left and reform politics. At last, in reaction to the cruelty of society toward women – wife-beating, compulsory sex in marriage, prejudices against women in factories and professions, unequal pay, and women's general lack of status – she made a life-long commitment to feminism.

Substituting the ideas of the Ethical Society and a passionate belief in the feminist cause for her abandoned religious faith, TBG attempted to shape her life on the basis of reasoned principle. Her sensitivity to violence had always made the cruel stories of the Old Testament repellent to her, but the curriculum, even in non-sectarian schools, required her to teach these stories to her young pupils. Her conscience finally dictated that she explore alternatives. She offered herself as a teacher for the Ethical Society and applied for a position in one of the Technical schools where she would not be required to teach the Bible. Finally, she approached the District Director, suggesting that teachers be exempted from teaching religion on the basis of conscience in the same way that students could be exempted from studying religion if their parents signed a conscience clause. He sent her to talk with a member of the Manchester Board, Mrs Emmeline Pankhurst, who helped her find a temporary position in a Jewish school.

The year was 1903 and, two months earlier, Mrs Pankhurst had gathered a few Manchester women about her and formed a new suffrage society, the Women's Social and Political Union (WSPU). Mrs Pankhurst, apparently recognizing TBG's formidable talents at once, soon recruited her and sent her out as one of the fledgling group's major speakers. In April 1904, TBG brought together a small group of teachers to form the Manchester Equal Pay League. Shortly thereafter, the problem of her employment was resolved when Mrs Pankhurst persuaded Keir Hardie to see that TBG was hired as an organizer by the Independent Labour Party (ILP).[4]

## The Autobiographical Fragments

TBG originally intended that her own story should be a medium for viewing the history of the women's movement in Great Britain so that what she had long perceived as the proper goals of feminism might engage the attention of a generation of women fully enfranchised since 1928. Though she began the work in the late 1940s, it was never completed, but the manuscripts describing her childhood and

young womanhood, along with notes, minutes of meetings, news-
letters, and some correspondence, have been preserved in the Fawcett
Library in London.

At first her scope was truly grand, embracing descriptions of the
political and social movements of her youth, and she made extensive
notes on personalities and events. In what she had intended as the
introduction to one version of her autobiography, she explained:

> A life that has covered the great part of a century and has taken
> on the colour and atmosphere of that century in its small way
> must be recorded in terms of the external environment as well as
> in personal terms . . . Seeking to crystallise the individual
> pictures . . . I can compare them as first a time of beginning, in
> revolt and hope, & then a time of age and ending, in revolt still,
> but without any single certainty of hope remaining.[5]

As she grew older, never able to take the work past the year 1907, she
made outlines for a more limited work. For the period 1903–1907,
there remain only brief characterizations and scattered short episodes. She seems to have been unable to write of her marriage and
the birth of her child, although her outline contains this chapter
heading: 'Personal Triangle – Husband, Child, Personal Purpose.'[6]

What she did write of herself and the Billington family is mercilessly honest. Rather than presenting herself as a frustrated genius,
struggling up on a path marked out by instinct, she described a
wayward, stubborn, loving but somewhat clumsy child torn by
conflicting values, who found her way only by making mistakes.

## TBG: Champion of Militancy, 1903–1907

After her appointment as an organizer, TBG worked almost two
years for the ILP, successfully handling several election campaigns in
the north of England while continuing to dedicate much of her time
to the Women's Social and Political Union (WSPU). In the autumn
of 1905, the WSPU saw the General Election as an opportunity to
gain attention for the cause of woman suffrage. Considering several
different tactics, they decided to have Christabel Pankhurst and
Annie Kenney attend a Liberal Party meeting scheduled for the
Manchester Free Trade Hall and interrupt the main speaker, Sir
Edward Grey, who was expected to become a cabinet minister after
the election. Mrs Pankhurst at first assigned TBG to go with
Christabel and Annie and be arrested with them, but at the last moment, changed her mind. Instead, TBG was charged with organizing

the protest meetings and speaking in defense of the women after their arrests. She also published a statement defending the action in the Manchester *Guardian*, thus making her debut as apologist of the militant women's movement.

The following spring, as militancy intensified, Mrs Pankhurst sent TBG to London to work with Annie Kenney and Sylvia Pankhurst as a paid organizer for the WSPU. Within a month the newspapers had picked out TBG for special attention, calling her 'the redoubtable Miss Billington' and 'truculent Teresa.' Among other activities, she had thrust a white flag proclaiming 'Votes for Women' through the grille of the Ladies Gallery in the House of Commons, organized demonstrations in support of Dora Montefiore's tax protest,[7] and spoken to a massive gathering in Trafalgar Square along with other suffrage leaders.

In June 1906, she took a deputation of working women to the residence of Chancellor of the Exchequer, H.H. Asquith, where they intended to wait politely for an opportunity to present their case to the Minister. When policemen struck several women with their fists, TBG objected and was herself seized, struck, and throttled. She slapped an officer in the face and kicked his shins, whereupon she was arrested. In the Magistrates' Court, she refused to testify, claiming the Court lacked jurisdiction because women had no part in making the laws she was accused of breaking, an idea she developed in later writings. She was sentenced to a term in prison, thus becoming the first suffragette to go to Holloway.

During this same time, the WSPU was undergoing significant reorganization, having attracted to their ranks the wealthy and astute Emmeline and Frederick Pethick-Lawrence; Christabel Pankhurst was completing her legal studies, and her mother planned to have her take command in London. Soon after her early release from prison, TBG was given the responsibility of organizing branches in Scotland.

In October 1906, she had returned to London to take part in a demonstration involving hundreds of women at the House of Commons, where she and several officials of the WSPU were arrested and sentenced to two months in Holloway. Also among those arrested was a woman well-known to the British people and deeply respected: Mrs Cobden-Sanderson, daughter of Richard Cobden, a nineteenth-century reformer. So great was the outpouring of public sympathy that the non-militant suffrage societies honored the prisoners at a banquet upon their release. TBG's prestige among the suffragettes at this time was probably at its zenith. According to Mary Gawthorpe, imprisoned at the same time, TBG and Mrs Cobden-Sanderson were the two who were singled out for formal toasts at the banquet and replied with speeches on behalf of the prisoners.[8]

A sketch of TBG written by Frederick Pethick-Lawrence in July 1906, characterized her at this time as a natural politician who 'can distinguish the right from the wrong, the wise from the foolish'; who had 'the gift of "speech" ' and 'moral courage'; a leader with 'assurance' who 'loves the joy of battle, and means to win, one whom . . . ridicule does not annoy, . . . but who can afford to laugh at opposition, make capital out of criticism . . . ' She had, he thought, 'that rare power of judgment of character . . . '[9] A portrait by J.J. Mallon who first knew TBG at Ancoats, offered with gentle irony additional insights into her personality: 'She cannot whittle down or compromise, because her principles are absolute and have immortal validity . . . The defects of such a character are easily guessed. There will be quick loves, but equally quick repulsions.' Commenting on her impatience with those who lacked her vision, he prophesied that she would become great if she could learn 'a larger toleration.'[10]

The only visitor TBG had been allowed in Holloway that fall of 1906 was the ruggedly handsome, witty socialist and businessman Frederick Lewis Greig, whom she had come to love before she left Manchester. Sometime in 1906, he had been appointed manager of the Glasgow Branch of Burroughes & Watts, a manufacturer of billiard tables. Family legend has it that TBG's close friend Edith How-Martyn, Honorary Secretary of the WSPU, had urged him to persuade TBG to marry before the movement absorbed her totally. Fred must have been very persuasive, for they were married on February 8, 1907, in Glasgow – not long after TBG had drafted *Towards Women's Liberty*, with its denunciation of male brutality and oppression. The nuptial agreement was a statement neutralizing the marriage and property laws of Great Britain; Frederick Greig became Frederick Billington-Greig; the wedding reception was held in the WSPU office; and TBG was campaigning again after a three-day honeymoon.

In addition to campaigning, she was again organizing branches in Scotland and writing prolifically. In the June 27 issue of *Women's Franchise* (1907), she told of the 'progressive organisation' in Scotland where the branches formed a Scottish Council of the WSPU to avoid 'the faults of the system of a single central body as the sole link between widely scattered branches.' The July 11 issue carried a notice that she had published in the *Fortnightly Review*, 'Suffragist Tactics: Past and Present,' an article based on two essays she had written in prison the previous autumn, 'The Militant Policy of Women Suffragists' and 'Woman's Liberty and Man's Fear.' The

August 8 issue of the same periodical showed that before June 30, *Towards Women's Liberty* had sold a thousand copies for the benefit of the WSPU. Beginning in May 1907, a series of TBG's articles began to appear in *The New Age*.

## Essays: 1906–1907

'The Militant Policy of Women Suffragists'
'Woman's Liberty and Man's Fear'
'The Woman with the Dog Whip'
'Socialism and Sex-Equality'

The young woman in Manchester TBG described in her autobiography had been irresistibly drawn to the multitude of reforming ideas swirling among the young intellectuals of that city, 'The sort of movements and people who gave one hope,' she wrote.[11] She recalled reading 'Joseph Mazzini – with his worship of humanity and his vision of universal and continuous "natural" progress'; the poets Byron, Shelley and Francis Thompson; Milton's 'Areopagitica'; Ebenezer Howard's discussion of Garden Cities; Robert Blatchford, William Morris, Robert Owen, William Wilberforce, Elizabeth Fry, Florence Nightingale, and 'pamphlets on Socialist feeling'; F.J. Gould's discussion of ethics; and probably in this period also, Bergson and Tolstoy, Locke and Mill, Darwin and Huxley.[12]

Her notes also reveal the impression made by events of protest and passive resistance which took place during her Manchester teaching days: the Boggart Hole Clough ILP protest where numbers of speakers allowed themselves to be arrested for holding open-air meetings; and the tax-resistance of the non-conforming religious groups who refused to pay taxes to support Church of England and Roman Catholic schools. She also noted that the Boer War had intensified her revulsion against the violence in the Old Testament.

By 1905, when she became an apologist for the militant movement, she had arrived at the basic assumption that human beings can achieve a decent life through their ability to reason; that if human beings were educated to reason, individual human liberty would produce the best possible world. This basic assumption underlies her ethical approach to politics, her insistence on democracy in organizations, her socialist ideas, her view of the state as a patriarchal institution, and her concept of feminism.

TBG's feminist principles appear in most of the works in this collection, but the clearest statement of her goal for the feminist movement appears in *The Militant Suffrage Movement* (1911):[13]

> I seek [woman's] . . . emancipation from all shackles of law and
> custom, from all chains of sentiment and superstition, from all
> outer imposed disabilities and cherished inner bondages which
> unite to shut off liberty from the human soul borne in her body.
> (p.137)

Translated into specifics in a set of notes probably made in 1912 or
1913, her feminism welcomed reforms that would bring equal rights
under the law to women, but absolutely demanded fundamental
changes in women's dependent role. For example, she supported
recognition of women's rights in the workplace, but questioned the
traditional idea that all labor is sacred and wanted to dispense with
sex-defined economic functions. Essentially, she asked for motherhood by choice, the elimination of traditional and repressive marriage customs, rejection of the family as the unit of society, changes
in attitudes toward prostitution and what she called 'unrecognized
sex relations,'[14] and a complete revision in every custom or attitude
that kept women subservient.

The essays she wrote in 1906 and 1907 focused, like most of her
writing, on the politics of feminism – the ways in which people
might act in order to achieve its goals and the reasons for their
actions. Three themes seem to be particularly important to her at this
time: women's right to use militant tactics; men's hostility towards
women and the implicit violence of their laws; and sex-equality as
more fundamental than the vote.

'The Militant Policy of Women Suffragists,'[15] a signed and dated
manuscript prepared when TBG was in prison in the fall of 1906,
concentrates on defending the tactics of the WSPU during the
preceding year. Although she presented the traditional arguments
for enfranchising women, her ethical sense demanded that she also
search out the most rational bases she could discover for militancy.
One reason was that it was inhumane for women to wait longer, for
they carried 'additional burdens' because of their sex. Another was
that the protest actions would expose the 'bigotry of men,' and thus
create sympathy for the cause in fair men as well as women.
Returning to the claim she made when she was first arrested in June
1906 – that the court hearing her case had no jurisdiction because
women are outside the law – she developed a third in an informal set
of syllogisms arguing women's right to rebel. Rebellion, she
claimed toward the end of the article, is in fact the 'duty of believers
in equality and liberty.'

Another handwritten essay, also probably composed in prison,
'Woman's Liberty and Man's Fear,'[16] arose out of a second

preoccupation of TBG's at this time: the violence and hostility of men toward women as they became militant. As an activist, TBG had herself experienced physical abuse more than once. A few days before the beating she received outside Asquith's residence, she had been dragged from a meeting, her hair pulled down, and her clothes torn. It is characteristic of TBG that she would seek to explain the violence that she and other women had suffered by contemplating the deeper – perhaps unconscious – reasons for misogyny. The essay is a much more emotional one than 'The Militant Policy.' TBG calls men bullies, cowards, tyrants who force women into marriage by keeping them impoverished, uneducated, and politically powerless. She exposes men's faulty logic in limiting women's opportunities in education, in industry, in society, and in marriage in strong terms: women's claimed 'incapability' is called 'balderdash'; she refers to men's 'coward policies'; she speaks of 'the robbery of women workers,' and 'the cloak of marriage' being used to 'cover unspeakable horrors.' The essay gives a valuable insight into the relationship between the powerful and the powerless:

> There is always for . . . [the oppressor] the fear that the end may come, and rebellion carries with it not merely the throwing off of the yoke but, alongside of it the dread of such vengeful retaliation as corresponds to the oppressor's tyranny. (p. 120)

And because man has oppressed woman for so long, TBG warned, man had good reason to fear 'woman freed.'

TBG's preoccupation with the hostility of men is developed further in the chapter 'The Woman with the Whip,' from *Towards Woman's Liberty*,[17] published in the spring of 1907. The book combines a brief history of the women's movement in Great Britain with the arguments TBG presented in the two prison essays. This chapter begins with a defense of what TBG admits was her 'aggressive' behavior in using a dog whip on the stewards at a Liberal Party meeting in Northampton: the injuries men had visited on the suffragettes in recent months had included sexual violence, and TBG decided that 'Insult of this kind could come only from curs, and for them the dog-whip was the fitting punishment' (p. 126). These personal insults impelled her to lash out at the double standard of morality and the unfair marriage, divorce, parentage, and prostitution laws that arise from it, claiming that it creates an evil environment for the human race.

'Socialism and Sex-Equality' appeared as part of a series in *The New Age* on June 20, 1907 (pp. 117–18). Primarily an argument against the Labour Party's attempt to substitute universal adult suffrage for the women's suffrage drive, the article presents a third direction TBG's ideas took in the spring of 1907 – the concept that women's full equality with men was more important than the vote and more necessary even than 'Socialism or Democracy, for without it . . . [women] cannot benefit by either' (p.132). Social change could not take place without sex-equality, for 'The exploitation of women by men . . . incapacitates humanity for Socialist thought and organisation . . .' (p.131).

## TBG: The Non-Violent Militant, 1907–1910

TBG's differences with the Pankhursts also began to surface during the spring of 1907. By June she had felt it necessary to resign as a paid organizer but volunteered to continue her work on an honorary basis.[18] Letters of Emmeline and Christabel Pankhurst written in the same month imply that they feared TBG's influence in the WSPU[19] and perhaps were worried about the strength of the democratically-organized Scottish Council. Not three months later, on September 10, 1907, Emmeline Pankhurst informed the London Branch that the plans for further militancy demanded a para-military organization and publicly tore up what she said was the WSPU draft constitution, a document TBG had prepared a year before. In October TBG chaired the Annual General Conference of the WSPU, convened without the blessing of the Pankhursts. There delegates from most of the branches ratified the democratic constitution and elected Mrs Despard Honorary Treasurer, Edith How-Martyn Honorary Secretary, and TBG Honorary Organizing Secretary. This Conference marked a split in the movement as two militant societies emerged, TBG's society becoming the Women's Freedom League (WFL), which remained a viable organization for over fifty years.

All of TBG's amazing energies were tapped during the next year and a half, as she lived a divided life – working to eliminate rigid roles in her marriage with Fred; providing educational opportunities and a home near Glasgow for two of her nieces; leading the WFL toward innovative, non-violent direct actions on several women's issues; traveling and speaking constantly as the WFL's main organizer; and publishing her periodical *The Hour & the Woman*.

In the summer of 1909, however, she had a serious operation requiring her absence from several National Executive Committee meetings, and when she returned to attend the Annual General Meeting in January 1910, she found dissension about the nature of the WFL's militancy. A back injury TBG sustained in a train accident

11

a month later while in Ireland to consult with Parliamentary leaders separated her further from the inner politics of the WFL.

TBG's inability to travel for several months was most unfortunate, because 1910 was a critical year for the suffrage cause. The Conciliation Committee for Woman Suffrage composed of members of the House of Commons from all political parties had been created early in the year to propose a suffrage Bill the Commons could support. Because suffragist members of Parliament were optimistic about the Committee's chances of success, the leaders of the militant suffrage societies had agreed to cease all militant actions while the Committee wrote the Bill and then guided it through Parliament.

Despite her recently-formed reservations about the ability of any government to affect the status of women, TBG wrote forceful articles supporting the work of the Conciliation Committee for *The Vote*, the weekly newspaper of the WFL, and exerted all her influence with WFL members to honor the Executive Committee's policy and maintain the truce. When it became clear in mid-November that the Conciliation Committee's Bill would receive no further consideration for some time, and WFL members joined the WSPU to break the truce in a demonstration at the House of Commons where numbers of women were brutally attacked and seriously injured, all of TBG's distress with both militant organizations burst into open expression. She resigned from the WFL in December and began to write *The Militant Suffrage Movement*.

## The Militant Suffrage Movement, 1911

Published as a series of articles in *The New Age* in January 1911, and appearing as a book in March, *The Militant Suffrage Movement* is a confession of disillusionment with the suffrage movement and a profession of faith in another kind of feminism, one using revolutionary tactics for social change. It represents four more years of considering the ways by which the goals of feminism could best be achieved.

As a leader of the WFL, TBG had learned the difficulties of combining political idealism with practical organizational realities: democracy had not worked in the WFL. The members expected the officers to take the burden of responsibility, yet insisted on the right to make decisions even on militant actions in which they took no part. The honest and essentially non-violent actions had not been well-supported by the rank and file, and after one action had backfired, they had voted not to start any action in which innocent bystanders might be injured, even though TBG had argued that such a stand would make any effective protest impossible. TBG also felt that many of the members yearned for the emotional satisfaction of following a charismatic leader. Furthermore, as a political theorist writing articles for *The Vote* in 1910, she faced a conflict: though she saw the Conciliation Committee as a new instrument of the people – an innovative constitutional change that might undermine the Cabinet's oligarchic powers – and therefore supported the limited woman suffrage Bill, her position was a retreat from her earlier one demanding nothing less than sex-equality in the legislation for the enfranchisement of women.

'I saw clearly my duty was to act as a critic,' she wrote in a letter dated February 2, 1911, to the editor of *The Vote* in response to the furore aroused by her resignation from the WFL.[20] She had lost confidence in the League because it could not remain 'standing firmly to a course of its own,' and had tended to follow the WSPU lead.[21] In *The Militant Suffrage Movement*, the course she had hoped the WFL would follow forms the set of standards against which she judges the actions of the militant societies – a set of standards for direct action that resemble those Gandhi was working out at the same time. Basing her ideas on the ethical assumption that the end does not justify the means, she held that the means used to reach a revolutionary feminist goal must be examined so that whatever actions women use do not destroy the basic values they seek to establish. If their means – persuasion, protest, non-cooperation – conform to the values of their goal, women gradually will change those ways of believing and acting that condemn them to cooperate in their own oppression. If, in addition, they really seek to reconstruct society so there will no longer be an oppressed group and an oppressor, they must try to change the attitudes as well as the policies of their opponents. Avoiding self-righteousness, they recognize the human needs of the opposition and incorporate negotiation as one of their means.

Trained as a speaker and journalist, TBG tended to organize her material in spiral fashion, with all her points stated in the beginning and subsequent sections or chapters focusing on one or more of them. Yet the nature of *The Militant Suffrage Movement* is essentially chronological. For this reason, the standards appear here and there throughout the book, in flashes of insight or prophecy, or underlying irony or polemic. The discussion that follows gathers material from several different chapters under three general headings, supplying additional information from TBG's notes.

TBG had always assumed that the goal women wanted was

liberation from the restrictions of the tradition that kept them in subservient and dependent roles. In her book she claimed that the means used by the suffragettes were not designed to liberate anyone: first, the protest actions, conceived to make use of women's emotional subservience to their leaders, were unrelated to feminist goals and created unnecessary antagonism in the opposition; second, the internal politics of the organization, which she saw as an integral part of the means, kept women accustomed to tyranny; and, third, their political dealings with the Cabinet and the Liberal Party demonstrated self-righteous refusal to negotiate.

When TBG first met Mrs Pankhurst, she had been convinced that working women, like working men, needed the vote to get good industrial legislation. Though she did not consider this initial demand as the final goal, she believed that the means used to get this intermediate goal 'would undermine the servitude of women in all other human relations' (p. 147). As she pointed out in her 1906–1907 articles, conventions restricting women would be outraged by militant actions, and true feminists would be delighted by that outrage.

According to her autobiographical notes, she had very early thought that ends should be incorporated in the means. She said she had proposed to the core group of the newly formed WSPU several forms of action that would outrage convention and were directly related to the franchise:

> Claiming the right to vote we would use every sort of endeavour to exercise that right in any form we could devise: an individual woman slipping into the polling booth and dropping a voting paper . . . a half dozen women rushing the door to cover a real or simulated voting attack; a raiding crowd of women creating confusion by demanding entry; the introduction into the count of an extra ballot box of votes given by women. . . . (p. 197)

This advocacy TBG called constructive protest, doing what women had been barred from doing.

But TBG's counsel was largely ignored – even her suggestion of having Mrs Pankhurst stand for Parliament. One of the WSPU's most frequently used militant actions was like the first one in Manchester in 1905, interrupting a meeting at which Liberal Party leaders were speaking, with the intention that one or more of the militants be arrested. According to Sylvia Pankhurst in *The Suffrage Movement*, these interruptions were more disruptive than the heckling common to British political meetings. She described Annie Kenney wailing out again and again the question, 'Will the Liberal

Government give women the Vote?' so vociferously that no one could hear or speak until the wailer was ousted.[22] In *The Militant Suffrage Movement*, TBG called this tactic 'a very inadequate outlet for the expression of our rebellion' (p.150). To provoke arrest and then claim to be an innocent victim was, she pointed out, not protest, not revolution – it was fraudulent advertisement. This strategy, she observed,

> is neither revolution nor consistency, nor does it show a high standard of honour. Revolution should never be ashamed of itself. It should never evade its responsibility. . . . One cannot at the same time be the aggressor and the innocent victim. (p. 187)

Militant women 'are rebels . . . ; they should stand frankly forth as rebels . . .' (p.164).

Worse yet, concentration on this type of protest ignored the real victims of society's male upper-class: the unorganized working women, especially those starving in the sweated trades; the ill-fed mother of too many ill-fed babies; women forced into prostitution in order to feed themselves; women denied justice and protection in the courts of Law. TBG believed there were

> dozens of cases daily of unfair laws and laws unfairly adminis-tered. . . . A system of protest against these . . . evils could have been devised. The obstruction of legislation and interference with its administration might have been developed. The great natural forces of emotion could have been more legitimately aroused by protests against the real victimisation of women in our law courts than by the creation of artificial victims. (p.188–9)

In other words, not only were the protests inappropriate to the real emancipation of women, they took time and energy and attention away from legitimate, effective protests and foolishly ignored the opportunities to use another form of non-violent direct action, non-cooperation.

TBG admitted, as she had to, that for a time the WSPU methods and tactics gained the attention of the public and the press, but essentially she saw that the same sorts of protest actions repeated month after month for five years were failures. Under what she called the Pankhurst-Pethick-Lawrence 'directorate,' the movement became 'political revivalism – that, and nothing more' (p.181).

Emmeline Pankhurst, as the high priestess of this revival, played upon the emotions of the rank-and-file members for years, working them up to a state of fanaticism; they were 'befooled' and, by the end of 1910, the Pankhursts were leading them on to new kinds of vio-lence which, TBG prophesied, would 'condemn a large number of

women to personal sacrifice that in some cases amounts to suicide. . . .'
This kind of violence, she charged, 'is victimisation' (p.211).

At the same time as militant actions escalated in both the number
of events and degree of violence – except for the 1910 truce – the
leadership narrowed the goal even further. This process began after
public sympathy shifted to the suffragettes in October 1906. Suddenly the movement became respectable; the women of the upper
classes decided that the rebels were really ladies after all; money
poured into the WSPU treasury; and members of the press became
somewhat more friendly. TBG's judgment was that 'under these
influences of rehabilitation the movement became conventionalised
and narrowed and hypocritical' (p.165). By 1908 the WSPU had
even changed the motto on its stationery from 'We demand the
Parliamentary vote for women on the same terms as it is or may be
granted to men,' to 'Taxpaying women are entitled to the Parliamentary vote' (p.179–80). Concern for the plight of the woman
worker under industrial evils disappeared from major speeches, and
advocacy of such elementary feminist principles as equality between
the sexes was 'reduced to the vaguest generalities' (p.165). In effect,
the WSPU, in order not to offend its new upper-class friends – rich
friends – had silenced discussion of all feminist issues but one.

These shifts were possible in part because the internal structure
and politics of the WSPU were basically undemocratic, though this
characteristic was not as obvious in the early years when their
numbers were small and their activities centered primarily in Manchester and the north of England. In these early years, TBG said in
one of the autobiographical fragments, decisions were made in
informal discussions, after many members had spoken. But, by late
1906, decisions were being made and orders given by what she called
the 'triune directorate,' consisting of Emmeline and Christabel
Pankhurst and the London Treasurer, Emmeline Pethick-Lawrence.
A cult of personality was assiduously encouraged by the selection of
speakers at mass meetings, by press releases before and after each
action, and by other tactics which today are called 'media hype' but
which TBG called 'booming.' TBG began to see 'cause for fear in the
excessive growth of emotion and excitement. Under the cover of
this emotional condition the will of the leaders rapidly came to be
substituted for the will of the members . . .' (p.167).

Next, TBG said, the leaders abandoned attempts to develop their
campaign into a mass movement. Although women rebels and
reformers, urban working-class women, educated and wealthy
women, and a few aristocrats had joined when the WSPU moved its
headquarters to London in 1906, the working class, the rebels and
the reformers were driven out by the end of that year; the 'hopes of a

union of women of all classes . . . was one more of the dreams that were to end in sudden disillusionment' (p.162).

The failure to ensure democracy within the movement TBG saw as failure to effect change within the oppressed themselves. The movement 'has given women chains that it may win for them a weapon that it has taught them not to use' (p.180), she wrote. 'Militancy as designed and carried out by Miss Pankhurst and her mother has not tended to work a revolution by the enslaved woman much less to work a revolution in her' (p.185).

TBG viewed the policies the militants used with regard to their antagonists – the Cabinet and the Liberal Party – from the perspective of a protester willing to be fair to the opponent and ready to work rationally for a change in his attitude before resorting to insurrection. The militants' refusal to take this approach she considered one more proof that they took every stand possible simply to antagonize, a method certain to lead to increasingly futile violence.

TBG also found the opposition to all Liberal Party candidates at a general election political stupidity, if it was not, indeed, calculated to gain more Conservative money for the WSPU. At a by-election, voting against a candidate who would only support the Government in power made sense, she admitted, but at a General Election, no Government was in power, and all efforts should be concentrated on defeating the opposition to suffrage, particularly those Members of any party who might be elevated to cabinet rank in the next Government. The suffragettes, she believed, had 'disposed of their claim to political independence' (p.159).

Finally, the militants demonstrated their serious lack of good faith by deliberately breaking the truce with the Government in November 1910, for the Government had made a pledge more positive than ever before. Rather than continue to negotiate, TBG said, the militants chose 'to destroy their own followers' (p.211).

What the militant movement ought to have been, TBG summed up:

> A movement of reasoned revolt, aggressive, and, however small in numbers, large in methods, working with clean hands, and without the employment of hustle and advertisement, employing no aids of artifice and emotion to carry women beyond their depths, and seeking ever to apply the principles [of democracy]. . . . (p.170)

Further, women should not look for 'Emancipation in a Hurry,' the sub-title of *The Militant Suffrage Movement*. If women intended to pursue militant strategies, they should support the persuasive and educational tactics she had been trying to put into practice through the WFL, like the protests in the Police Courts against unfair laws and the treatment of accused women; the passive resistance of the Tax Resistance League and other forms of non-cooperation; and they should try once more to create a mass movement which would include the poor, working women, trade union members, professional women, and married women of all classes.

## TBG: Revolutionary Critic, 1911–1914

In the next four years TBG supported herself as a free-lance journalist and speaker on socialist and feminist topics, working from the home she shared with Fred and her young nieces. In addition to a regular newspaper column called 'Women's Wider World,' she wrote articles for such periodicals as *The Freewoman*, *The English Review*, and *The Contemporary Review*. Her notes indicate that this was also a time for reading and study, a time to synthesize the ideas and experiences of the last ten years. She began but never finished a book on the patriarchal family, insisting that people should be considered as individuals and not be forced by the state into rigid roles largely based on sex. Influenced to some extent by the writings of the guild socialists and the French Syndicalists, she moved from criticism of government to an almost anarchical distrust of the state; she hoped that smaller units democratically organized on the basis of economic function, could replace it. She published *The Consumer in Revolt* in 1912,[23] translating these ideas into another plan for a mass feminist movement based upon woman's oppression by a capitalist patriarchal society; but the book did not have wide circulation, for she had alienated her natural audience by criticism of the sexism of the Labour Party, the Fabians, and the Trade Unions. At the beginning of World War I, TBG was working on a book opposing the White Slave Acts on the grounds that they were an unnecessary interference by the state in women's personal freedom.

## Selected Publications, 1911–1913

'Feminism and Politics'
'Women and Government'
'The Feminist Revolt: An Alternate Policy'
*The Consumer in Revolt*, 1912

The two articles appearing in late 1911 after publication of *The*

*Militant Suffrage Movement* further develop the ideas set forth in that book. 'Feminism and Politics' (*Contemporary Review*, November 1911, pp.693–703) solidifies TBG's view that true revolution takes place apart from the state, which in a democracy responds to the ideas of the average citizen, not to those who would create a new society. In order to establish the feminist revolution envisioned by Mary Wollstonecraft and John Stuart Mill, women should have a feminist program that would 're-make society, would set up new standards, would destroy old customs, would establish a new morality' (p.227). The purpose of the campaign should be to change the minds, then the habits of all people. If the vote only were won, it might lead to reform by compulsion, 'the last ditch of the modern reformer' (p.234). Foreseeing the destructive potential of protective legislation, TBG said that the vote might work against women as Parliament passed measures 'opposed to the root-principles of sex-equality and that upon the demand of newly enfranchised women' (p.230). Appearing in the December 21 issue of *The Freewoman*, TBG's article 'Women and Government' attacks the state which has such coercive powers through its bureaucracies and party politics that even universal suffrage cannot change it nor help the feminist cause. 'The Feminist Revolt: An Alternate Policy' is a typewritten draft of an article found among TBG's papers.[24] Commenting on the martyrdom of the suffragettes as militancy escalated, TBG agreed that propaganda and protest were necessary to the movement, and that the British public can only be aroused through sympathy with victims. But in one long passage, she explained in detail the kinds of non-violent direct actions that she would approve – all of them centered upon the real sufferings of women under male oppression.

Ever the political realist, TBG had recognized that the feminist reconstruction she sought would be a work of many years. Thus, searching for the broadest possible base for her revolution, she turned again to one of the root causes of women's oppression – their role as consumers in a society that denies the value of that role. Possibly in response to Olive Schreiner's *Women and Labour* (1911), where women in modern technological society are viewed as parasites, TBG shifted her focus in *The Consumer in Revolt* from the need for a general feminist program to one which would gather the forces of women of every class and interest to restructure the economic life of her society.

Although her analysis makes use of some of the ideas of guild socialism, she imposed a feminist point of view on the original ideas. She agreed with the guild socialists that society should be organized on the basis of functions, that no function be considered superior to another, that concepts of status and class be eliminated, that individual liberty was more important than the state, and that society could be organized in small, democratic groups of many different kinds, each contributing its voice to decisions affecting the common welfare. Under the influence of the socialists, she said, the Labour Party had failed to achieve anything in their concentration on gaining political power and, in fact, had lost their effectiveness in industrial wars. The Fabian socialist idea that the state could represent the consumer, she argued, was false. Like A.J. Penty in *The Restoration of the Guild System* (1906) she saw that government ownership would be like ownership by a corporation and the pursuit of profits would alienate the worker and emphasize quantity in production, not quality.

Taking a feminist view of economics, TBG claimed that women's function had been ignored. She observed that there is a large group of human beings, including children, the elderly, homemakers, artists, professionals, and service workers, who are not engaged in what the leftist thinkers call productive work. Neither are these people necessarily profiteers or capitalists, but they all function as consumers. Modern society, however, has divided production and consumption artificially so that capitalists can play the producers and the consumers off against each other in order to make a profit. This division cannot be bridged as long as men falsely idealize productive labor and see themselves as the only producers. Women, most of whom have been prohibited from serving as producers, have been also prohibited from the public world in their function as consumers. If women were to organize in their function as consumers, unite with other so-called non-productive groups and create a balance with the organizations of producers (e.g. Trade Unions), they could work toward a new society where the interference of capitalists could not take place. Reviewing the experiments of Robert Owen, the syndicalists, the Co-operative Societies and various socialist or communist colonies who tried to bring 'the consumer and the worker into a natural material harmony' (p.282), she reasoned that these did not last because they existed apart from the whole society. What was needed was a mass movement, involving the whole nation and taking place without the state, using education, 'action through existing agencies and institutions,' 'peaceful pressure,' 'aggressive protest and boycott and strike,' and the 'invention of new systems and methods' (p. 282). She maintained, 'It is the one movement which will awaken the average woman to her relation to the rest of the community, and to the vital matters affecting her which call for her presence in public affairs' (p.289).

## TBG: An Infinite Variety, 1914–1964

At the very end of *The Militant Suffrage Movement*, TBG made a prophecy about those former militants who like herself left the movement: 'We shall drop to the level of the common-place and do our common-place work' (p.222). Compared with the period 1903–1913, TBG's life after 1914 may indeed have seemed 'common-place' to her, but what she meant by 'common-place work' can only be defined by a brief review of her next fifty years.

In late 1913 or early 1914, she had to cope with a crisis in her relationship with her husband. Although Fred shared most of her socialist and feminist ideas and supported her writing and speaking, they separated because of differences of opinion never explained, and TBG spent some time in England. Whatever the difficulties, they were somehow resolved, for TBG had returned to Glasgow by December 1914, when she lectured the Clarion Scouts on birth control. In December 1915, she gave birth to her daughter and only child, Fiona Billington-Greig, who says her mother told her she was 'a reconciliation baby.'[25] Whether because of the demands of motherhood or the pressures of a nation at war, TBG appears to have found little time to write until after the Armistice. Then she discovered that there was no market for her consumer-oriented and feminist writing.

Nevertheless, she did not give up her attempt to model her life on her own feminist principles. During the war, when Fred was made a fuel controller, TBG substituted for him at the billiard company office in Glasgow. Experimenting with communal life, for several years she organized guest houses in the country for students and young professionals run on what she called 'co-operative' lines. Shortly after the family moved to London in 1923, she again substituted for her husband, this time at the London branch of Burroughes & Watts. Quite characteristically, sometime in her association with the billiards table firm, she conceived the idea that women should be encouraged to play billiards and founded the Women's Billiards Association, which sponsored exhibitions and tournaments for women. Burroughes & Watts also encouraged another of her interests – the Sports Fellowship, which she hoped would interest underprivileged girls in athletics and foster camaraderie.

On her return to London, TBG did take some part in a few women's organizations, but in the early 1930s Fred lost his position, and she was forced to direct almost all her efforts to earning money. She tried writing fiction, but none was published. She helped her husband with the small stationers shop he established in Carnaby Street, and at the age of fifty-nine she suffered the usual fate of older women as she applied for a variety of jobs. In 1936 she had hopes of earning money as a paid organizer for the Business and Professional Women's Club, developing a grand scheme for uniting in a national organization all working women, including those who worked in the home. Finally, at the age of sixty-two, just before the outbreak of World War II, she obtained a temporary appointment as a teacher of small children at a private school in Hampstead.

TBG's brief association with the Business and Professional Women's Club seems to have re-awakened her desire that feminism could become a mass movement. Although there is no commentary on the matter in her papers, her activities after 1935 suggest that the years since 1914 had convinced her that elimination of women's disabilities – necessary changes in such matters as marriage and divorce, employment, and equal opportunity in every sphere – required the active involvement of women in government. Further, she may have seen the Labour Party's rise to power in those years as having captured the minds of ordinary citizens to such a degree that they would find the ideas set forth in *The Consumer in Revolt* less attractive. Or she may have perceived that the complexities of post-war society were so great that her earlier ideas simply would not work. Whatever the reason, in 1937, she returned to a position of leadership in the WFL, concentrating eventually upon its Women's Electoral Committee, which, by the end of World War II, she had managed to carry over into Women for Westminster, a national organization devoted to electing women to office at every level of government.

For two years she served as national chair of Women for Westminster, with the goal of establishing a headquarters in London as a center for all national women's groups. But the post-war atmosphere in Britain, as in many other nations, put feminist issues low on almost everyone's list of priorities. Women for Westminster encountered financial difficulties. Refusing an offer from the much smaller, but much wealthier feminist lobbying organization, the Six Point Group, TBG arranged for Women for Westminster to merge with the National Women Citizens' Association. By that time more than seventy years of age, she never again attempted to lead a national organization but continued to play an active role as a feminist, lobbying Bills in Parliament, testifying before the Royal Commission on Marriage and Divorce, helping in women's election campaigns, working with the Married Women's Association on a Bill to strengthen the rights of divorced women and their children, participating in conferences on the feminist agenda, and traveling frequently to speak on topics that ranged from her unsentimental approach to love and marriage to the history of the suffrage movement. Ever the prophetic and constructive critic, seeing herself always as a kind of conscience of the cause, she refused to give up hope that the movement would continue and grow stronger, and in her eighties urged on those who appeared to falter in the struggle.

In the late 1940s, recognizing the need to educate a whole new generation of women, TBG had turned to her writing again. In addition to working out her ideas on such topics as patriarchal language, male deities, sex relations, women's fashions, nuclear warfare, and the examples of 'women pioneers,' she attempted three major projects: her own autobiography, a history of the suffrage movement in Britain, and a biography of Charlotte Despard. For the history, she received little encouragement from the publishers she queried, from the few surviving suffragettes, or from younger members of the organizations in which she was involved. The autobiography was never completed. The Despard biography, begun after TBG was eighty, she abandoned in her grief over Fred's death in 1961.

To her personal grief in 1961 was added the distress of witnessing the failure of women teachers and civil servants to pursue the cause of equal pay for all women after they had won it for themselves, the final dissolution of the WFL, and the obvious senescence of the Suffragette Fellowship. Within a year, she was stricken with cancer and with characteristic courage and clear-sightedness refused surgery. She died in 1964 at the age of eighty-seven.

For TBG, perhaps, her work after 1914 seemed commonplace, and, given her gifts of courage, percipience, and determination, she could believe she had failed herself and her cause. As a writer, she had turned from her first dream – poetry – to become instead a propagandist and political theorist. Though her ear for rhythmic language and her talent for transforming insight into apt phrases had served her cause well, she had moved from writing to leading, first in an effort to live her life as a practical feminist and then in an attempt to put political theory into practice and inaugurate a mass feminist movement. As a leader of women, she had not allowed herself to be successful; for she would not compromise, and she refused to be the kind of leader described in *The Consumer in Revolt* – she who ceases to lead as soon as holding on to leadership becomes more important than principle. As a lifelong analyst of the feminist movement, one who hoped 'to make the instrument . . . more fitted and more fitting for the task,'[26] she had been misunderstood by those incapable of realizing that her real objection was to a divided movement, and that what she proposed was a revolution in the minds of all women over several generations.

But to those of us who serve the cause of feminism one hundred years after her birth, if her accomplishment was 'common-place,' then let us all do commonplace work. For, as TBG added to those final words of *The Militant Suffrage Movement*, 'If we do our work as well as we can, what else matters?'

Carol McPhee
Ann FitzGerald
San Luis Obispo, California
1986

# Part I
# *The Genesis of a Feminist:*
## *Autobiographical Fragments*

### Prefatory Note

TBG began to make notes for her autobiography sometime in the 1940s and continued to work at it intermittently until about a year before her death in 1964. Beginning with descriptions of her family background, she presents a fairly complete picture of her life through her meeting with Emmeline Pankhurst in late 1903. After that date, the fragments contain the descriptions of only a few isolated episodes.

The autobiographical fragments are in rough draft form with many of the flaws of such drafts: material for insertion written in margins or sometimes on separate pages; inconsistencies in spelling, punctuation, and capitalization; missing words and incomplete dates. Therefore, to make the fragments as readable as possible, the material has been edited to incorporate marginal notes where they seemed to fit; to eliminate inconsistencies in matters of mechanics; and wherever possible, to supply within brackets necessary words or dates.

TBG wrote several versions of some episodes in her life. The editors' selections were made to present a continuous narrative, as far as possible following her many outlines, and to emphasize the topics they believe were most important to TBG. Some sections move between two or three versions of the same story, such shifts being signalled by a subheading. As a result of the use of several versions, there is occasional overlap and contradiction in matters of detail.

Cuts within the texts have been kept to the minimum to avoid as much as possible the distraction of ellipsis marks and brackets. In these selections, as in others throughout the collection, the omission of an entire paragraph or more of the original text is indicated by three asterisks.

The necessity to make selections, of course, means that some interesting fragments are not reproduced here and await the attention of scholars in the Fawcett Library. Most of the fragments which appear now reside in the TBG Collection Boxes 397 and 398; two are in Box 375 TBG's notes for a Biography of Charlotte Despard. The editors cannot be more specific in citation because most of the autobiographical fragments were uncatalogued when they copied them in 1983. Therefore, to identify the different TBG versions of the same event, they have used the subheading 'From . . .', and TBG's title for the section or the first few words if she did not provide a title.

# My Mother

## From 'Birth and Childhood'

[Helen Wilson, TBG's mother, was the daughter of John Wilson and Mary Orrell, who had founded a department store in Preston, Lancashire. Mary Orrell Wilson died after having given birth to three children, George, Margaret, and Helen.]

. . . My mother first. All her childish memories were happy ones; even after her mother died, the first stepmother gave the family a sense of unity and comfort . . . Helen [said she] used to 'talk to my mother after she was dead. It was like praying. And Stepmother Ann understood.'

. . . The stepmother's child in turn was expected and both died. And the father, twice bereaved, with two girls approaching their teens and an older boy, found his remedy for homemaking in sending them away to school. The boy, and every boy he fathered through his long life, was sent to the Marist Brothers' College at Dumfries. The girls [attended] . . . various convents of the Sisters of Notre Dame. With intervals and holidays in Preston with him, these institutions became their permanent homes, far more of the years of their youth being spent away from home than at it. He was a genial and generous father to the three, and home had a glamour for them. They had only short intervals for its full enjoyment, for there was another marriage, another stepmother, another child and another twofold loss; by which time the son and daughters must have begun to feel fear and distress about the juxtaposition of their father and re-marriage. Questions or criticism were impossible in those days to children brought up as they had been, but forbidden expression did not remove deep-down anxiety.

There was a period of widowerhood this time; years went by; the boy George came of age; Margaret and Helen went from their

Manchester Convent to the head house of the order at Namur in the valley of the Meuse. Margaret applied to be received as a postulant for the conventual life. Helen had a holiday at home, filling with delight the position of hostess in the home – temporary hostess, but full of delightful anticipation; for in the following summer her long convent schooling was to end. She came home then, unwarned, to find her father married for the fourth time. Once bitterly she said, 'I came home to find I had no home!' The quick-glancing Irish maid, dark-eyed, dark-haired with the sunny skin – the Spanish type of Irish beauty – had changed over in her absence to become mistress of the house, and her father had not warned her. She never called this place-usurper anything but 'Mrs Wilson.'

She was approaching her eighteenth birthday and from then until she was twenty-one and claimed her right to decide for herself, she was the young pendant female in her father's or her brother's households, kept in lady-like impotence while the relatives looked around for a husband. It was the 1860s. Her desire at this time, almost her passion, was to return to the convent and become a nun like her sister, who progressed through the white-veil novice stage to the full acceptance of the black veil, and with a new name of Sister Mary Beatrice. But Helen's plea to join her was rejected. She was judged to have no vocation, and no other reason was ever given, or is ever given (unless customs have changed in conventual matters since my own youth). But of the two, Margaret had the sturdier mind and the more practical equipment. Her temperament was more equable. She had been received with warmth. Such young women, especially those with a *dot*, are always of high value in a teaching order of nuns. Sometimes they receive flattering encouragement even before they have given their future careers serious consideration, and the whole atmosphere of a residential convent school is such as to exalt the conventual life. Perhaps too, knowing nothing of the fourth marriage when Helen left them, they might have felt that it was more Christian to leave the poor father one daughter to manage his home. They were justified also in remembering that so very recently Helen had anticipated with pleasure this very same way of life and that the rebound to the call of the convent was probably the measure of her disappointment rather than a vocation to the religious life. They were wrong, however. There was never a woman born who was, by this time, so shaped and moulded for a quiet life of service, prayer and contemplation . . . [as] poor Helen.

These two heavy blows shaped and darkened her life. To the sympathetic few among her circle she was 'Poor Helen.' The old aunts and a friend or two chorused together in my hearing, 'She could be so gay.' 'She had a lovely laugh.' 'In the country she was uplifted.' 'She ran on smiling and chattering like a little river.' 'And so kind as well when her proud heart did not remember.' All these things were said to her daughter and at her daughter's ear, and they were true . . . .

What was left for her to do with her life after these two rejections? In the 1860s the better class woman educated by the standard of her time and with narrow means had no openings but marriage, governess employment or residence with a family of relatives in a sort of dignified semi-dependence, sometimes a cheap servant. Helen early decided that she would have none of these. She would follow what had now become the family pattern. As soon as she was of age she would open a shop. When the time came, she won agreement from father and brother and was introduced to the counter for a time in both Friargate businesses. She enjoyed journeys to the Manchester warehouses with one or the other of them, learning the way to choose stock and the business of keeping accounts. Then her father passed over to her a sum that he deemed sufficient to start a business and keep her going until it was established, making the wise condition that she must not live or run the business alone.

This was no handicap to the eager girl. The Literary Circle to which she belonged had given her pleasant contacts. The congregation of the church she attended contained relatives and friends and the friends of friends. Her demure smallness, her pretty dignity, her fierce flashes of momentary protest, her laughter when the clouds were thrust away – they all endeared her to those who knew her. It was easy to find two other young women who would share her independent life. All this to them, in that day, was a wonderful adventure.

There had to be a certain element of the irrational in their choice of a place to open this shop . . . They chose Blackpool. Of course it was not the Blackpool that we know today. It was a small seaside town then, a little boisterous perhaps when the Lancashire towns had their 'Wakes Weeks,' but otherwise neither noisy nor flamboyant.

There was the great attraction of the sea. There was also the prospect of a few months' heavy labour in catering for the visitors and a longer stretch of near-leisure in the off season when the refreshment of sea and country could be enjoyed and literary interests could be cultivated. The first shop was opened there with anticipation amounting to glee. No such mundane first start ever gave greater happiness. Three emancipated *femes soles* set their barque afloat on the front – actually on the Promenade – all tensed up to win their battle and enjoy the venture. The names of the colleagues come to me as Miss Boileau and Miss Matthews, but there were others named at times and some changes, so such details must be taken as just recollections, a little indefinite. I can vouch, however, for the truth of the general picture.

The shop of liberty was opened. 'It did very well,' said Helen, with a half sigh, 'very good takings indeed during the season, but the off season was too long.' The lovely rest, the walks, the jaunts, the literary evenings could not be enjoyed when the bank balance and the rent and rates were totalled up against the almost microscopic daily sales. The young venturers had to face a change to a town where there was a possibility of more regular trade.

That the new site should include the possibility of refreshment for the spirit was a prerequisite, but they were determined to be very practical indeed. They chose Barrow-in-Furness where an industrial boom had created a mushroom town 'with furnaces and foundries and factories,' [and] as my mother wrote, 'all their wage-earners needing underclothing for themselves and their families. This must bring good trade,' and 'for refreshment to keep us healthy and content the Lake District is within a few miles, some mountains actually in sight – and a great wealth of sea air.'

It was a good choice but proved impermanent. The independent young lady shopkeepers attracted more than custom. Admiring and interested young men began to appear: local schoolmasters and clerks, men who had made business contacts with the three incomers, young men coming to jobs in the new town – some from Preston with personal introductions – local young men of the farmer class who had forsaken the land to win fortune in this expanding town . . . . 'It was embarrassing,' said my mother. 'Even if I had wanted to marry, there were too many. They changed the quiet harmony of our lives.' But she was to marry one of them after all.

One colleague succumbed first and married, as my father said, into 'what became a first class job with the booming Prudential Society.' The two left reacted differently to the new conditions. My mother was still subject to family pressures that she could not escape, and Grandfather controlled her finances. Money for carrying over, for removal, for shop fittings – the new capital – all had to be obtained from him and could only be obtained by strenuous effort. And he had never much believed in the business start which included consideration of literary relaxation and the Lakes. These were boons to follow after success. He found her habit of mind impractical; her future was an anxiety to him. And he had other anxieties: his new young wife was presenting him very regularly with a new family of healthy children. She, and they, all survived.

It was now the 1870s and at this opportune moment William . . . Billington . . . came to the mushroom town from Preston, via America, and he lifted up his lovely tenor voice in the chapel where my mother worshipped as he had done some years before in the grander edifice in the home town. He called with a letter from her father. 'William has returned from America,' he wrote. 'He has hopes of making a good future in Barrow. As he has no other friends there I am telling him to call on you,' and as a P.S., . . . 'You will remember him. He sang in the choir – very fine tenor. Surname "Billington," Mrs Thomson's brother.' This 'William-surname-Billington' was a source of laughter for Mother all her life. Though after the spontaneous ripple she would fall silent. William did not find the joke so amusing.

Here, poor lady, was her fate, though it took some time and pains to subdue her. Her protestation that she did not wish to be married to anyone was repeated *ad nauseam* and considered as almost sinful, especially when it emerged that the families on both sides were united in the young suitor's support. She refused, and consented, and refused again; she would not see him, would not be touched, would not read his letters. Any young man who was so treated would have taken himself off had he not been deeply in love, wanting in imagination and misled by supporting relatives from both sides. 'She was too long in the convent,' they explained. 'The nuns make girls prudish and fearful. She has never been awakened to her own natural needs. There are many such cases. With marriage to a loving husband they become happy wives.'

He believed them enough to carry on. She actually fought to the last day, but they were married. Her last straw of resistance had been taken from her by the withdrawal of her business colleague who had endured the time of wooing and was harassed beyond endurance by the storms and tension which enveloped them all.

## From untitled fragment, beginning 'The prudery of that day . . .'

The women of the family were as urgent as the men in overwhelming the reluctant Helen. [William's] . . . sister Margaret and [Helen's] . . . stepmother were charged later by the desperately unhappy bride with having made an unholy alliance against her, and with having magnified to William the value of her little business and her expectations from her father . . . so as to confirm his sexual attraction with a financial one.

Be that as it may, the unsuitable match was accomplished and the unhappy marriage consummated in an atmosphere of strain, tears and hysteria. Poor groom. He had no imaginative insight; the tone and texture of his attitude was wholly that of his day; even the respect and admiration which he always showed to his wife in their periods of peace were not for her as a woman but for a more talented and better educated person who was thus entitled to recognition.

## From 'First Portion Life'

Their eldest child, Beatrice, was born in January, 1876, a nine-month-bride's child to a reluctant bride. In October, 1877, I was born and two years later my brother. There followed a period of ten years or so in which four other infants were either still-born or were miscarried; and the birth . . . [of] another girl . . . complete[d] the family. This was either the end of Helen's fertility or the end of her acquiescence.

When Fate, through my father, burdened Helen with me, she made her first effort to escape. She ran away from William and her Preston home to Manchester and sought refuge with the three spinster sisters of her dead mother, with whom she thought she could live and bring up her babies, earning her keep by helping them in their refined millinery business in what was then the better class suburb of Ardwick Green. But loving her and pitying her unhappiness, they were too religious and too law-abiding to resist Church and family pressure and sent her home again with loving, reluctant tears. It was much less difficult to send her home again when she reappeared with a two-year-old and a baby in arms. A callous cousin who saw humour in everything used in after years to chortle about Helen's return. 'It must have been really funny,' I remember him saying, all agrin. 'It took three fathers to bring her back home – her own handsome father, your injured father and the holy father from the adjacent church. Poor little Helen, just trapped she was!'

Poor Helen indeed. For years thereafter her running away had to be only symbolical – long periods of prayer and peace in one of the Catholic chapels or churches in the home town or stolen days in the country alone or with a child or two, away from what had been from the beginning a prison house with its alien standards.

## From 'Last Version. Birth and Childhood'

The next stage she called Calvary – marriage, sex relations, pregnancy, children. 'Poor little victims,' she called us . . . . 'His victims and mine!' and then she would fall to praying for forgiveness, being specially tender with us, and speaking gently of William. 'He does not understand. He means to be kind.' With a flash of defiance, 'If all men are so driven, God help them! They need help.'

I was more with my mother than any other of her children while this rebellion lasted. In my later teens, just before I left home, there came a mellowing of spirit, and the rare laugh and the dancing merriment of her blue eyes came more often. There was a new shadow on the home at that time but it was not the overwhelming domination which was the prevalent atmosphere of so many earlier years, which threatened even in the intervals of sunshine. I felt it as a crouching threat always there even when her laugh was merry and William's jokes called forth the united family laughter. I would love these interludes, almost praying for them to come and to stay. But the same evenings I might be sitting shivering on the stairs, as I did so often, in a flannelette nightgown, out from my bed when the raised voices clanged and rattled in my ears and I was all tensed up to rush down to them and defend my mother. I never dared. I knew she would have forbidden it, resented it. As the storm died down, I would slip back to bed generally weeping and chilled to the bone. My cold shivering body would awaken my sister, who would murmur protests. 'They are quarrelling again,' I would blubber. But her philosophy was to join with them when they were happy and not to hear them when they were not. Certainly it saved her a lot of suffering, and probably contributed to peace in the house. No antagonism flashed between her and Father after a night of marital dispute. I never learned to hide the flame.

# My Childhood and Education[1]

## From untitled fragment beginning 'There are three . . .'

There are three close-contacting groups in a child's world: the mother; other adults in authority; and other children; and from a beginning in which my words ran like a river in spate and my vocabulary was astonishing, they all helped to make me a silent child. I see Helen and me talking when I was too young to talk. My extensive range of words were picked parrot-like from her. With her there were no inhibitions, the to-and-fro current of thought and words was like a pulse beating in the two of us. I did not know any other person – ever – so closely as I did her in the days before the child is expected to know anything.

But this communion of spirit, the interchange of words, this giving and receiving began to fade . . . Helen withdrew. There were questions in the wide blue eyes, checks to speech, admonitions in stern words. The sensitive religious spirit was disturbed by the questioning child who asked confidently the impossible questions and made without fear the infant judgments on the world around her. They were said, it would appear, before Helen had expected them, before she had prepared for them, before she quite knew what line to take in dealing with them. It was obvious, however, that the child had been talked with too much and that it was developing an undesirable precocity, . . . leading heaven knows into what kinds of danger.

So the talks grew shorter and less mutual, and would be abruptly stopped. Odd shreds of talks survive: there were a number of 'Why's?' thwarted sometimes with 'Hush!' or 'That is not a good thing to say!' or when a strong view was stoutly expressed, 'Don't talk like a grown-up, child,' or 'You are much too young to understand.' So the wide communicating current was dammed up in some measure . . . [Others in the family] understood, . . . respected, . . . shared, even if they did not agree, but the [cutting down of] full flow and range of the current between them . . . was a deprivation to the young Teresa.

The child's confident expectation of contact, of interchange, is a magic possession, bringing nourishment and enlightenment and courage to the small adventurer. The breakup of that confidence throws the child's development into interior darkness. It leaves the little individual mind much alone . . .

I was early classed as a stodgy, silent child at school, and one whose few words were not always easily followed or approved. The nuns were kindly and quiet, like Helen, but they were a little awesome and mysterious and their kindness had a different quality. The natural tendency to confide and question stopped bubbling out of me. I watched and then chattered to my sister and brother all the way home.

Except for Little Sister Agnes and Big Sister Agnes, the teaching staff of the day school was very impermanent. All kinds of nuns – straight from Ireland with pink cheeks and blue eyes and strong brogues; little plumpy smooth nuns from Holland; black-eyed, hardy ones from France; and heavy handed and footed large ones speaking with an accent which made their words incomprehensible to me. I sank into silence there before I was seven. But when I spoke, I found I said something startling. So I spoke seldom. This became the atmosphere of school, and I was variously classified as a dreamer, a withdrawn, somnolent child, an odd little thing, secretive and rather odd in speech, who wasn't always satisfied by the most reasonable of answers. During all my convent years I loved two nuns only and they are so much shadows to me now that I do not remember their names. One was old and almost abrupt in manner, but we seemed to understand each other. She talked with me, not to or at me, and I had no fear of responding to her. The other was a novice with a white veil, and I met her again years later when I had a brief try-out as a candidate for pupil teacher. She was the only one who understood my awkwardness and won my confidence. The last and most daring thing she said to me was, 'Don't be a nun. Don't let them make you into a nun. Your mind ranges too far afield . . . . No good would come of it. God bless you my child!'

## From 'Mother and Business'

One became conscious of being planned for very early. There were two simultaneous futures indicated as desirable . . . by a word here or chance comment there, a hope expressed, a criticism of some objectionable way of life. The great first dream of my mother was that we should all four dedicate ourselves to religion – three nuns and a priest or at least a monk would have given her almost too much happiness and glory. Before and above everything else she watched us with that hope for years. But when, children-like, we began to play at religious ceremonies in the back garden – the three elder ones – and were found posing as Great Holy Ones, or reduced to vulgar laughter by the antics of would-be angels, . . . doubt and dismay crept in.

The alternative future crept more and more to the front, as the cherished first dream was dissipated. The second was a common-sense down-to-earth one.[2] It was the dream of a family business in retail drapery and clothing. My mother was definitely unfitted both by temperament and training for a business career. But to the end of her life, she did not realise this. Her business ventures before she married could be considered as partial successes, brought to premature end by external circumstances before they were firmly established. But she saw herself as the head of a family shop-keeping firm, the manager and buyer, with her four children – later it became three when she reluctantly realised that her son had no business-aptitude whatever – . . . specially prepared to start and run departments. She regarded her father as having been in his small way the inventor of the departmental trading shop – the general store – in which both men and women and children could find their clothing needs supplied in addition to household linen and drapery.

So we were all to learn how to run a shop and have a special trade training for one department. My [elder] sister was to be fitted to take charge of a dressmaking department, I of a millinery one, my brother of the gentleman's section of the business – while Mother managed and acted as buyer for 'the firm.' The bookkeeping and financial side was rather vague, . . . beginning in plans for a book-keeping apprenticeship for my brother, and then transferred to an additional job for me.

There was an entirely unanimous and unvoiced rejection of this maternal dream by the three elder children – Beatrice wished to be a musician, and I a writer of books and a fighter in great causes, while my brother, left-handed and inventive in small practical ways, wished only to be allowed to show what a left hand could do with a pencil or a tool.

. . . [Nevertheless] Mother's gallant effort to realise her dream ruled our home life for years. She had a number of elderly relatives, in the Orrell connection, chiefly, all of whom seemed to have warm feeling for her and some small legacy to leave. She inherited small sums three or four times. Also she drew on her share of her father's allotted inheritance – his share-and-share-alike plan, leaving it open for any child to claim during his life a part of what they would otherwise inherit at his death. During our childhood such lump-sums served to open little drapery and children's wear shops four times, every one of which having too little capital lasted . . . only a year or so, after which we were back in our cottage-type private home. Three of these shops were in the best streets in town and could have succeeded, if it had not been for the unrealistic optimism displayed by both Mother and Father – especially Father – who expected the new business to begin contributing to the support of the family before it was on its feet. . . .

## From 'Mother in Business 2: From Pillar to Post'

There was more than one reason why Helen would never make a good shopkeeper. Seven years of convent school influence had their effect, but there was also lack of the common touch. She greeted people with genuine and charming friendliness when she knew them and approved of them. The ordinary working-class shopper found her distantly polite – not at all the type of the brusquely genial Blackburn type. A rude or facetious customer would freeze her to ice. One who was vulgar or foul-spoken would be ordered off the premises. And she had a failing she passed on to me: we would much rather give than sell.

She hoped for the custom of the convent. With some sixty nuns, boarders, pupil-teachers in training and the small secular staff, there must be quite a large consumption of drapery goods which could be obtained through our business. But after only one trial, that hope was abandoned. The nuns put in charge of this department were either chosen because they were natural cheese-parers, or the financial stability of the convent depended on their being so. The chief practice I remember was the demand for second-quality job lots of towels, dusters, print remnants, which, having been passed on to them with a charge that barely covered the costs entailed, were then gone over by the nun concerned and all items which were not 'firsts' in quality either rejected or used to cut down the charge until the transaction was a gift, not a sale. . . .

The second King Street shop was the most successful and might possibly have succeeded but for a flash of particularly unreasonable optimism in which [Helen] . . . actually opened a small branch shop in Ewood . . . then an outlying village. I remember it well because I was the allotted victim who had to serve in it. It was one of a row of cottages with ribbon strips of gardens and had had its front window altered in a minimal degree to fit it for showing goods for sale by an earlier optimist. But it was presented to me as my chance to make a beginning for the family business and for myself. After a month there, the customers averaged about two per day. Then a bright little leaflet was printed which I carried round the neighbourhood handing to people I met in the street and popping through letter boxes. This increased the custom to about four a day and a high level of six or seven on Saturdays. The empty cottage behind and above the shop front room was then sublet and the communicating door fastened up and barred. That enlarged the income by 3/6 per week. The end, of course, was inevitable.

The venture had only one advantage for me. I carried books with me and read the hours away. Under pledge to Mother not to study or write lest I should not know a customer had arrived for a reel of cotton, there was no objection to Thackeray and Dickens sharing my incarceration. I had a new volume from the library every week and discovered my lifelong preference for Thackeray.

## From 'Mother and Business'

. . . The poor lady, defeated again and again, persisted indomitably in the training of her two elder girls. Whatever else they got in the way of further education, they must have practical knowledge of the trades which would equip them for running businesses, and though concessions were made to us both – Beatrice's music training and my writing ambitions – [we] were advanced as far as was judged necessary and narrow means permitted. [When she had] . . . passed her second examination, my sister's tuition ceased and she apparently rested content with her dressmaking job and the extra money giving piano lessons brought her. But there was no clear avenue of advance for me, with certificates to be won or positions to be secured. From ten to seventeen I was in rebellion against the shop idea, and there was no clear way open so far as we knew by which I could escape it into literary, even a journalistic, life. The first stage could be accomplished by becoming a pupil teacher. But here the impractical type of education then given at the Blackburn Convent Day School and its low standard even of that type, were against me.

## From 'Blackburn Convent of Notre Dame'

There were reasons for the deficiencies of this little establishment. The teaching orders of monks and nuns had been back in England only for two generations . . . and had had to build up their institutions from the ground: two or three nuns at first in a room of the small house they rented, then a larger group, as the children [from] . . . families [of] the old faith were brought to them for education. At the beginning [the nuns] . . . were mostly of foreign birth – French, Belgian, Dutch – and their most pressing need was to secure postulants for the order from the young Catholic women they reached. As the national determination to create an educated nation increased, so did the problems of the Sisters and their advisers. They were poor and presented with problems requiring much expenditure, and their only reliable income must be self-earned. Fees from the pupils of their day and residential convent schools never made a large total. There were too many Catholics still in the lower income groups who had to be permitted to pay what they could.

The only reasonably large item of income came from the state education grants which were given to the schools which were inspected by the Board of Education officers and adjudged up to the required standard. The school attached to the Roman Catholic parish churches came into this category and were in general staffed by nuns of one teaching order or another. The school managers received the grant and from it paid the nuns, mistresses, teachers, and pupil teachers the salaries which kept the convent going.

Hence the convent's first need was to get as quickly as possible as many religious-minded young British women to become nuns, to prepare for and pass the three qualifying Board of Education examinations and so to become . . . partner[s] in providing the income on which the convent could live. Its own schools within its own walls [i.e. those schools not attached to a parish church] were the latest to be brought under national control, first because there was the fear of national interference with the atmosphere of the religious instruction arrangements, and second because there had for years to be some provision to employ the many foreign nuns who were learning our language before they could hope to qualify and for those who failed to satisfy the examiners.

The school within the convent, therefore, in such cases became the dumping ground for the unqualified and unready and willy-nilly carried the atmosphere of the old amateur Dames' School into the later period. My mother had been much better educated than we were by the same order of nuns working under different conditions.

There was much anxiety among the responsible clerics about this matter, as I was later informed by Canon Richardson, one of the special inspectorate appointed by the Bishop of Salford to raise the position of their schools adequately and so reach security for them in the national system. He told me that the school I had been unlucky enough to attend was rated then at the lowest rung of the ladder. . . .

## From 'Mother and Business'

We were taught there to be Catholic young ladies on the lines of the education given to our grandmothers. There were no oral lessons, no demonstrations, no analysis or breaking down of problems. We sat quietly in rows of desks, learned from books, and our work was corrected by the nun who was mistress of the moment from the answers at the back of a similar book.

. . . We had long periods of devotional instruction – reiterative and unenlightening – and Friday afternoon was devoted entirely to Behaviour. 'Manners make the lady,' we were taught, 'not money or learning, not beauty.' So we were practised in opening a door, entering and leaving a room, bringing in a letter, a message, a tray or a gift, asking the mothers of girl friends to permit their daughters to attend a party, receiving a caller in the absence of parents, and so on! As I noted then, there was one item of instruction which stamped the whole lady-idea as snobbishly outrageous. We were mainly the children of upper working-class people – black-coated employees, 'tie and collar men' and . . . local shopkeepers, with a small element of professional men's children. There were only three families who owned a carriage in my day. Yet there was a lesson given at intervals (which occupied the whole of a Friday afternoon) on entering and leaving a carriage, leaving cards or gifts and instructing the coachman as to your next destination, during which I was either a dreaming absentee, a caustic critic or a clumsy conscript. These performances, I believe, gave [me] a taste for honest, gruff crudeness; though my mother's natural, quiet dignity pervaded our home, this wasteful and insincere school snobbery strengthened the Robert Burns 'A man's a man' attitude of my mind.

Such a foundation was no good when it came to the standard of elementary education required of a candidate for the teaching apprenticeship, the one easy way to learning open to the poor!

My mother made two efforts for me: [first] an examination in which I failed – writing a four-page essay instead of the five hundred words prescribed and failing to recognise the meaning of arithmetical terms, thus reversing the problem to be solved, and . . . answering history questions at an argumentative length which indicated strong views rather than sound knowledge.

This first reverse, as my parents saw it, shut me out of the only chance of pupil-teacher training available while living at home, and to them the matter was settled. There was a weary interval in which I was sent to work in a shop and then in a warehouse as elementary beginnings for the family business destiny, during which my ravenous reading turned into a personal fight for knowledge. The reading appetite became more disciplined and was fed by any enlightening book I could lay hands on and by looking out for and picking up information from newspapers and magazines. Thus I constantly reminded the family that I still had my cherished ambitions. Also, though much less usefully, I spent laborious hours trying to learn how to make my sums come right.

## From 'Blackburn Convent of Notre Dame'

My infatuation with books and eagerness for study were regarded as a childish addiction to reading, selfish and unsociable, rather than admirable, until I began to write. [TBG sent a story to a Catholic weekly and it was accepted. Her family arranged] . . . lessons of one hour each on English literature with the headmaster of the Catholic boys high school – who set me an essay one week and corrected it the next. My spelling appalled him. I worked hard at that and at a primer on syntax which was brief and bright . . . and registered where my old school grammar book had failed. But after the school holidays interrupted the course, it was never resumed. Perhaps it was the 1/- per lesson fee – poverty pursuing us – or perhaps a new shop was under discussion. I cannot remember.

## From 'Mother and Business'

. . . I was nearing the prescribed age at which the pupil-teacher training then began. So after the tale appeared, a new approach was made to the school authorities of our parish, where a most understanding nun was headmistress. On the strength of my writing they took me in for a trial period; and this time I satisfied them as to my ability to learn as well as demonstrating an unsuspected capacity to control a class of forty girls only a year or two my juniors and to

41

awaken in them new interest in their English and history, subjects on which I had fed my hunger even then for years.

But this effort was doomed to fail too. The teaching order of nuns known as the Sisters of Notre Dame had to keep their convents financially afloat by making every branch of their activity pay, and the training of teachers could only be conducted without financial loss to their house if it were done on a collective basis and with each student-teacher serving half time receiving tuition and half time imparting it. By housing all the area candidates, they received the government grant for them all and could manage to cover expenses of keep and tuition with a very moderate contribution from the parents. In our case, the parents had to clothe their child, support it during the holidays and pay a sum of about £26 a year to cover board and residence in the convent. This was an appalling amount. It simply could not be managed. The aunt who was the headmistress of the Wigan Convent Girls High School was approached for advice and possible help. She had to say 'No.' Nuns who inherit or expect to inherit do not dispose personally of their inheritances. The disposal may sometimes be in accordance with their wishes – or it may be contrary to them. In our case Sister Mary Beatrice had already supplemented our mother's payments for the fees of the three of us at the Blackburn Convent Day School – 'and had not this child failed in such and such an examination?'

\* \* \*

Four years were to pass now before I found a way out, and if at times my hopes almost died and my personal efforts became desultory – I wakened up to resentment again and to self-contempt that I was letting the years go by. I was not quite without practical ideas as to how I could find my way, but they were not definite and covered such points as the opportunities for getting sewing or domestic jobs in schools or colleges on terms which included a very low pay and a right to tuition . . . But generally I had no way mapped out. I wrote a little in the hope of publication – with very sparse success. I eased my heart with poetry, reading it – and writing it. I read hungrily the wildest assortment of books. I began a great novel three or four times. I gave up and viewed the world resentfully. I set up as a critic at large, held forth to any listener on the deficiencies of men and women and especially of the powerful, criticised preachers and statesmen and was ribald about the Saints, questioned the morality of the Old Testament and the efficacy of the New, enthralled by my daring the small group of friends who shared our leisure time walks and talks – and all the time read avidly.

. . . The immediate duties expected of me – the millinery, the shops, the round of household tasks – they were not a living part of my life at all. The family business didn't exist for me. The employments I was put into were of no interest to me, just a part of the convict routine to which fate had committed me. I was a sort of puppet-person serving a sentence of imprisonment – but some day I would be free. Yet all this time waiting for my own real life to begin, I loved my mother passionately, shared many mutual interests with her, resented her lot, its wastage . . . and planned ways in which she could be sheltered and comforted. Without this tie, I might have run away from home too early and perhaps disastrously.

## From 'My Job and Education'

It was then that Mother had an attack of conscience. It stemmed, I think, from her step-sisters being actually sent as boarders – the high-level resident – into the same convent which we attended as Day Scholars, a much lower-grade institution. The days in which this had happened were long gone but . . . [were] recalled to her by a visit to Preston when she realised that they had remained . . . [at the Convent School] for three years after we, at twelve or thirteen, had been regarded as sufficiently educated to begin training to work.

There had been one or two embarrassing incidents while the step-sisters and the daughters were – both sets – in attendance and there had been meetings undesired by either. The 'rich' girls had no desire to have their shabby relatives looked over by their schoolfellows, and the shabby relatives had no desire to be seen. But the goodhearted nuns had on two occasions arranged a meeting at which no one of the four of us had behaved naturally.

Helen had written to [the] Mother Superior after the second event asking that it should not be repeated.

It was on that occasion only that I ever heard her say one word of judgment on her father. 'That they should be sent here,' she exploded, 'to humiliate my girls! All they have has been built up on *my* mother's money and her own grandchildren have to take the lower place!'

It was two years later, when Beatrice had passed her first pianoforte examination and I had been prematurely removed from school to learn to be a milliner, that the visits to Preston rekindled this resentment . . . .

And out of the blue . . . Beatrice and myself . . . were informed that we were going back to school, this time as boarders, for a further stage in education and a chance of teacher training that at first

43

I thought was specially arranged for me. But we found it was a matter of economy. Our aunt, . . . because of my mother's appeal, had arranged that we should be received as probationers in the pupil-teacher department for a period of two years with the opportunity of continuing throughout the course if we worked well and were found suitable. The charges for this type of boarder were much reduced. Beatrice stayed a year. I only about eight months. She was approved and could have continued. I was uneven in scholastic achievement, a misfit in the classes because I was so far behind my years in routine matters and so far beyond in the literary subjects. Also I was not responsive to the small scale, literally-to-be-obeyed routine discipline which I often ignored, not always consciously. To crown my ill-luck, I was at the age for a natural change for which I had been ill-prepared.

## From 'Birth and Childhood'

I came home from St Helen's silent with resentment, not at Helen, not at the nuns – by all but one of them I had been kindly received and assisted. The door of my desire was opened, and I was only unhappy with them because I did not know why my physical condition was disturbed and my nerves and temper on edge. The only guidance I had was vague and hence alarming. 'You are a girl still,' said my mother, 'but you will soon begin to turn into a woman. It isn't a change to be afraid of, and you have Beatrice with you. She will help you.' That and some strange items packed in my trunk only thrust me more deeply into a shamed and estranged silence. Three years of thwarted hopes and now, at this moment, these threatened bodily changes in myself. I did not want these changes. I hated them. Probably the resentful anxiety showed itself in taciturnity and just tipped the scale against the authorities helping me over the period of strain. As it was, I was sent home, though permitted to call on my aunt at the Wigan Catholic Girls High School on my way. She comforted me with pledges that I was only a little more disturbed than was usual at my age, that a few months at home was the worst to be expected, that I must keep up with the subjects in which I was weak and be ready to return without losing my class rating. 'You are two years younger than your sister,' she said, 'and now in the same class. There is no need for you to worry.'

I went on home still cowed, yet ready for any effort within my reach, but the parental attitude was that I had had my chance and lost it. 'We'd do better to send her to a mill,' growled William. 'No child of mine . . . !' stormed Helen; but she did find a dressmaking workroom in which I was to get inside knowledge of this side of the business 'for the future' and where I was known by the friendly Catholic owner as a very good odd job girl!

\*　　\*　　\*

So Beatrice had the full first term of this 'higher education' – not caring much about it, not seeking or treasuring it, for she had no desire to earn her living by teaching, unless indeed it was teaching music – preferably the piano. She was a much more placid child than I, without resentments against the calls made on her or any planning for her of her way of life. . . . She was much more the type of girl the convents welcomed, merry, responsive without any clumsiness or shyness, willing, engaging and useful on the musical side; fair, blue-eyed and rosy. But she had a capacity for going her own way quietly. The convent had no charm for her; to nuns and priests and other clericals she gave attention and respect, but she did not expect of them any outstanding super-human virtue, as I did. To her their dedication to a religious life left them still fallible human beings who could be met and judged as one would judge any other person. So she enjoyed her period of living and learning at St Helen's; but left without any expressed desire to change from the home way of life. Indirectly, the convent view of her musical ability assisted her, since it was immediately thereafter that her piano lessons were not only resumed but definitely aimed for the qualifications which she secured and which served her well as piano teacher and organist until old age approached.

## From 'Blackburn Convent of Notre Dame'

About this time came the visit from the U.S.A. of my Uncle Charles and his delightful Irish-American wife, who became very fond of me and I of them in the short few weeks they spent coming and going among the Billington relatives. I counted their visit as a major turning point in my home life, for they proposed to take me back to Philadelphia with them, got the consent of my father – and of my mother – if I should myself agree. The aunt had an 'artistic temperament' and an 'artistic business,' and as I was so unsettled in any way of life or employment at home, I might find an outlet for my handiness with tools in working with her. This was a suggestion based, so far as I could see, on the toys, decorations, knick-knacks and small garments which I had the habit of assembling out of the most unpromising of materials. One of the home relatives said, 'There is that girl buried in books, and she could cut her way to fortune with a pair of scissors!' But the scissors and the needle, the paste or paint brushes were play with me, not a vital need. I was deeply hurt that mother had been persuaded to agree to my going if I should decide to. But I thought about it for two days before saying a very decided, if friendly, 'No.' Both Uncle and his wife wrote to me later and renewed their offer – they were childless; but I could not accept. . . .

## From 'Mother in Business 2: From Pillar to Post'

The details are blurred now, but in the following few weeks, Mother and I somehow reached an understanding. My father, it seems, regarded the conjoint policy of gathering experience for the family business while studying in my spare time as a concession long since proved worthless. He entirely ignored the fact that I was carrying, as time passed, a greater and greater degree of the work of the house. He knew that for a long time I had risen between six and seven to clean and wash and cook so that there would be some hours left for books. He knew that I was on short call to do emergency sewing for the shop where Beatrice was employed. But the husband who had expected to enjoy his wife's monies and had been disappointed, who had been brought up in a Lancashire in which the work of children not yet in their teens had been an established custom from earlier days than the industrial revolution, could not see any justification for years wasted on a search for scholarship – a blind sort of search anyway in my circumstances – when the years of his single support of the family continued. It was easy to forget the series of temporary relief periods to which Mother's relatives had treated him, and the earnings of the elder daughter were countered by the expense of keeping a 'great growing apprentice lad who would not earn his keep for seven years.' . . . After all, he himself had had to be put to work at nine by a father who was bitterly opposed to the child-slavery system!

This revelation showed me that I had been foolishly self-absorbed by my own grievance against life. I offered to go willingly to work in some business in which my series of short experiences in our own and other employments would secure me a sort of 'half-qualified' position. This plan was delayed by a call for help from our emigrating relatives [Helen's widowed brother George and his family, who had returned from America almost penniless], now home for the last time and settling in Manchester, where it was imperative for each member of the family to find a job in order to re-create the vanished home in the shortest possible time. There was one child still of school age and no one to keep house, to shop and to prepare the meals. Everyone shared in the housework, which was done in the evenings. Everyone had a job. Could my mother spare me, now the King Street shop was closed, to keep the house open for young George, to do the shopping and to cook the evening meal for the returning wage workers?

Such an appeal from a widowed and unlucky brother could only be refused by my mother when it was absolutely impossible. My father would temporarily be relieved of my support. I said to myself grimly that it would be experience and that they, poor things, were more sorely tried than I, but having a vision of a house empty of almost everything, I begged that there would be a bed, a single bed, for me.

I was in North Manchester, near Queen's Park, for more than two months. In the daytime, in spite of my attempting much more than was asked of me, I was able to devote some time daily to Milton, both poetry and prose. I had a volume including his 'Areopagitica' and 'Tractate on Education' with me, which I read and re-read, and I had Green's *Short History of the English People*. Entirely unexpectedly, I was happy there; I had expected penury and perhaps sordidness, and found instead a little community of keen rebuilders of the family fortunes, united in every way, lively, expectant and keeping fear at bay by energetic co-operation.

In the two months I stayed, the house furnished itself: every weekend saw an accession, an armchair this Friday, a wash tub as well, a sideboard, a mattress, three yards of print to cover two orangeboxes serving as a temporary dressing table, or a travelling trunk to serve as clothes chest – or to make a wardrobe supported by a triangular top fitted carefully into a corner. The quiet house I knew by day became a hive of industry, feverishly keen and happy, every evening and every weekend. And every day it was insisted upon that I filled in my reading and took at least one walk in Queen's Park. This visit was more than experience; it was a humanising education.

## From 'Mother in Business 2: From Pillar to Post'

This was no home of superficially preserved union, no family of artificially cherished harmony. There were gay times and quick quarrels, . . . but beneath all surface disturbance, there was this united effort, this completely accepted common job. There were contrasted laughter and tears, days of storm and of sunshine in my own home, but not this foundation of united purpose and complete acceptance of the common burden that was the lack with us . . . .

I had learnt much when I was called home. My uncle and cousins were grateful and acquiescent. Five people working in united effort can do a great deal in two months and even in those days could earn the price of many necessaries and some small comforts. It was felt that now one of the girls could be housekeeper; indeed, that with her needle and a paint brush and her home cooking she might reduce some of the future expenditure. The linoleum was down and the curtains were up. The little cousin stop-gap girl could go home.

Since I came back elated rather than depressed, and Father had rather enjoyed the financial relief of my absence, both Mother and I were receptive to the idea of another move. Had the American opening come then instead of earlier, I would probably have accepted it. What did come was a chance to take what was a sort of undefined drapery shop 'improvers' job offered by an old friend of Mother's youth whose family ran a three-shop business in three adjacent towns in Cumberland. Cumberland itself was a name to conjure with – to me it meant the Lake District, in which so far I had spent only two blazing afternoons, the highlights of holidays, with the narrowest and most limited contact with mountain and water beauty. Also, my Manchester episode made me eager to learn from another group of humans in action, even in shops!

I was to live with the family, bread and board free, and a small wage. I was to work in the millinery room when required and at the counter. I was to come and go as required from Worthington to Whitehaven or to Maryport, and I was to have anything I wished to buy in the shop at 25 per cent off. That was going to mean a lot to me in my long-endured shabbiness. I was a little ashamed of myself for this feeling until Mother said firmly to me, 'You will need to buy clothes. You must not send any money home. You will probably find it little enough.' And after a pause, her blue eyes slightly mocking, 'Of course, I must advise you to learn to save!'

I was some six months away from home, making contact with new people in new circumstances, learning, observing, and in some definite ways, sharing in a new way of life. The business of the family was on a longer-settled basis than anything my mother had been able to do. It was run by the wife, but owned by inheritance by the husband, who did not find that the drapery trade fulfilled his needs, indeed filled only his pockets. His neighbours regarded him as cranky and selfish, living a life of comparative self-indulgence while his wife managed both the business and the home. And he did indeed indulge in a variety of practices and beliefs that marked him off from the ordinary man of business. He was a vegetarian and while he was present, his household had to be vegetarian too. He was a cold-water enthusiast who bathed in the sea daily and carried off any followers he could influence to the same practice. Every infant of the large family had a cold bath at home or in the sea daily. His ideal medical guide was an old German priest. . . . For colds, you rolled yourself in a wet sheet and then a couple of thick dry blankets and arose in the morning free from all the germs that were distressing you, took a cold plunge or shower or washdown to close the pores, and the cure was completed. A sore throat or a bruised limb had a wet cloth of suitable dimensions over-wrapped with a great thickness of woollen scarves. And a full supply of cold water would cure most internal troubles. Walking barefoot in the wet grass we practised quite shamelessly in the nearby open country. . . . Drugs were anathema – all medicaments must be herbal. Beginning half on the laughter line against him, I too became a vegetarian and, in my own approved way, lived out some cold-water cure remedies. Sometimes they worked, sometimes they didn't, but I never dared to apply them to anyone else. Also, I shared his passion for walking in the near-mountain district between the coast and the Lake District. If there was ever a walk projected, I was willing to join it. But his age and longer legs, his practice and untiring vigour were too much for me at the end. Finding me unwilling to give in, . . . [he would encourage me to lengthen the walks] by a tempting name or vista, and I would arrive home crippled for the next day with the aches and pains of over-exertion. I came to content myself with the sea-plunge and walks with more moderate pedestrians.

I was there six months, and I bought myself some presentable clothes. I remember well a summer straw hat and a long light coat which I wore for years. And I had more than two nightdresses and unmended gloves. . . .

### From 'Blackburn Convent of Notre Dame'

The convent try-out failure and the Cumberland interlude were over. My position in the household was becoming that of the 'general convenience,' the standby for emergencies, the odd job girl. The Manchester expedition had partly fixed my status. I was making no profits, or at least earning nothing at what I wanted to do, but I had certain abilities and a willing industry. At home, therefore, I could be popped into a job which would give me some training that would be useful later, however unsuitable the job itself might be, or I could be kept as deputy housewife at home because Mother was sick or depressed, or I could be divided between the two, housewife and very amateur nurse, helping out on occasion in an overbusy dress-making workroom in the season or selling goods in a store two days a week or running alone a little 'branch' cottage-type shop while Mother was in her most sanguine business venture.

The only common denominator of these last three years at home was the complete annihilation of any chance of study. Lack of the actual time was not the worst element of the dreadful interval; much worse to bear was the complete exhaustion which made serious reading impossible, and the slow certainty that 'the girl's craze for education' was regarded as a closed episode. . . .

The break came when I realised that my chances were slipping away, that this hateful assignment of myself to the post of the useful spinster drudge of the family was becoming established, that the waste and the tragedy of it to an ambitious and intelligent youth was not apparently obvious to William and had become dimmed in Helen's more sensitive mind. It is a common occurrence. When the effort to force a round peg into a square hole ends in failure, it is the poor peg that is held to blame. 'A difficult child,' they said. She had begun to echo them.

# My Loss of Religious Belief

### From 'My Loss of Belief at 13'

No home over which Helen presided could be anything but observant of religious ceremonial and duty. It would have been so whatever the creed in which she had been nurtured; with the heritage of recently won Catholic emancipation, the Orrell tradition, and ten years of convent school education, her religious fervour was a burning flame. She heard Mass every morning unless illness or family mishap intervened. She made her confession and received Holy Communion weekly. She was a member of the Third Order of St Francis, the fraternity of laymen and laywomen enrolled to follow his precepts in everyday life. . . .

We were not preached at or governed with any sanctimonious injunctions. The times for church service – Mass, Benediction, and the sacraments – and the meatless Friday were a part of life, as meal times were and the set hours for going to bed and getting up. . . . There was censorship of reading, which to some extent we resented and which at other times has caused us amusement or approval! Sex crimes, gory murders, disgraceful happenings in the locality or in society, whispers of scandals – these were all neatly cut out of the daily and weekly 'lay' papers which came into the house. The Catholic papers were never suspect. I read them, for I read every available line of print, but there was no competition for *The Catholic Times*, *The Lamp*, or *The Catholic Fireside*, until we began to search in them for the scraps of verse, little stories and 'pieces' which I began to send to their editors when I was eleven. *The Tablet* was too learned for us.

It was, I think, this effort to write in the Catholic spirit that made me examine my own personal faith. All these small juvenile efforts were paeans of praise of the Virgin, the child Jesus, or the saints whose Christian triumphs had been courageous, rebellious or ecstatic. Most of them never saw the light – happily! – but a few got into print, sometimes as I sent them, and sometimes remodelled into a useful shape, but never paid for and rarely giving the author. There was at about this time bloody warfare raging in [the Sudan], there were evictions and murder in the dark in Ireland and great disasters, and in our own town there were wives kicked to death by drunken husbands, a girl-child raped and killed and a few other horrors, such as [a] . . . malformed infant born and whispered about in our neighbourhood.

It was the malformed child that brought me up against the presentment that had [been] given to me about God. No child of Helen's could be blind to the beauty of the natural world, the skies, the seas, the green glory of the countryside; the wonder of living things great and small moved her to an adoring worship. That is one of my clearest pictures of her. Taking a group of children for a picnic, and while they were gathering flowers, wading in streams, plying bucket and spade or gathering white pebbles, she would be found motionless with head lifted, eyes worshipful and smiling as she contemplated the beauty her God had given us so bounteously. All my puny efforts to praise the Lord for the glory of miracle and beauty in our inheritance had come from Helen. It was the rebel spirit in me that saw the other side of things and was just as deeply moved by them – the evil, the harshness, the waste and cruelty of life, the mercilessness of the Omnipotent behind it all, the blundering brutality of humans to each other. The child born crippled and incurable threw it all up into highlights of vision and conviction. . . .

## From untitled fragment beginning 'The Billington brothers . . .'

. . . Though we had few contacts with neighbours, the children's tale . . . [of the deformed baby] reached us at home and awakened in me a sense of . . . rebellion. Transported beyond tact, I burst in upon Helen and poured out my tale of horror. 'This baby was born deformed. It could never stand or walk, but must lie on its face as long as it lived,' I told her.

'Poor infant! Poor mother!' she murmured, busily washing dishes from the last meal.

But pity and acceptance were not for me. 'Do you mean, Mother, that this could be true?' Followed by, 'Does God let such things happen?' There was no answer that did not finally mean 'Yes,' however many words of explanation Helen's piety put forth to wrap up the truth. Indeed, the final explanation that the sins of the parents were visited upon the children served only to increase my distress. This discovery was a nightmare to me, for it destroyed for ever for me the phantom consolation of a Good God. Later I refined this conclusion, deciding that God might be almighty and not all-good; or all-good but not almighty. This was enough at the time to give me some ease of mind as to God himself. Of the two possibilities, I preferred the Good God doing his best against the forces of evil whatever they were – accident, the natural results of misbehaviour, ignorance or stupidity, the animal streak in humankind. I rejected the Devil very early as a personification of all the causes that might lead to pain, horror and evil. Then angels had to go too, and all the heavenly hosts sitting singing on damp clouds.

## From 'My Loss of Belief at 13'

This was a devastating discovery which for a time felt like a blight on my inner self. I was tossed incredulous and afraid into a ferment of questions and doubts and fears much beyond my scope. I had to give Helen some hint of my doubt and distress. Beatrice and I prayed together nightly that I might find a way out and be saved from the damnation inescapable by the unbeliever. I found a mesmeric condition of sham relief could be induced by prayer. I prayed hard.

Before this turmoil of reasonable doubt was allayed by prayer and fear of hell-fire, I had been sent to confer with Canon Lonsdale, our pastor at St Albans, and had tried in humble spirit to escape from my reasoning mind. There were many added points to be laid before him, and he showed no contempt or unkindness because of my presumption.

The chief points of his advice were that I must sincerely wish to get rid of my doubts and questions, regarding them as pitfalls for the trapping of the immature, that I must not forget that I was too young and uninformed to formulate the real values of the problem, which, I must remember, had been resolved in the opposite way by generations of greater and holier people than myself. That until I grew up I should refuse to think about these fundamental matters, but should pray humbly for faith and grace. He solemnly recited a little prayer which he suggested I should use to keep the Devil at bay. 'Lord I believe. Help thou my unbelief.' Finally, he asked, 'Does it really matter whether the Devil of evil is a permitted power in our lives, or whether he is a lesser rival of God – if we live and work according to the highest teachings of our Mother Church?'

53

He lent me books. After a time the interviews were of his, rather than my seeking. My mother, I knew, carried the burden of my scepticism to him in appeal. I was never convinced, but the . . . self-treatment, self-brain-washing in its mild form was for years effective. Live the good life according to the teachings of Holy Mother the Church. Refuse to confuse your immature mind with problems immeasurably too great for you.

All this could not but mark me off from the rest of the family, practising and unquestioning members of the Church. My father kept just within its sheltering arms; I came to wonder if, married to some less religious woman, he might not have fallen away, and indeed whether the joy of his weekly singing did not hold him more firmly than any element of faith. But there was no conclusive evidence, unless it was provided by his invariable practice of giving only the strict minimum of observance to the sacraments.

## From untitled fragment beginning 'The Billington brothers . . .'

This was the period of what Helen described caustically as my 'gaggle of girls' – four or five of them only – who dropped into the habit of the Sunday afternoon group walk. Our short routes were around the park and the Revidge Road area; a longer one took us on to Billinge Hill and the longest a round route that ended via Pleasington Priory in Cherry Tree. The length of the walk was commonly determined by whether or not there was an evening attendance fixed for Benediction. With a high Sunday tea to fit in between, this meant that the longer walks were impracticable.

At this distance of time, I cannot myself see why these group walks should have turned into discussions not of the trivia of our daily lives, but of big fundamental issues – of religion, of morals, of the big problems of society, of war and peace, of all aspects of the multitudinous mess that life spread before us. All I know is that I became the critic, the questioner, the flyer of the wild kites of free thought, the voice of the critic of all things great and small.

. . . the group . . . described their afternoon as 'a nice walk around the Park and Revidge district while Teresa talked.' There must have been a great deal of crude criticism of things established in the talk that Teresa was responsible for – on religion and church usages especially – for we were all fresh from morning Mass, the later-hour-attenders at a sermon which could be full of points to question. Apart from the creed, morals and faith which might emerge, there was at this time another cause for comment and criticism among Catholic congregations . . . [A] result of the prohibition of Catholic practice . . . [had been] a real decrease in the membership of that Church, and a shortage of fully-educated priests and preachers. The growth that began after the Repeal[3] had to be met by the importation of priests from other countries, and these in the industrial centres of population were mainly from Ireland, Belgium, and Holland, who were largely hampered by their ignorance of English ways and conditions and by linguistic barriers. . . .

The keen eyes of the young could see that those guides were not equipped to lead us as they ought to have been. We envied . . . the churches and chapels which had a full supply of adequately trained English-spoken clergy, and there was a spice of venturesome irreverence in a lightly amused criticism of the sanctified persons' inadequacies. The latest ga[ffes] were commented on quite openly in small circles. Pietists like Helen discouraged them, more realistic Catholics admitted them, even a little cautiously deplored them. An irreverent Teresa made fun [of] or bitter comment on them. . . .

Applied to these unsuitable and primitive pastors, comments from the fluent girl critic could be acceptable and funny to the gaggle of girls without the black heretical backgrounds becoming too obviously damnable. The apprehensive Catholic child might have been expected to refrain from forming part of the gaggle, yet this did not seem to occur. One of its steadiest members, who remained an earnest Roman Catholic all her life, remained also to the end a dear friend of the heretical and irreverent critic of that early group. Yet there must have been a number of near contacts who uttered warnings while we still enjoyed our explorations into the rights and wrongs, the fors and the againsts, of the great issues of religion as they were presented to us.

# Running away from Home

## From 'I Leave Home'

By New Year 1894, it was recognised that I was a rebel against the family authority. My older sister was nineteen and interested in a future embracing husband and marriage rather than a family business. She was quite content to continue in dual activity, for her sewing ability, with a new Singer in the home, was very useful to us all and gave her the chance of dressing much better than would have been possible on our limited income, but this entailed a lot of home dressmaking in addition to job and piano. Her dressmaking wages went to Father, but her music-lesson money was her own, and she was working much too hard. The young men of our own area did not appeal to her; our betwixt-and-between position in the local Catholic world kept us somewhat isolated . . . from the industrial workers, . . . the successful small tradesmen and workers, and the better placed clerical grades of more literate families. But when Beatrice was temporarily free of her threefold burden, she was the brightest and gayest of companions; and this lightness of heart and bearing, added to her blond, blue-eyed beauty, made her very popular. These off-the-chain opportunities, however, came seldom and always came away from home, so that her little following of interested young men were either in Preston or in Manchester. . . .

Meanwhile, Mother had become more than willing to pass over to me the burden of the house, and I had been at home for some three months, in sole charge of its work and responsibilities. It was then suggested that while continuing in this duty I should act as emergency dressmakers' assistant . . . where Beatrice was employed, which would leave me no time at all for study. I saw that this was the last step. Up to this time I had claimed and had been permitted the time and privacy for reading and writing – and must have been one of the most constant borrowers from and readers in the local Free Library. (What I read would have raised an educationist's laughter and my Catholic Mother's fears. But I acquired fragments of know[ledge] and fed an avid curiosity about times and people and places which sustained me.) But part-time housemaid, cook, and washerwoman plus part-time dressmaker's assistant would just swallow up my life And I knew from the life around me and from my reading what sort of life loomed ahead for the family drudge, the spinster sacrificed to family needs and living at last as a despised dependant in whichever family group could give her refuge – for benefits unacknowledged. My dream of achieving an education, . . . of grappling with problems in the learning, science, and mechanics which faced my generation, was to be utterly broken. Only . . . that lower step of an unlettered amateur could be mine if I agreed, having only a litter of crumbs of knowledge on which to feed. Crude in judgment. Baffled in argument. A hand to give, not a head, for my contribution to the world. The capacities *I* knew I had – the capacities *they* knew I had – to be wasted. It was utterly impossible for me to submit. And Beatrice, silent, but having her own need for release, agreed with me.

Our duty to our mother weighed heavy upon us. This was the first time in which she had shared actively in the effort to cut out my chance of study . . . But if there were reasons of her health which would make my sacrifice the only way, . . . then I might have to yield until a new opportunity could be found. But a consultation with the family doctor by the two daughters removed that fear. It would be better, he said, for Mother to be less free from home duties at this particular time; she was brooding and praying too much – hours were spent in church daily, the early-morning Mass, the daily afternoon pilgrimage to at least one church, the days of contemplation and abstinence. So far as she could, she was being like a nun . . . How far our rebellion would go we did not put into words, but first we planned a break for her, a holiday with two of her old friends in the Lake District, two of that group of young women who had formed their little Literary Association some quarter of a century earlier . . . the same group from which her assistant and partner had been drawn when she began her independent existence as a business woman. She was welcomed and made comfortable there at Grasmere. Little excursions suited to more elderly ladies became the order of the day, old times were revived, but there was only one R[oman] C[atholic] church within reach; and it was closed most of the day; and the gap of years was too great and the development of hosts and guest were at variance. She stayed only a few weeks, and then returned, brighter and with reawakened pleasant memories;

obviously, she was unfitted now for the inactive . . . life they lived. 'Living like a vegetable,' she called it. 'And the church open only at fixed times!'

She came home with a brighter eye and colour of cheek and a recaptured little gurgle of a laugh which I had always loved to hear. After a few days I told her that I had managed to continue to study a little even while she was away. 'But that is all over,' she said. 'Father points out that this cannot go on. I thought it was all settled. This studying is time wasted. You cannot hope to make a living this way. None of your stories or poems have brought you a penny, but with the sewing you hate, you can earn and help to repay us for all we have spent on bringing you up. And when my next money comes, we may start our own business – for which you are quite necessary. Or you might study bookkeeping. That would be a worthwhile plan. You could be ready for that side of the work? Or perhaps cutting-out. Cutters get good pay, and we would develop according to all our abilities. Your clever fingers would be an asset.'

I remained obdurate, silent and rebellious. For the first time the home division was dominating. There was nothing that was not tinged with its bitterness. For the first time my mother and I were on opposite sides. I realised the position was hopeless. Beatrice became involved on my side. There were ultimatums issued by both sides. And while my mother was on one of her church visitations entailing a morning of prayer at three separate shrines, we packed our clothing and personal possessions and departed, leaving the usual note of regretful defiance. Our plan was that I should make a place for us in Preston or Manchester while Beatrice lived with some friends in the home town and financed me while I got on my . . . feet. She would continue to work and earn as [a] qualified dressmaking hand and would give her music lessons at the pupils' houses for a time. Released by this co-operative effort, I parcelled a toothbrush, comb, a nightgown and a change of underwear, made it firm with seven flat exercise books containing some of my writing and a 'primer of English,' . . . [wrapped it] with a strong brown paper cover and put an old belt from a rainproof in my pocket with which to strap the parcel on my back when I got tired of carrying it and set off to my new life.

Beatrice and Mary, . . . [a friend], and I carried the trunks of our joint possessions up the hill to the home that was to shelter my sister, and there we had eggs and tea cakes and tea. Then the two of them, anxious, excited, but assured, 'set me on the way' to the nine-mile walk to Preston, all the money we could raise amongst us, eighteen pence in all, being in my pocket. We parted where the 'new' Preston road crosses the way from Revidge Hill above the park to Billinge

Hill . . . I went on toward Preston, and they after kisses and a few tears, turned back into the town. That afternoon saw my sister at work in her dressmaking workroom, where she stayed late to make up the time consumed by our preparations.

Along the way at first I was much occupied with gratitude to them both and thankfulness that we had cut the ties which had been increasingly imprisoning me. There was an element of faint amusement as well . . . in my contemplation of the co-operation of Beatrice. I knew that in either of the two towns in which our near relatives were to be found there was already the nucleus of a friendly circle for her with admirers already in the places, whereas at home there were perhaps three old girl school friends in touch – only Mary close enough to come and go to our home – and no young men at all! I did not share Beatrice's need for this wider social circle, nor for the young men who were an essential part of it. The only men I was interested in were men who could teach or men who could open to me the way to a life on an educated level – and though I knew not where I should find them, I was certain that they existed and could be found. I went on my way to a new life without any qualms and now without any bitterness. . . . I had to make my own new life. I walked easily and with pleasure in the exercise. Our holiday and leisure restriction to country walks and picnics had become an asset. I . . . [passed for good] the two long-legged Scots lads I . . . [met] on the road. . . . Only the brown paper parcel – the paper was the shiny kind – slipping in my arm or on my back, irritated me. I was ashamed of it anyway. Some day I would have a nice little brown briefbag!

## From 'Home Rupture'

I reached Preston in mid-afternoon, and I walked along Friargate until I reached my grandfather's shop. It was an 'old-established' business, a sort of 'gentlemen's emporium' . . . with a much more recent Ladies' Department up a broad stairway in a raised gallery at the back.

The windows were very neat and shining – ties and gloves and socks and day and night shirts and the woollen underwear which men wore then all the year flanked round by tidy stacks of good quality materials for the made-to-measure underwear in which the business specialised.

I was not neat. I was dusty, tired, thirsty, conscious of my shabbiness and my need for a wash. I hesitated. I looked up and down and across the road – especially across the road where my paternal aunt's stationery and printing business faced the end of Orchard St, but it was even a more unpleasing sight. Yet there was no avoiding this visit one side of the road or the other . . . of the two possible temporary refuges, Grandfather's was the least repellent. He might help to give or to find me a temporary job. I stepped inside and stood waiting just inside the door, an obvious suppliant. There was a neat boy about fifteen packing up parcels of socks in the corner to the right. He stared at me and went on packing. . . .

\*     \*     \*

There was an air of politeness and quiet in the place – almost derogatory to call it a shop. No crowd, no rush, no noise, no pushing obtrusiveness about anything. Three decently competent men serving behind the counters. Four or five customers, a little murmur of women talking up above. But my grandfather, no-where.

My step-uncle John had seen me at once and nodded a surprised face at me. He was serving shirting for made-to-measure shirts to a plump matron who knew what she wanted to the last button and gently made sure that he knew it too. He gave her all his attention, with a little air of irritation newly showing on his face. I stiffened into immobility by the door, sensing the no-welcome. Then he made secure a moment to question me.

'You want to see your grandfather? Sit down by the hosiery counter. He is busy in the counting house.'

I moved and seated myself as told and fixed my eyes on the little office under the gallery where the light of a gas-jet behind a window showed an outlined head with a beard.

To his grandchildren – and they were numerous – my grandfather was a brisk, handsome man, intelligent and kindly in manner with brilliant, dark blue eyes . . . I never reached beyond that in my own personal contacts with him. . . .

We had our interview in the office, and I made my statement.

'Your poor mother,' he said. 'Think of her.'

'It is too late. I have tried for four years. I have waited obediently two years. I will soon be too old.'

'What do you think I can do?'

'You can employ me in the shop or the workroom until I find some way of getting into a school; while I work here in the day, I can study at night getting ready. I cannot study at home – scrappy reading in scraps of time, nothing more.'

'But what have you to offer?' he asked, eyes coming back to my face. 'Good penmanship, very good, good composition – you write the best letters of any of my children or grandchildren. But these won't carry you far. No examination; no training.'

'I know I could do it,' I said doggedly. 'I like study. I have ideas, and lots of general information. I have read so much these last two years, but it needs to be systematic – a regular study course. I can do that in the evenings.'

He went out and consulted Step-Uncle John.

The decision was negative.

'You couldn't live on the wage I could pay you here,' he said. 'I could only give you a beginner's wage – 7/– a week. You couldn't live on that, even if you could manage to get time for study. I am not at all sure that it could be done. Your books and your teacher would cost money. You couldn't pay for real lodgings, you'd have to live with someone who needed your help in the evenings and so you couldn't study. Much better if you go home. Have you enough money for your fare?'

I stood up. 'I am not going home,' I said firmly, 'not ever,' and then like a flash, 'How much do you pay the boy who was packing parcels?'

It was so quickly flashed at him that he answered, 'He gets 10/– a week.' And then it was an excuse – 'He's a boy.'

The tears vanished and I rose. I bade him good-day and turned to leave.

He became fussy and uncertain, 'Where are you going? What will you do?' he asked, holding my arm lest I carry my heated spirit into the quiet shop.

'I will ask my aunt Thomson, across the street,' I said. 'She will let me sleep there a night or two, I hope, until I try elsewhere. And I shall have some money by the weekend from my sister.'

'You mean she is rebelling too?' he asked, startled.

'She has left home with me,' I said. 'We planned it together. She will stay in Blackburn and earn money as she does now and keep me going until I get on my feet. Then she will join me. She is staying with a friend who understands why we are breaking away.'

He spent some minutes in silent thought. Then very firmly he said, 'Come to me for help here or at the house if you decide to go back home. I will write to your mother at once. I cannot give you any help in your plan for running away.'

I could only mumble, fearful of tears. Then I felt anger, and though my eyes brimmed, I felt I must leave with . . . quiet dignity, but my going I fear now was a very clumsy effort.

I walked up Orchard St and down, fuming and humiliated. . . . A boy of fifteen – a common, ordinary boy, a boy content to work in a shop all his life. Three shillings a week more for being a boy. If he were the same age, perhaps 5/- a week or 7/-. I did not feel my grandfather was admirable anymore. To the distaste about the four wives there was now added the stupid injustice of sex privilege.

\* \* \*

[TBG's paternal aunt who had the stationery business across Friargate 'ungraciously' said she could stay at her house for a few days.]

I went up to the aunt's house to deposit my parcel. Both relatives lived in the Avenham area, the aunt nearer the park. I passed my grandfather's grimly on the way and [upon arrival at my aunt's] was given a snack of food and drink by my cousin. It was my intention to go forth at once, after a good wash and a tidying-up, to begin my calls on the drapery, dressmaking or millinery shops asking for employment. But my aunt arrived before I was ready. She was armed for battle. There had been, I saw, a conference of paternal and maternal relatives. Someone had crossed the street which had served so long as a dividing line between, denying them . . . any closer contact than a formal greeting.

And the conference had not been to my advantage. It was evidently agreed that I should be forced to go home.

There was a ten-minutes' undignified face-up, and the same ultimatum, 'When you have decided to go home, you may come here for help. We can't help you to run away.'

So I had my parcel under my arm again, and my half-cleaned boots re-laced; but fed, a little rested, clean and tidy, except for the feet, I declined the terms and set out again.

The parcel was a burden and a handicap. I decided to deposit it in the park before beginning my painful procession of enquiry. This plan I carried out and was back in Fishergate to seek my job while it was still late afternoon.

But alas! too late for my purpose. I started with the best – an emporium – and it was my last that day. The superior shop-assistant brought the superior manager, who fixed my status by a harsh negative before I had stated my case, and then said as he waved me to the door, 'But you surely know that all applicants for employment must call before ten in the morning?' So the planned canvass was useless that day, and there was nowhere at all to go for the night. I trudged, appalled, along the streets, trying to solve my problem. Mother's people, no good. Father's people, no good. Well why should they be? They know you have just enough money to take you home. They expect you will go home and make your peace and submit. With the mother you have, they think you must be in the wrong. The thing for you to do is to wait until the last train is gone and then go back and let them choose whether you are to sleep in one

of their homes or in the park – where there might be tramps or police
and a scandal. This was the only way out that I could see, and much
as it hurt my pride, I felt that there was nothing else to do that would
be possible to me.

There was not money enough to pay for a bed in any sort of
lodging. I did not know how to find such a place except through the
police, to whom I could not possibly go. There were of course
convents; by appealing to one of them I might be found safe shelter
in a 'good Catholic household' and returned under escort to my
family in the morning! That was no good. So the appeal after the last
train had gone was decided upon, and meanwhile I wandered
restlessly about that side of the town, viewed Winckley Square
garden as a good hiding place, if hiding became necessary and as
dusk fell, took a seat in a secluded little grove in Avenham Park and
sat listening to the subsiding noises of the town and the vague
murmur of the Ribble.

It was a long evening. No one approached my corner. I tried to
thrust thought out of my mind and rest, but the anxious churning of
anger, fear, and argument spun round and round inside, and though
it was July, the chill of evening stiffened my tired body.

It was very late when I suddenly yielded to fright. I had begun to
fear the noises in the dark. They were suddenly malignant. One
moment sitting there quietly, and the next I was up and away parcel
and all, ready to climb gates if they were locked or even to hammer
on them and scream in order to get out.

I made for my grandfather's house and hammered at the door – a
torrent of words ready to pour out in resentment.

They must have been waiting – perhaps anxiously – hoping that if
I had not gone home I would come, for there was my step-aunt
Fanny at the door almost as I knocked. My step-aunt Fanny was only
six years older than myself and had been, in a few slight encounters,
the most human contact in that house. She pulled me into the hall.
'We have been waiting,' she said. 'Have you a bed for tonight? It is
too late for you to go home. What are you doing about it?'

I sat on the hall chair. She did not ask me to come further in.

'What am I doing?' I asked. 'Nothing. Not any more. I waited in
the park. I thought I might have to sit there all night. But you will
have to take me in. My mother would hate you if you didn't.'

She almost wept. 'We are all in trouble through you,' she said –
but it was said kindly – 'but Father has arranged for you to stay a few
days at Arthur's – until he has seen your mother and everything is
explained. But we can none of us have anything to do with helping
you to stay away from home.'

That was the end of the runaway's first f[l]ight. Arthur and his

63

wife gave me shelter for some two days and on the third I received simultaneously a postal order from Beatrice and an urgent telegram from the Manchester relatives which I preserved for years, and still brings a mist of tears. 'You are welcome here. Come at once. Uncle George and Polly.'

# Study and Work in Manchester

## BECOMING A TEACHER

### From 'Manchester: The Break In'

There were five cousins at home, Uncle George, two commercial gentlemen in the two best rooms, and their poor waif – me – without an asset which would make me a contributor or anything but a charge upon the little community. But I was invited. I was welcomed. I was supported materially and in spirit, and I was assisted in every possible way to find my feet.

I arrived about noon having walked from Victoria Station carrying my brown-paper parcel and my three books. From the determined but forlorn suppliant in Preston, I had become the determined and grateful but self-confident co-partner in Manchester. I knew I must make my way. I had the certainty of friends behind me, offering me refuge, believing in me. With the few shillings coming from Bea – even without them if the worst befell – I would have as much a chance as they could give me. And when I reached the house I strode up the steps and rang with a sense of certain success.

Lord Polly[4] was as sure as I, and more generous. Full of certainty for me and of suggestions . . .

### From untitled fragment beginning 'Now I had to face . . .'

. . . There were three or four most depressing weeks of useless perambulation about the Manchester central area. What could I offer in my search for a job? Years of over-youthful contact with small

drapery businesses, all short-lived and unsuccessful except one, a
. . . half-training in millinery in what central Manchester would
classify as the lower-class trade, a useful acquaintance with the
sewing machine and a speedy needle on plain dressmaking jobs; and,
in my mother's eyes, a genuine talent for cutting-out. I got very little
chance to tell my tale, being politely or casually ushered out after a
broken sentence or two in most cases.

The first day was utterly wasted. I walked to town from the
Crescent and began my calls in Oldham St – one call only, indeed –
'The staff manager cannot be seen after 10:30,' I was told curtly.
Then the calls began as soon as the shop opened, and I was too early
and had to call again, or new staff was only interviewed on Tues-
days, or vacancies were always advertised and no applicants considered at other times, or the holiday season was a useless time to
apply. I moved from the centre to the radiating lesser roads, where I
generally got a hearing but no encouragement. My name and
address were taken at two minor shops whose owners might have
occasional part time work to offer when there was a rush. 'It might
be convenient to have someone with a little all-round experience,'
said a stout, short-sighted lady in Oxford Road. This was the only
encouragement I got. Drooping but dogged, I walked back to find
Lord Polly night after night (it was a hot summer) and confessed my
failure. She answered my every need. She looked at my heavy,
shabby, only coat and insisted on lending me her best light one to
make a better impression; she preached the gospel of a cheerful
approach and an air of confidence. 'Remember you have been born
into this type of trade.' I shuddered but remembered. It was a bitter
boast.

And Polly knew that whatever I lived by at first, the essential
objective of my effort was to lay an educative foundation for my
future life. She had said little about this when I was searching for the
'rag trade' bread-and-butter jobs, but as empty day followed empty
day, she dropped a casual comment or question now and then into
our conversation and must have gathered a general sort of picture of
bookish self-indulgence and the futile efforts so far made to win a
beginner's foothold on the educational ladder. I had reached the
stage of watching the papers for any kind of shop or domestic job
which would give me evenings free, when the elementary schools
re-opened after the summer holidays. This brought Margaret
[Polly's sister] and Edmund, her husband, back from . . . [their]
holiday and there was coming and going between the Crescent and
the newly-marrieds' home in Queen's Park, which had no special
significance to me until one grey evening, when I was trying to
remake a jacket and skirt into a dress and so to improve its appear-

ance, Lord Polly [arrived] home with a length of neck frilling in her bag. 'Sew this into the neck of that dress,' she said. 'You will need it tomorrow when you go to see the Rector of St Edmund's where they want a temporary assistant.' And St Edmund's it was, where the sisters had discovered an opening, and where at 10/– per week I made my debut as an untrained, unqualified assistant teacher under Article 68 of the Code of that day which required no other qualification than a birth certificate showing that you were or would be eighteen years of age when appointed or would be within six months.

The Rector was a little, precise Belgian priest who made it clear to me that the post was temporary and that my cousin Margaret's introduction had secured it for me. It was thus that I became a 'supply teaching assistant,' and until I achieved the first grade in qualification at Christmas, I moved from school to school, a few weeks here and a few weeks there, getting a variety of experience packed into weeks or days, finding my feet as a teacher by luck and quick imitativeness, and spending literally every minute of my time in study for the Queen's Scholarship Examination in December.

At that time there was a four-years' pupil-teacher training course with this Queen's Scholarship Examination at its close, by passing which the trainee became a fully-fledged Assistant Teacher. I had four months and six days to cover the ground, and when Lord Polly and I gazed at each other and doubted it, Margaret pointed out, 'But you can go on trying once a year, still working as a Supply,' and, awful as this sounded, it at least saved me from desperation.

There were three of my old school fellows ending their four years' course at that time, and the knowledge that I had for pride's sake to equal their achievements helped to stiffen me in any moment of relapse. There were not many of these. I dare not permit them.

I did not study unguided. The headmistresses of the upper and the infant schools at St Edmund's both offered to tutor me. They said later they were impressed by my approach to the job as two-fold: to learn everything needed; to make a confident start in teaching. I had to be helped.

Miss Sullivan took me for private tutoring. Knowing that I could not pay, she bargained with me to help some other beginner when I was qualified. . . . She was a miracle of helpfulness, giving guiding tuition in the subjects covered by the syllabus, in the selection of books and the ways and means of proceeding as a candidate; and when the great gaps of ignorance and imperfection in my knowledge became obvious, Miss Sullivan toiled strenuously over elementary arithmetic and the technicalities of history and English grammar and geography – all of which should have been supplied at the elementary stage in school. One day she declared that my education had no foundations: neither dates, nor tables, nor any framework for systematic study; and when thereupon, for the first and last time during these months I wept, she added, 'But you *can* hammer all those things into your head; *we* know you can.'

So hammer them I did, in all those numberless minutes which we waste in ordinary times, letting a few physical movements shut the door on our minds. As I dressed and undressed, as I ate and washed and scampered from home to tram or train, as I was carried to my school of the moment, and as I returned, I revised and read and murmured dates and definitions, and set myself problems to solve. I had scarcely any other consciousness of the world around me and cannot even now remember what happened to anyone else in my circle in that four months.

*        *        *

[Miss Sullivan] . . . had to tackle not only . . . covering . . . the set syllabus for the Queen's Scholarship Examination but also all the elementary underpinning which ought to have been done at school. 'It is a good thing,' she said, 'that I specialised as a teacher of infants. We must start to make bricks and build our castles at the same time.' And penmanship must be seriously tackled; the antique Italian script of the nuns would certainly not do. It was a great comfort to her that, ignoring all these handicaps, I could write her a thrilling adventure story or an essay on the Lake District or the Romance of the Railways of any length she required at any time at a moment's notice.

'This facility will be a great help,' she would murmur, looking over the last essay. . . . At the other extreme, she foresaw and armed me against pouring out a plethora of interesting knowledge in reply to questions in history or literature or any of my pet interests. 'Three super-excellent replies out of eight spells failure,' she said. 'You want eight adequate replies.'

To give form and limit to my history and shape and reason to my arithmetic she sent me to the Mosley St Evening Institute where, through the interest of the class leader, I made my first contact with Charles S. Lodge, who controlled the classes devoted to study for the external degree examination of London University, and he became another generous guiding benefactor in the following years.

## From 'Manchester Study Begins'

Within myself I was at peace. I had escaped from the net; I was on the first step of the stair I had to climb; I never doubted that I could climb it. I could keep myself meagrely on what I was paid. I had a refuge and a kindly welcome for some time with the kindly uncle and cousin who had befriended me. I missed Helen, my mother, my jailor and the lost love of my child world. But I put her out of my mind. I could not carry any burden of remembered grief to interfere with the task of achievement. I had to make good – or admit myself an empty vessel, a humbug self deceived.

. . . There were three weeks at the end [of the August-December employment as a supply teacher] to cover the examination which would give me my first qualification: . . . first, an hour-by-hour slogging at my books and then the examination hall itself. I had Christmas in bed with neuritis and a new job to go to out of the Manchester area at a school on a high hillside in Darwen. I was classified there as 'qualified' for by rule of that time, the Board of Education recognised a candidate who had sat for the Scholarship Examination as being qualified until it was proved otherwise. This, no doubt, was to provide a better atmosphere during the months of delay before the results were announced.

I was inured to change now and still confident. In Darwen . . . I was slightly amused to discover that I had been engaged wholly because of my handwriting, the new upright hand which was putting up a fight with the cursive Civil Service hand so long established. The head mistress and the school rector had suffered from the criticisms of H.M. Inspectors on the penmanship of the school and were quick to see that my upright product could be taught on a more systematic basis. I worked one out on request, a matter of straight up and slanting strokes in which the curves were added at the third stage. It was very ugly for a first week or two, and then it evolved into a clear consistent calligraphy within the reach of 99 per cent of learners. In the few months I was there, we revolutionised the handwriting of the whole school and struck H.M. Inspectors dumb with what I felt entitled to claim was not so much surprise as admiration.

But any town which had no evening classes for ambitious beginners, no library for reference work, and therefore no opportunity for firsthand advance through study could hold me except for the minimum time. Immediately the examination results were published, I gave notice, applied for and got a new job in Manchester again and left the handwriting triumph and Darwen behind me . . . .

## From 'ıst Exam Passed'

I made my 'thanks visits' first to my cousin and my two kindly tutors. In the first stage of study Miss S[ullivan] and Miss P[arke] wished me to apply for admission to a recognised teachers' training college, for a trained certificated teacher naturally ranked higher and was paid more than a mere certificated one. They touched my heart with their generosity. They were prepared together to loan me the money to tide me over the two years. We worked this out at £20 per year (which seems grotesquely inadequate now). It was to cover clothes, holidays when the college was closed, all incidentals and pocket money. Jobs as governess-nurse or companion, or shop assistant might possibly be obtained in the summer, but there was no certainty. Girls who could go home for their holiday periods might have risked it, even penniless ones, like I was, but with home absolutely barred by pride and poverty, it would be madness to take the risks. But I turned it down with real gratitude – and real tears.

But before we actually turned it down we had an interview with the Chief Inspector of Education for the area, Dr Cornish, who thought it would be better for me to wait another year, sit for the scholarship examination again in order to come out 'near the top,' whereupon he indicated that there were funds that could be called upon to carry a student through.

The delay of a year partly subsidised by my relatives . . . created a centre of unwillingness within me, and there was the further know-ledge that my sponsors would expect me to apply for training to a Catholic training college, in fact our old college, governed by the Notre Dame nuns. And I, being now eighteen, did not want to be under convent rule ever again.

There was another argument against this kindly plan for my good: I did not regard teaching as a future life-work. It was not my goal, only a stepping stone on the way. It seemed to me something less than honourable to win my way to the literate life, employed in some form of service yet undefined, by the service and the money which were intended to produce teachers. I had to say 'No' on all these counts.

## From 'Manchester Study Begins'

I lived with my relatives until the Darwen move, but my return was to a post too far away from North Manchester for this to continue – a new Catholic school in Plymouth Grove – so that I had to find a lodging in that neighbourhood. First I paid 7/- a week for a room and bought and cooked my own food, but found this wasteful of both time and money. From the £26 per year of my first post I was now receiving £45. The first-year teaching certificate was achieved while I was there and the second in due course. For another £5 per year I moved to Ardwick with a very useful testimonial – the best I ever had – from the head mistress at Plymouth Grove. She saw in me more teaching ability than I found in myself. A little humbled, but proud of her praise, I transferred to a post with the same petite and vividly competent Miss Parke, under whom I had made my gate-crashing debut at Miles Platting. I needed the extra fiver because my way of life meant a continuous expenditure on books and footwear.

In those days I walked everywhere. Looking back I see myself, shabby, happy and absorbed, swinging away into town to evening classes, having already done the walk between school and lodging twice on days on which I carried my lunch, or four times when I returned to cook it for myself there. I lived in a shabby little house in a shabby little street between Stockport Road and Plymouth Grove with the family of a disbarred solicitor now earning a pittance as a law office clerk. They had a quiverful of children to which every year or so another was added in a spirit of cheerful incompetence, resulting in dirt and disorder. The neat spruceness and clean smell of my mother's house made this lodging a repulsive trial to me, which I managed to endure for almost a year by keeping to my own front room, doing my own cleanup and cooking and leaving everything securely locked when I was not on the premises. This slum interlude ended when the poor, cheerful incompetent died, and the school authorities, pleased to see one of their teachers in a more suitable home, found me a room in a quiet, refined home in Newton where everything was at the directly opposite pole. But bad luck pursued me. This comfortable, quiet and clean refuge was sold-up when the man of the house failed in his venture to start a business of his own in opposition to his old employers. For some time Lord Polly had been willing to take me in again, but the distance had discouraged me. Now I accepted her offer, decided to ignore the strain of the daily to-and-fro walk across Manchester and to make my home with my two rescuers again. A greater deterrent than the cross-town walk had to be overcome before I joined their household. . . . My decision to subdue my personal probing into religion, to suppress my doubts and assuage my conscience by refusing to accept that I had made any real decisions had carried me on in a sort of detached somnolence of conscience. But I was living by teaching in a Catholic school. I had to observe the routine of the Catholic way of life. I had to teach it to children. Only by conforming could I persist in my life effort to find security with the life of study and intelligent contacts that were necessary to me.

I had one conscientious self-enquiry of my position which continued for a matter of three endless-seeming days. I had begun, it seemed ages ago, to refuse to think about religion. It was no matter for a ferment leading to any hasty decision. It was no light matter to be casually dismissed without deep and devoted concentration. And every moment of my thinking life was committed to doing my teaching job and preparing for step after step of the scholastic ladder of qualifications. In a grim way I was compelled to endanger my soul for my day-by-day earthly salvation. I argued with myself that this was no crime, no sin. I did not feel that I had chosen study and teaching with its involvements of a superficial religious conformity: it had happened to me. I had to make terms with my life. I alone was responsible for keeping myself alive. Fate, luck, chance, had opened the door to me to make a living in the school. External conformity was forced upon me – or the securing of some other way of making a livelihood. I had not even knocked at this door. It had been opened to me by Margaret and the Miles Platting School Manager. Once inside there was no possible present chance of studying seriously the rights and wrongs, the faiths and fantasies, of religion. Make your terms with the conditions that have arisen. Isolate your inner self from the surface of the life that has happened for you. The problems of survival are enough for the present. The greater part of what you teach in many subjects is based on the untested statements of other people. You pass on the accepted dogmas. Then you can fairly do the same with religious teaching. By so doing you will keep faith with those who employ you. Supply to your pupils the information they are expected to receive and commit yourself to being in school only a channel of accepted data and theory.

This theory worked itself out in my mind in those intervals between study and teaching in which I still indulged a roving imagination. As night after night I swung my way to my classes, enjoying every moment of being myself in a world of books, this was one of the lines of thought which assured me of the rightness of my choice, and having solved the problem to my satisfaction, I could and did live and teach and study with a conscience at rest. For years I did not ask myself if I believed in God, or if the creeds which divided the peoples of the world were necessary for the attainment of human moral living. I gave my mind to the binomial theorem, the elements of psychology, the histories of kings, countries and industries, the make-up of languages, the shape and size and production of the countries of the globe we live on, and a dozen other elementary knowledges which go to the creation of an educated human being . . .

## From '1st Exam Passed'

I had visited at home now two or three times, the olive branch having been offered to me by a forgiving and slightly proud mother. I found then that she and my aunt in the convent at Wigan had compared notes and found that, among the group of girls from my old school and the group from which I had been turned down, I had actually been placed higher on the Queen's Scholarship list than any other. They had enjoyed – or suffered? – four years of tuition and half-time study; I had been pressed into several forms of preparation for a loathed retail-trading future, used as an unwilling housemaid, judged as a graceless and ungrateful child to whom all possible help had been uselessly given. Now, it appeared, these two at least recognised that my addiction to books and my 'scribblings in corners,' when the family would have preferred my company at music or cards or some other game, were not merely selfishness but a worthy-enough effort to reach the most suitable way of life of which I knew.

I was happy to see Mother from time to time and to receive her letters, but the strain of the conflict on religion which was burdening me at this time and which had gravely interfered with my studies kept me to short mid-week visits at holiday times and some deliberate evasions. Two things I felt Helen could never forgive – unchastity and the rejection of the Catholic religion. I was never to disturb her with the first, as she and I already knew, but there had been evidence of 'heretic tendencies' in my youth and there was always a consciousness between us of her anxiety.

## From 'Teacher Conscience Period'

It is possible, although I am not at all certain of this, that I might have gone on steadily teaching and studying, at least until my final was passed, without making any change. I knew that I was supersensitive in conscience and created for myself, or at least enlarged, any deviations I had ever made from the strict and narrow path of principle. I held myself guilty in accepting love and confidence from my mother without confessing to her that I was an agnostic, believing no longer in any church or creed, nor in a God as she knew

God. I had reversed the statement that God had made man into its opposite, that man had made God for his own comfort and in his own image. I saw the Catholic Church . . . as only one of many institutions grounded on tradition, making super-human claims and imposing on the human mind and on human conduct beliefs and compulsions that restricted the human mind in its free development and imposed codes of conduct, some of which were trivial disciplines and some immoral impositions. All my dear Helen knew was that I was a 'questioner,' a 'doubter,' passing at this time through a period of temptation to disbelief. But she knew that many great saints had suffered so, and . . . I, of all her four children, . . . was the one with the kindest heart and the clearest sense of duty. Against all the evidence and against my silent withdrawal, she continued to hope – and to pray – for me. And the silent withdrawal was a permanent one. Religion and the state of my immortal soul were excluded from our communing for the last thirty years of her life. She spoke her last words to me just before she died, when I rushed north to her bedside from our new home in Northwood. They were 'Teresa, my dear, from Middlesex!' Tears and gratitude for the love came with smiles for the odd exhalation of the county from which the black sheep of the family had come to be beside her. She did not speak again. Some time later very softly her breathing ended in a sigh.

## From 'Study Days until I Left the Church'

. . . release from mental discipline and regulated routine gave the dammed-down questioner its chance. The free-time reading became more and more the reading and examination of the claims of religion, especially the claims of the Catholic Church. I read again all I could trace of the recommended list of books presented to me so many years ago. I read also all the rationalist and free-thinking literature and pamphlets I could find. I dipped into the breakaways, schisms and heresies which make up so much of the history of the older religions, got a glimpse of the religions of other peoples and other ages – and then found it was all in vain. Many of these investigations had great value. They proved without any doubt that humans have had to have something greater than themselves to explain their world, that they have admired and feared someone or some thing greater than themselves, that . . . they have needed hope and help, and that they have devised ways of comforting themselves.

The old fever of my earlier struggle was over. I was no longer a tempted and bewildered believer drawn by Satan into apostasy . . .

In the quiet under-mind to which the problem had been thrust down, it had resolved itself. I was no longer personally concerned. Here was the wonderful world which humans inhabit; here were the humans who inhabited it, with all the lesser kinds of creatures; and here, in the multiplicity of religions were 'the explanations' of the great mystery of the how and the why. There was no shame or sin in declaring that these explanations through religion were to me no explanations, that the great mysteries of the universe and of life were still mainly unsolved, and that while there had been and was an urgency toward the good, a hope of elevation and love embodied in religion, there were also all the lower primitive hates and fears there too. All religions are marked by the characteristics of the age that produced them. They can safely be left aside as the creations of the human spirit seeking explanation and comfort in a mystery universe, beautiful and fearful.

This meant of course that my Catholic school teaching days were over. I must move, if possible, to a post where I could teach without being false to my trust and to myself. I transferred to the Municipal Education School Service, hoping that the compromise religious instruction agreement which had been accepted after much consideration by all the recognised churches, would give me the opportunity to teach morality, explain religious thought and history usefully without disturbing the pupils' minds or criticising what were accepted as fundamentals by others.

I applied, was immediately accepted, and took over a class in the Lower Crumpsall school, leaving my old sponsors in distress on the religious aspect; they believed me a sincere but misled enquirer, and showed none of the usual rage of condemnation which the apostate usually has to face. And they amused me rather by rejoicing that I would at least better my financial status. Usually this would have been an added sin! And indeed the salary position was greatly improved; from £45 to £65 at one jump was almost miraculous.

# 'SOCIAL AND POLITICAL AWAKENING'[5]

## From 'Settlement Period'

. . . The faces of the saints are masks, achieved in the devotional exercises and ultimately worn all the time. Sweetness, humility and dedication on the surface, self-satisfaction and implacable and immovable judgment below. There are some elements of this in many benevolent institutions and among persons who devote themselves to 'good works.' It had always nauseated me and I walked warily to avoid it.

But I did not find it in the [Manchester University] Settlement.[6] I liked their faces. They were quiet and attentive faces, kindly and responsive, neither smug nor superior nor sanctimonious, not actually welcoming, but accepting in kindness. A sound, healthy, practical outlook prevailed; nobody preached or prayed at you. Two Saturday evening Toynbee debating opponents would go rambling in the same group on the Sunday, discussing *Selagenella* (see Scotts botany) . . . or the distribution of plant life on the chalk soil of Derbyshire, or they would jointly carry the cripples to the Santa Fina Social or work the lemon peeling machine for the Associates' evening drink. Even the friction was firmly friendly. One did not impute evil intentions to a trouble-seeker – one jollied him a little or turned his eyes in a different direction. And there was no fuss and no scared avoidance of difference, and no sense of dominance. Ancoats Hall, Carr Meadow, and the Round House had the atmosphere of tolerance – of that . . . acceptance of all who were members and of their opinions, which should be the essence of the home and which, because of the sense of property-relationship in the family, is so utterly absent there. I entered all this slowly, feeling my way, savouring the new atmosphere while escaping from loneliness, awakening gradually to the reality of the tolerant quality of the kindness which permeated the place – and finally yielding to it. 'The family,' I had written once to my sister, 'is like a chain-gang. Its members may be kind to one another, may share experiences and the feelings they arouse, but the chain forces a unity and agreement based on force. Each one must do as the others do or penalties are incurred; [there are] restraints and struggles, in which one may be the cause or the victim, but all will suffer.'

## From untitled fragment beginning, 'Free from some of the old loneliness . . .'

. . . released from some of the old tension, I was not only growing and deepening my knowledge, but was actually becoming a better and a speedier student from the quicker pulse of life, the new vigour of my mind.

I ceased to commune unendingly with myself and to write sonnets to ease my mind, and found contacts, even superficial, with Alice Crompton, and her fellow wardens and the some two hundred-strong ranks of Associates an exhilaration and a release. At Ancoats Hall and Carr Meadow we gave each our great or small mite of service and drew each the large disproportionate reward of a particularly kindly and intelligent co-partnership.

Personalities that remain as well as Alice Crompton herself are Jimmy Mallon, to whom I became the woman Co-Secretary of Associates, H.P. Turner, R.C.K. Ensor, Helen Fisher, Fred Halliwell and his wife Frances, Mr Clement, of the William Morris printing venture, the botany circle Ramblers, including Robinson, and Eva Gore-Booth, sibyl-like at her Poetry Circle.

\* \* \*

By now teaching for 27½ hours in the week, . . . still covering the same class and syllabus, had become an easy routine, and the actual time spent at lectures and classes as a student myself was much reduced. The chief commitments left for my final were at Owens College laboratory on Saturday mornings with Professor Weiss and on two week nights at the Mosley Street Institute at the tutorial classes for London University degrees, which were run by Dr Charles Stewart Lodge . . . .

\* \* \*

The mathematics and mechanics courses I had only to keep on revising, and this was most economically done by two allotted periods weekly in which nothing else existed except textbooks, pencil and paper, sheets of old examination questions and my notes from the previous years' lectures. Practice piled on practice with guaranteed checks by experts' answers. This was was the way I worked.

I had been especially indebted to Dr Lodge for long sessions of private tuition in the earlier years, and he . . . sought to give good counsel and practical guidance to earnest and promising students handicapped by circumstances. . . . I fear that he was at the end deeply disappointed with me and had sound reason to be, when I threw the whole thing over to devote myself to my own idealistic and rebellious socialist dream, which was compounded largely of ethics [and] humanitarianism, to be fulfilled in a dual society which would destroy masculinism and cast aside all creeds and crutches to rely on reason, love and fair dealing. I was one of the idealists who saw as the hopeful dawn, not the political Labour Party then coming to birth before our eyes, but a great missionary movement for mental and moral uplift based on the solid foundation of an equalitarian economy.

I remember when a group of us joined the Central Manchester ILP[7] and were welcomed at an early private meeting by Keir Hardie,[8] how naively and earnestly we ventured to argue against the propagandist socialist groups joining up with the Trade Unions. We were so crude and new that we did not realise that this union was the very dream of his heart, from which he believed that the great reforming agency of the next age would be born. We, without this knowledge, argued for the missionary body, urging that the Trade Unions were just as much a class protection body as organised employers and must use their power to carry out this object . . . .

## From 'Social Conscience Awakens'

Religion now was gone. Any contentment I had enjoyed from that suppressed source had long evaporated. So also had my anxious effort to find supernatural support for myself or my way of life. There was left from my childhood training a sense of the selfishness of my solitary way of life. I had learned early to enjoy the wide world of books; no daughter of my mother could fail to find pleasure and profit in the natural beauty of the world around and, with the interest of an observant mind and eye, in my fellow creatures. But I was giving nothing. I moved alone, full of the possibilities of useful service, but doing nothing.

Actually before the consciousness of this lack began to trouble me, some of the old indignations had re-awakened to enquiry about the manifest imperfections of the world around me. I was yet a rebel against things as they were and, being logical, against those who presented them as acceptable.

On the religious side, questions were presented to myself no longer. They were now analyses of observed facts – nearer to statements of reality – observed scientifically. In the Lord's Prayer we said, 'Lead us not into temptation,' . . . word[s] which stumbled

78

unwillingly out of my young mouth. It was clearly evident to my child's mind that the world was paved with every sort of temptation, and these being created by God, it must have been constructed on quite the opposite principle from the phrase . . . in the prayer. The truth seemed to be that He created every sort of temptation to try and test us, and those who resisted most frequently and firmly found their way to a reward in heaven. How utterly illogical therefore to ask this Super-Being to do something contrary to the great existing plan!

Awakening sexually very late and inhibited from thoughts about sex by the attitude and atmosphere of the convent-minded Helen, I did not at that time include any survey of the Creator's arrangement of a sexual nature in my naive investigation. Much later I did. My conclusions then were even more emphatic. Here was the great universal urge and the greatest of penalties for yielding to it. The fever existed in the poor, possessed human for a large part of a lifetime, but it could only be beneficial to the person or to the race if strictly limited in time. It was an urge which might awaken passion and seek expression with any number of persons of the opposite sex – even as I learned almost a lifetime later with persons of the same sex – yet those who claimed to interpret the Creator to the world, after the period of Jesus's history in which the leaders of the nation were permitted wives and concubines in multitude, set up as the only sanctified union a one-pair life marriage that entirely ignored the hungers and physical pressures and emotional fevers with which this same Creator had endowed them.

## From 'About 1901'

The early general aspirations were coming to be recognised as requiring the justification of deeds. And it was obvious that the method of generally campaigning against all evils which disfigured our civilisation was a presumptuous impossibility for any ordinary human and was unlikely to achieve any substantial permanent change. This policy was the one to which the various churches and congregations, missions and apostolic movements had devoted themselves. Generalised to the point of vagueness, it led people to pray to renounce their besetting sins so far as they were recognised and probably to apply their new humane principles in a vague attitude of greater benevolence.

\*    \*    \*

The uneasy seeker had therefore to make a choice – to begin somewhere – and choice must be to some extent determined by practical considerations, something near to hand, something within my scope, something that was so worthwhile that taking risks for it was justified, but that would not necessarily destroy my chance of earning a livelihood.

The recognition of this problem brought under mental review the happenings and usages of the day to which I found myself opposed. There was the war in South Africa in which Britain, her best case stated, had still much to be ashamed of: fundamentally the British and the Dutch were two Western tyrannies struggling one against the other to gain profit from the native peoples of the land. One could campaign as Pro-Negro, or Pro-Boer, or Pro-Peace. But all these were too big, and I could do no more than add my mite and my word in season on the side of justice and mercy.

Nearer to myself and open to the lesser range to which I could reach were the vegetarian [and] anti-cruelty movements, and still closer reforms touching education and the educators. My interest began to centre here, and discussions with fellow teachers and fellow students, with the Settlement mental attitude as background, began the crystallising-out process in my mind.

The Carr Meadow weekends were prolific of wide discussion and there, initiated by some of those troubled about conventional religion and the new Ethical Church movement,[9] . . . began a spontaneous series of week-end explorations, earnest, if scrappy, and confined sternly to the general terms. One hardly mentioned the name of a denomination or considered at all the strange and often puerile ground of difference that separated them. The thesis would seem to have been: 'Considering the religions that persist among us as institutions, do they achieve the object of elevating the human race and inspiring it to personal and social advancement?'

\* \* \*

The booklets of lectures of F.G.[J.] Gould[10] on moral teaching in schools won my wholehearted approval, and I saw possibilities there for a useful line of service. But at this stage very little beyond optimistic first-stage mental planning could be achieved.

Running alongside this experience there was the growing resentment all intelligent women were beginning to feel at the multiple ways in which they were penalised. The growth of the Labour associations, exposing the exploitation of the workers as a whole, could not but turn the enquiring eyes of women upon their own condition, which they found was always at the bottom economic level of their class. A newly-engaged shop assistant boy would find himself poorly paid, but it would be taken for granted that he should receive half as much again, or even twice as much, as a newly-engaged girl.

## From 'Settlement Period'

My venture in opening a debate on marriage [under the auspices of the Settlement] was as advanced as any at that time and was deeply deplored by one of the Settlement supporters. My chief crime, and that of Miss C[rompton] in permitting me to commit it, was not only that I wanted marriage to be between equals, . . . [but] that I used a vulgar but descriptive word like 'guff' to describe the ocean of emotional poetic and romantic sentiment with which 'love' and 'marriage' were presented to the young.

But I denied the morality of the promise to 'love' until death, when character and development and all the circumstances of a mutual life of the most intimate nature yet unexperienced, might make love impossible. I denounced the promise of the wife to 'obey' as being utterly immoral and originating in slavery.

. . . [A] lady brought to the debate I opened two younglings of her circle who were obviously in love, expecting them to benefit by hearing the sort of innocuous sentimentalities and advices with which the benevolent outsider tries to give emphasis to the social and human aspects of the married partnership in order to counterpoise its sexual urgencies.

At the critical moment when I concluded and the chairman was rising to open the meeting to debate, the disconcerted matron rose to her feet and . . . hurriedly and noisily shooshed her younglings out. It was the most eloquent contribution of the evening! Miss Crompton first consoled me for the rebuff and, lest I should fear damage to the institution through my address, . . . then made peace with the patron.

We had other venturers open debates: 'Moral Instruction in Schools,' entirely apart from the creed and dogma of institutional religion, was another extreme subject and there were [discussions of] innovative anti-sweating legislation,[11] the growing of beet for home production of sugar, housing reform, garden cities, the Single Tax,[12] abolition of the gold standard, old age pensions, the paucity of public lavatory accommodation for women, education for the worker, school journeys, and Norman Angell's *The Great Delusion* – all figuring on the agenda or flowering from the floor during my Toynbee days.

Miss C[rompton] showed her understanding also in one move made before I departed: noting that among the women members of the Toynbee there were only a minority who ventured to speak, she formed a debating society for women – the Fawcett – which gave them the confidence and practice to attempt expression in the larger body, a task which is still largely neglected except by some women citizen groups and in partisan societies for partisan reasons.

## From 'Teacher Conscience Period'

There was now no alternative. The gradual recognition of the divergence between what I was supposed to be teaching [Bible studies] in the first daily school period and what I was teaching became too obvious to be ignored: morals; the thinking out of right standards of behaviour; the sound practical reasons for living a good life, for dealing fairly with others, . . . [for] refusing to hurt or rob or degrade them, for giving to them in all fairness a fair deal; truth and honesty and kindness, and a hatred and rejection [of] greed and cruelty and the many forms of dishonesty; and high among all these the humanist charity rule, so hard to learn oneself – if ever learned – not to judge others and especially not to assume the right to condemn.

Just to state this aspect of my problem was to demonstrate clearly that I could not go on teaching as Holy Writ sections of an old inherited Jewish Saga and a collection of more recent sermons and epistles written by the first reformist zealots who had attempted to remould it nearer to the spirit and conscience of the evolving human creature.

*   *   *

There was little hope of finding employment in the 'higher education' type of school where the class teacher was replaced by the teacher of special subjects. The degree in science would almost certainly have to be completed before I would hope for such a post, and this meant almost a year's delay with every school day of this period committing me to a double trespass in the religious instruction hour. But I made one effort in answer to a Stockport advertisement issued when it was found that the younger entrants to the Technical School were in need of a strengthening course in English and Mathematics. At the first interview the applicants for this post were reduced to two – myself, the only woman applicant, and one of the men. After the others were dismissed I was called in for a second interview . . .

\*    \*    \*

. . . Two questions only were put to me by the Chairman. Did I intend to remain in teaching in the Manchester area or had I other ambitions? To which I replied that I had strong attachments to the area especially because of the Manchester University Settlement. He nodded and smiled and next [came to] the crucial danger point: what salary would I expect if appointed? My courage ebbed out of me. I had to find a new voice. I heard it say, 'The standard salary, sir. I believe in the rate for the job.' Then there was a shuffle of papers round the table, and . . . one man laughed. It was all over. I was bidden a very courteous 'Good morning,' and dismissed. The little angry man in the waiting room moved impetuously towards the inner door as I left it. I caught at my courage and wished him joy of the job.

So this was my second lesson of the practical advantages of conformity and the price which one might be called upon to pay for making an individual judgment contrary to that generally accepted. The torment was momentary, for after all I was already aware of all that particular experience had displayed to me. There was nothing in any way extraordinary about it. Conformity to the accepted standards was the line of safety for the individual, and of stability for the group, the class, the State. It was to be expected that innovators, or heretical individualists should have to compromise with the established conventions in order to live or to seek ways of livelihood in which they were not called upon to sell their principles for bread.

\*    \*    \*

The high schools for girls, in one of which I would have felt it an honour to serve, were most strictly orthodox in religion and . . . they naturally selected their teachers chiefly among graduates from university-level institutions, women who had probably had a more cultured background and a full formal education before emerging with the equivalent of a university degree. An application from me – with a near-the-poverty-line childhood and the barrenest elementary education it was possible to envisage, followed by a penurious purgatory of seven years' devotion to the passing of Board of Education, Society of Arts, and London University External Examinations – would have been tossed out at the first stage.

At the other extreme were the reformist schools run by idealists who found the great educational machine repellent, and who called their small experimental groups 'new' or 'free' or 'progressive'; also there were the infant or near-infant teaching schools applying one or other of the theories of Froebel and Pestalozzi, and the Italian, Maria

Montessori, and the British Macmillan sisters. I consulted the written publications of the three first named and wrote to the Macmillans.[13] They had no vacancies except for trainee students and thought my qualifications fitted me for other teaching avenues, but they would welcome me as a student in the ordinary way 'which might improve my chances for infant school employment with an enlightened education authority.' This was no good. I decided against applying also to any of the single 'crank' schools which determined iconoclasts had established in a few instances at that time. Alice Schofield and I, bewailing the wholesale mass-methods of our daily work, had discussed opening such a school ourselves, but had achieved nothing more than discussion. The practical problem of starting such a venture had deterred us from action – getting money, getting 'backing,' living while we built the structure up, making ourselves known, working out a plan which faithfully expressed our aims – all these preliminary impediments considered from time to time during our day-to-day busy employments and studies loomed between us and the dream.

In my consideration now I saw that such schools, devoted chiefly to the ideals which sustained their founders, would be unlikely to accommodate easily anyone but a disciple. And there would be the precarious financial handicap, the sacrifice of all retired security and the almost certain encroachment on studying time or outside lecturing opportunities, both of which had become imperatives.

Journalism might be attempted, but with all my inhibitions and devotion there did not seem to be many doors of opportunity, while propaganda work would only be possible if it expressed at least some part, if not the whole part, of my own convictions and ideals.

\*    \*    \*

There might have been difficulty in fully presenting a concrete reply to the question of alternative education when I came before a meeting, a committee, or ventured into the press to urge the need for reformed religious teaching – my little whimper of protest against the organised roar of the congregations throughout the centuries! My tentative shaping of what could be put in the place of creeds and primitive sagas too holy to be questioned would very likely have been vague and incomplete. But there was guidance and inspiration at hand.

My contact with the Ethical Movement brought me knowledge of F.G. [J.] Gould, who was proclaiming the need for moral instruction in schools. So far as I remember, he was not presenting the case for this vital innovation as an alternative to the 'religious instruction' which I had found impossible; he had left that danger point alone.

The one time I heard him speak, his argument stressed the absence of everyday common-sense moral guidance for the children in schools; showed the need for direct rational talks on conduct, kindness, honesty, service, courage, patience and straight dealings; and drew his exemplars of these virtues from real everyday people of all types and races . . .

Here was my positive, practical, good policy to be suggested as the alternative to the indirect approach in which creed and tradition and the atmosphere of unreality and implied judgment of the non-Christian stood between the hearer and the acceptance of the moral lesson. I introduced Dr Gould's propaganda into the few beginner-type speeches that at that time I was making to small Ethical Movement groups which I was invited to address.

## From 'Settlement Period'

It had been in my mind that I would write to him [F.J. Gould] when out of the blue he wrote to me, via Ancoats Hall with which he knew I was associated . . . There was, he wrote, some suggestion that a propaganda effort should begin for moral instruction in schools on the lines he advocated.

\* \* \*

[The plan] would entail the employment part or full time of an experienced teacher who could be sent about the country to lecture on the subject and to give specimen lessons before audiences of educationists and officials. The plan would need a lot of working out, but there was a definite intention to go forward. Would I write to him and perhaps meet some of the Committee when it could be conveniently arranged? What about such a position for myself, if the plan progressed and the Committee approved? This to me seemed a very miracle of promise, and I responded in an enthusiastic way, although I did not feel sure that I personally was the best type of advocate for such a cause. There was too much heat in my blood; I was too much the fervid iconoclast. But I was an honest adherent of the plan and would discuss it in any aspect with himself and the promoters.

Two interviews followed. One in London with Mr Gould and his secretary, for which I had to scrape to the bottom of my post-office saving book, and one with a Cheshire lady Ethical Society supporter who was, I think, giving financial backing to the propagandist-teacher scheme. The London talk was pleasant and understanding, productive of serious practical suggestions and with anticipation of an opening door. The Cheshire one closed it with a bang. The lady was of the careful reformist type, with a vision of an inch-by-inch advance, correct and accurate, and free from all extremes of heat or argument, a rationalist without red blood. The interview and the plan ended together. It was not necessary to wait for a verdict. One knew it. 'The candidate was unsuitable. She spoke fiercely about the misdirection of the minds of the young. She read Ingersoll[14] and had listened to Foote. [15] Quite likely she would announce that she did not believe in God. She would arouse resentment rather than promote enquiry. Not the Ethical Society type at all.'

She was of course right. Youth in rejecting the established, the pontifical, may be expected to reject it utterly in hot blood. Middle life and age may count the cost of raising opposition. But the criminal imposition of creed, the ban on thought and enquiry, the exclusion and condemnation of the heretic, the denunciation of one institution by the other, the old records of persecution and the modern . . . 'missionary' ones and of proselytising – all provide youth with food for anger. There had been, there were still, indepen-dent thinkers whose conscientious scientific and philosophic work was more damaging to religion than any rebel eloquence . . . making tombs for old faiths, but the fire of zeal does not only bring such super-minds into action: the little people in revolt must make their rejection in common terms. A young crude creature escaping from religious credulity and hating it must be permitted to clamour and condemn. The careful cold criticism of religious reasoning, . . . by itself, would seem to have smothered the movement that devised it.

Churches may be half-empty, and increasing thousands live and die without contact with a church, but the Ethical reform movement meetings rooms are emptier still or have ceased to be born or survive, and the numbers detached from church religion know nothing of any better way of life, of morals, of aspiration. It seems to me a great opportunity was lost when the several preaching and protestant groups of those days at the turn of the century did not persevere on the more vital and popular lines of appeal to the common people. You cannot remove false idols without destruc-tiveness, and there were the freethinkers as dedicated iconoclasts. But they put nothing in the place of the faith they destroyed. This the Ethicists – in their societies, groups and unions and Labour churches – could have supplied, a teaching of morality on the basis of kindliness, fair dealing, service, equality before the law and the best human conditions possible to be created for all. Ploughing its way vigorously apart from politics, apart from the organised churches tied to their creeds and ceremonies, how far could such a movement have gone to permeate the world with a practical ideal, set a standard for the common people, and give at the ground level a consciousness of the best that science and philosophy was producing? Even it is possible that the presence of such a practical idealist element in the cauldron of these sixty years might in turn have reacted on the scientific mind and produced that humanising of research which we fear is entirely lost today.

# Mrs Pankhurst and the WSPU[16]

### From 'Settlement Period'

I did not at that time consider the possibility of transferring myself
from teaching to any other occupation, although this had been my
intention from the start. I felt that I was as yet ill-prepared for a sort of
missionary lecturing life, precarious if entered into on my own, and
unlikely to be offered me yet by any organised movement. . . .

There was some period of inaction as all these considerations
occupied my mind and, although I was conscious that the change-
over might eventually turn out to be exactly what I had intended, there was anxiety too – the anxiety of conscience – and of
finance.

Conscience carried me one Saturday to the Authority's Central
Office in Deansgate to put the position before the . . . Inspector of
our North Manchester District. He knew my story and had been
very considerate indeed when I entered the School Board employment and had congratulated me in his bluff way when I had recently
gotten my London Intermediate B.Sc. But he was visibly shocked
by my present approach. 'Tell me all about it,' he said brusquely
when I blurted out, almost before I was seated, that I had come about
religious doubt again. I made a muddled beginning. 'You think of
going back to the Roman Catholic schools?' he asked, eyeing me
coldly.

'No, indeed,' said I, getting to the vital point at last. 'I want to give
up teaching religion altogether.'

It was a long interview, and it ranged to and fro until the position
was quite clear. I could not accept the duty of imparting to the young
as guidance the moral standards of the Old Testament and the
authoritarian [interpretations] of the New. I found myself com-
promising in such teaching, putting a gloss upon the actual stories, a
humanist-ideal explanation rather than an orthodox Christian one.
This was not what was expected of me; even if I knew that such

88

interpretations were more morally valuable to the children, I was not teaching what I was engaged to teach.

It seemed to me that a teacher who has honestly set out to qualify and had all necessary qualifications should not be debarred from the teaching profession on the ground of conscience. There were conscience clauses in the Education Acts for the parent and children, why not one for the teacher? Could I be moved or my work in schools so re-arranged that I would no longer have to teach scripture?

The last presentment was too much for the officer. His composure disappeared. I was making an extraordinary request – one unheard of – one which might create much disturbance in the community. Had I any idea of the time and trouble that had been involved before the churches had been brought into agreement on this thorny question of religious instruction – was it five years of negotiation, or fifteen? And had I forgotten [the] tax resistance of the Non-conformists as a possible indicator of what in their turn the Roman Catholics and the Church of England might do?[17]

## From 'The Student away from Home'

[The Inspector continued] It was of major importance to avoid any disturbance of the precarious peace secured by this agreement, unwittingly entered into and cordially disliked by all but the Non-conformists. There were, therefore, only two alternative courses possible for him to consider: that I should be relieved of the teaching of scripture by some rearrangement in the school which was within his power to make, or that I should seek employment other than teaching where personal religious beliefs would not be involved. Here he stopped – I [was] deflated because I had nerved myself to a dramatic claim for religious tolerance, and he had made it a small personal problem. He would give me three weeks to think about it, meanwhile keeping the problem in mind. Finally, as I appeared unsatisfied, he sent me to see Mrs Pankhurst, who was a member of the Education Authority Committee . . . [18]

. . . Her name was a household word in Manchester, as Dr Pankhurst's had been years earlier in the local press. I had seen it too at election times placarded through the town, and I had read reports of her speeches and heard her praises sung by the young Labour element at the Settlement (notably the Boggart Hall Clough Free Speech agitation).[19] Also I had heard that her daughter Christabel had at one time accompanied Eva Gore-Booth[20] when she organised poetry classes at Ancoats Hall. I knew also that the late Dr Pankhurst had in earlier days rather flaunted his rejection of orthodox religion. I went to see her with keen anticipation.

She had asked me to call at the King Street shop she then ran to supplement her income as Registrar of Births and Deaths for a southern area of the city. It was a good type [of] arty crafty business in which Christabel assisted her between sessions of study and lectures at the law classes of the University. Owens College . . . I saw them both here for the first time.

Mrs Pankhurst [was] as gracious, lovely and dominant as she was always to be, Christabel unobtrusively attending to customers, moving in the background while we talked. . . . [I] . . . hardly noticed . . . [her] while [I was] in conference with her mother, who was much more outspoken than the official had been. Any public demand for relief from religious teaching was unthinkable. We could not know what it might lead to. Whatever was done, there must be no letter to the Clerk of the Committee, no letter to the Manchester *Guardian*, no canvassing of Councillors. A conscience clause for the teacher was utterly impracticable. An attempt to raise the matter on those lines was out of the question. Did I want to continue teaching, she asked, and I explained that it had been my plan to get my degree in science and then to look around for other openings – lecturing, writing, educative or social work of some kind where I could feel I was giving worthy service.

She applauded this and, considering a while, stressed the point that I ought not to move from teaching until the degree was secured, that some compromise arrangement might be worked out, and meanwhile I must stick to my books and make up my mind to agree to the compromise arrangement. I must not spend too much time at the Settlement. Such service was only a modern version of the old benevolence and not reform, not my type of work at all. This I felt was a superficial judgment, as also her belittling of the Ethical and Moral Instinct Movement.

[To this section, TBG appended a note: 'Mrs P's questions in the interview were more detailed, covering a) what I was doing, b) what I could do – speaking, writing, c) Equal Pay, d) Teachers Trade Unions.']

\*     \*     \*

She showed then what was to become known to me as her 'assumption of success.' She had spoken. You might have offered some variant of agreement, some indication of a differing view. But this was ignored. You left her feeling that without any definite committal on her part or agreement on yours, the line of action to be taken was settled, and I was expected to agree to it.

The conversation changed to more general lines and we parted in friendly fashion in spite of a last-moment access of courage which drove me to say that I could accept some form of compromise which left the principle unstated, but that I did not think I could agree to resign without raising the question of a conscience clause for the teacher. She frowned at this then brushed it away. 'It is too early to make decisions,' she said, and smiled her farewell.

She was at once recognised by me as a force, vital and resourceful. She had beauty and graciousness, moving and speaking with dignity, but with no uncertainty of mind or movement. Later I was to see her captivating the mob, turning commonplace men and women into heroes, enslaving the young rebel women by the exploitation of emotion. But there was always a moiety of loving admiration even when reason and judgment was against her.

When we rose from our conference corner among the green-stained oak and the Poole pottery that graced the simple-life homes of those days, I sensed that we had experienced together a meeting typical of those of any later association. Each time we met there . . . [were] further questions and further encouragements, and a closer approach, but I was never able to reveal myself easily and she would never argue or state a case.

## From '1903 – Atmosphere in 1906'

It [the solution to TBG's problem of teaching the Bible] was very simple. I was moved to a school near Strangeways, largely Jewish, in which the religious instruction was given to the Jewish children by accredited personnel of their church; . . . [non-Jewish teachers were] free . . . for other duties for such periods. I did the coaching of new immigrant pupils from other lands with other odd flotsam backward children. The duty of teaching scripture was no longer mine. The kindly pompous headmaster explained to me that only he and I knew of the reason for this arrangement together with the two persons 'in authority,' and so far as they could see there was no reason at all for anyone else to know it. I promised to do nothing without previous notice and had a most interesting year's work there until the WSPU called me, through the ILP, to lecturing and organising in the political world.

By this time I had got my Intermediate B.Sc. examination over and, because of some rearrangements of the University of London calendar had a choice of sitting for the final in some four or five months or toward the end of the following year. Mr Lodge favoured the early try. 'It will be a tryout quite worthwhile as practice,' he argued. 'You may pass. I would say it is possible: depending very much on the luck of the questions: if you do not, you will have a year to strengthen the weak places and you will know your way about better.' But there was the cost and the distaste for indulging in a gamble, and I held out for the longer preparation. This was probably a bad decision for the re-awakening crusading spirit on the subjection of women was preventing any absorption in science study.

This was really the end of my hope of a University Degree, although I continued steadily to give one half my 'free time' to books and classes and practical work. I continued to arrange for a fifteen-hour day, rising early for the pre-school study, carrying my 'notes and headings' on cards in my pockets to con in tram or memorize as I walked. I gave more than half of the two-hour midday break to my books, and I had three evenings a week at the tuition and coaching classes at the Technical College, Owens, or with Mr Lodge, and between four and seven also on these days I was a student reading up or revising. A good systematic period of overwork which was still my way of hope to the future of dignity and usefulness that I planned.

The Settlement activities loomed large in sentimental feeling, but occupied little but the weekends and monthly meetings. They were to expand when the studying was over. The other real effort was the insidiously permeating call to sex-equality protest and propaganda. In the growing WSPU the five or six women with speaking capacity were under immediate call to address meetings any evening and at weekends anywhere within range of return to employment or class. Only class or laboratory nights were excluded for me. Otherwise I snatched a tea-meal of sorts at school or on the way and, with suffrage arguments in one pocket and mathematical treatise in another, took train or tram to the many towns of Lancashire or less often further afield. One travelled there planning eloquent political demonstration and back conning formulae and working with the slide rule or struggling with the differential calculus.

Outside of these major interests I do not think I was fully alive. Things just went on and I with them. Only the Settlement friends and the few hours of moorland air with them kept a living pulse of being alive. The rest was doing – too persistently absorbing in effort to leave room for anything else but itself while it was being done, but with the door shut upon it for relief when it did.

The close connection between our movement of pressure [the WSPU] and the Labour organisations was demonstrated by the names of the societies and groups for which we spoke. Invitations

92

came unsolicited from Trade Unions, Labour churches, ILP and SDF[21] branches, Ethical Societies, Cooperative groups,[22] Nonconformist chapels and churches and Clarion Scouts.[23] They were called forth by circulars from the WSPU direct and from the reports of our addresses in the Labour press. We were definitely regarded as a section of the 'socialist forces of progress,' a sister organisation preparing a part of the sound foundation of the new world.

When in 1903 Mrs Pankhurst and I met, she was of the opinion that the new combined Labour Party would be the instrument of enfranchisement for women. She and her daughters, with some three or four other women within the ILP, were beginning the task of conversion in all the various groups of humanist thought. They were addressing meetings of all sorts to win support for the old Dr Pankhurst equal suffrage resolution with the intention to have the ground so prepared that when the Labour Party was formed and acting in the next General Election, it would be committed to put the enfranchisement of women on its programme.

This may not have had the same degree of support from Christabel as from her mother, but she worked hard with all of us and made no withdrawal, so far as we saw, while it continued. There were a large number of women in Left organisations lined up loosely behind us and even larger numbers of men whose sympathies we won. But there were opponents, from the semi-educated type of male always anxious to cling to his one area of mastership, from the class-conscious men and women feeling distrust for what they called the lady-type of reformer, from the stereotyped and the lazy and from the Marxians. The latter opponents were more than adequate to the task of counter-balancing our propaganda by turning the light of their opposition not on the principle of the Equality Bill, but on what would be its actual practical results – which women would be enfranchised? Around this point the struggle raged – we to establish the principle that citizenship should be on a basis of equality in law, and they to misrepresent the type of women who would be enfranchised and the immense majority of women, mainly working women and working men's wives, who would be left out.

Prominent Labour women were divided in the issue, but such trades union leaders as Mary McArthur and Margaret Bondfield laboured against us and made havoc of the support we had collected. The adult-suffrage movement,[24] instead of equality in the law of citizenship, began to carry the preponderate vote. Arguments of principle and the earlier women's suffrage history counted little to the uplifted members of the multitude seeing the wide door of opportunity opening before them.

It was not the Pankhurst way to accept defeat, or to discuss with

93

colleagues any change of policy, or any breaking of alliances. The co-operation continued. Its later form was to ignore the division to point further forward to full citizenship for all, but to emphasise [that] the Equality Bill would give a basis of equality in full adult suffrage. We were on safe ground here, for every previous extension of the suffrage had been advocated and worked for by women as well as men, but there being no franchise of women to extend, they had been inevitably left out. And wherever there was an outbreak of industrial unrest, there we appeared to link the economic degradation of the women workers with the lack of voting powers.

Our contacts with Labour continued steadily during this time of diminishing hope.

## From 'Emmeline Pankhurst. The Home'

I do not know what was the atmosphere of the Pankhurst home while Dr Pankhurst was alive. But when I knew it, [it] was a home of love and unity and confusion. Whatever they had been while the four children were juveniles, they were now a dedicated family, missionaries in unity in a home in which the mission came first and everything else existed on a lower level. The mission had not one aspect only – it had several according to the hopes and fears and circumstances of the time – but it had one aim, full political rights for women, as the essential foundation of a new world of sex equality. In this there was not only unity of purpose but unity of feeling; a slur upon women, a new trick of evasion, a sudden hope roused a five-fold flame at 62 Nelson Street [the Pankhurst home]. With this went a surge of mutual admiration. They worshipped each other. They believed in each other. They had a large enveloping ambition for each other. There was no position so high but it might not one day be graced by Mother or Christabel. And this family ambition and unity was strengthened by the nature of their mission – reformist, rebellious, revolutionary. It was a house from which five went forth, and cool judgment, bitterness and adolescent sentiment, ambition and the spirit of sacrifice – a house which was inevitably to produce martyrs, missionaries, fanatics, politicians, publicists, saints and dictators.

Emmeline Pankhurst was a very wonderful woman, very beautiful, very gracious, very persuasive. To work alongside of her day by day was to run the risk of losing yourself. She was ruthless in using the followers she gathered around her as she was ruthless to herself. She took advantage of both their strengths and their weaknesses, laid on them the burden of unprepared action, refused to excuse weakness, boomed and boosted the novice into sham maturity, refused maturity a hearing, suffered with you and for you while she believed she was shaping you and used every device of suppression when the revolt against the shaping came. She was a most astute statesman, a skilled politician, a self-dedicated re-shaper of the world – and a dictator without mercy. The handicaps in the way of her purpose – the dishonourable type of opposition, the inertia and home-isolation of the women she sought to elevate – all these not only convinced her of the grievous difficulty of her mission but of her own importance and that of her close companion Christabel in carrying an accepted responsibility – a duty laid on them and cherished in acceptance.

These impressions of the first two years of my close contact with her probably gave her personality too great prominence over Christabel. But this is to be recognised as the natural result of circumstances.

## From 'Early Days. 1903–4–5: Militancy in Plan'

There was in the strict sense no order in the WSPU proceedings. We came when we could to our weekly meeting after the first tentative vague months, settling down to planning visits to Labour and Left societies. Although we had named a secretary, she changed frequently, and the major part of the letter writing and booking for speakers was done at Nelson Street.

Mrs Pankhurst or Adela would arrive with three or four favourable replies, even at times with invitations *ab initio*, and the speakers would be allotted – one generally, but where a supporting sympathy had brought a larger offer of a special meeting, two or three of us might be sent. The mother, fresh from the NEC [National Executive Committee of the ILP] meeting and made more urgent than ever by it, would give us reports that increased our zeal. In my case, that generally meant that I sacrificed a class or a turn of duty at Ancoats to do another ILP or trade union meeting. I was reluctant to make the sacrifice for the latter. So often they were business meetings at which an appeal for a resolution of support for the women's equal suffrage bill was sandwiched in between routine branch details, letters from their head office, complaints about the working of some trumpery rule and a whole lot of stereotyped socialist phrases and ballyhoo about brotherhood. In my own case, more than once such meetings had to be reminded that I had come specially from Manchester by invitation of the Committee to speak about equal suffrage and that time should surely be allowed for that.

Sometimes we carried the vote without any opposition, getting warm support at the idealist-type meetings, but finding only a few friends at many times. The ILP, the Socialist Sunday Schools, and Socialist Churches along with the Ethical and philosophical groups were generally 'for' us, some of them quite emphatically so; the SDF, and the Marxians under other titles, and the self-interested trade unionists were indifferent or opposed, sometimes rabidly so. They held that the men workers had votes enough, once they were organised, to make a better world for the men workers, and that, at bottom, was all they were concerned about.

Our spirits were kept up by the general belief among us that our friends were the best, the most active and the most intelligent in the Left ranks and that they would carry to victory a real human reorganisation of both citizenship and industrial life. 'The heart of the common man is sound,' said Margaret Macmillan to me after a Yorkshire meeting rescued from futility only by its angry women. Pinning our faith on this, we spent our time and strength and argument on the effort to get their help and votes, which meant those of the new political party coming to power, for the admission of women to full citizenship.

Of course we were foolish and blind. All around us, all around them, these organised, angry, revolting men – revolting often in both senses – were [either] the evidences of the deeper degradation of women which they ignored or shared in imposing, or, at best, [they] uttered unwillingly a feeble, sentimental and half-dishonest admission of worse injustices than they bore themselves. These stumbling words of guilty admission were nauseating, uttered in half fear of their fellows and in half shame in consciousness of their lack of honest practical purpose.


# From untitled fragment beginning 'We were not then aware . . .'


We were not then aware, as we discussed the methods of protest in this little Portland Street office, that the only protest methods which we would be allowed to use were those promulgated from Nelson Street. With our draft constitution safely drawn up, and only awaiting the day of our launching out on 'national lines' with a London headquarters, many hours of eager discussion went on there. Before and after our more formal meeting periods – and they were never very business-like – the free-for-all range of anticipation went on intensively: the hopes and fears of a Labour alliance, the expression of protest at a new incident of insult, the recording of an unexpectedly good reception at a meeting, as well as the debating of the methods of protest we would have to use.

This last subject was of the greatest interest to me and provided others with a stimulus which had in it elements of constructive thought and also elements of hot rebellion in which there was more hot anger than logical thinking.

I naturally remember best the tactics I put forward myself, some of which I still feel would have justified themselves as valuable. My chief suggestion was that of intervention in elections. Claiming the right to vote, we would use every sort of endeavour to exercise that right in any form we could devise: an individual woman slipping into the polling-booth and dropping a voting paper – a symbolical one or a duplicated one – into the sacred box; a half-dozen women rushing the door to cover a real or simulated voting attack; a raiding crowd of women creating confusion by demanding entry; the introduction into the count of an extra ballot box of votes given by women at a special polling booth of our own. In all such action the women voting [were] to be some of those actually entitled to vote by existing law and debarred only by sex.

We reached the stage of listing those among us who could be the initiators of voting-action, and I carried it about in my WSPU folder along with notes of the constitution discussions and data about friendly contacts and opponents to be feared. I have never understood why this voting plan was not applied.

The only such effort made by the Women's Freedom League transformed a positive claim to vote into a negative destructive protest, which for all the bravery of the two women concerned, was a failure, marred too by an accident for which the Election officers themselves were responsible, but which might have been foreseen.[25]

There were a lot of lesser ideas discussed, some immediately dismissed as far-fetched and some as dangerous in that they would arouse prejudice on wider issues. A hotblooded Irish member promulgated the idea of a sex-relations boycott to pledge the young and desirable members on 'no engagements, no marriage, no babies' lines. But we thought this crazy and were fully behind Mrs Pankhurst when she so described it, indicating in no uncertain terms that if it were unsuccessful, as it would be, it would only bring ridicule upon us, and if, by an unlikely miracle, it succeeded in part, it would create not sex-equality but sex-war. A year or so later a woman of note who joined us in London put forward the same idea, based in her case upon the Greek model and planned neatly in circles of commitment so that every type of woman could deny men something until equality was achieved.

I always regarded this line of thought as essentially masculine and therefore doomed by its nature and its certain failure to remain in the fantasy stage.

What I did advocate, and believe in as a method of positive citizen-action, a publicity winner, and a demonstration of the standards of women's ability was the promotion of a woman candidate for Parliament – Mrs Pankhurst herself, of course.

I believed for a period that she kept the possibility of this method in favourable consideration. In putting it forward I, of course, had in mind the candidatures of pamphleteer [John Wilkes] and of Bradlaugh[26] and the intense interest both their candidature fights had aroused. I had come across also a brief record of the fact that the step-daughter of John Stuart Mill, Helen Taylor, had been nominated as a Parliamentary candidate for [North Camberwell] in [1885]. I made as much of these facts as I could and was naive enough to believe that I was initiating some items of what would become our movement's planned protest and publicity policy. I was quite sure that the fundamental idea of protesting constructively by doing the things we women were debarred from doing by the existing law, was sound in itself and would be dramatically enlightening to the world at large.

But like many other matters which our conspiratorial group discussed, there was little possibility of decision on them or any application at the then stage of the movement.

Most of us were living an intense life involving three or more simultaneous activities – converting the public mainly at streetcorner and market square meetings, urging action in our support upon all the varied sections of the Labour movement, earning our livings or shouldering all the burdens of homemaking for husband and children – or tied to school or university and their hours of study, as with the three Pankhurst girls and one or two others of the student-teacher type.

The months went by, these tasks filling them; the future plans were for the future.

In the midst of this ferment of action and planning there came a[n] ILP annual conference in Manchester itself – and I was elected one of the Central Branch delegates. Chief interest of the delegates was in the developing merger of the several Labour and Socialist groups from a Labour Representation Comittee into a Labour Party. But also with others on the agenda there were resolutions on education and on our Votes for Women claim – all three issues on which I was deeply committed in mind, but as a teacher and a member of 'this

Pankhurst Group' the Branch rightly saw no reason [for] which I should urge caution in the great political amalgamation ahead, so I was allotted to speak twice on the interests I was associated with and not to raise a lone argument of caution on the amalgamation.

I was well received and astonished at the close of the conference by an invitation to meet Keir Hardie and Mrs Pankhurst at the head-quarters hotel after the NAC [National Annual Conference] con-cluding meeting. I was told then that I had been nominated and accepted as the first official woman organiser of the ILP, and they would like to discuss with me the outline of the work I was to do and when I could take up the job.

I had had no previous warning of any kind from anyone of this plan, and while flattered, was not entirely free from a measure of resentment. We had tea together before I agreed, not because of the compliment involved, but because of the opportunity . . .

## From an untitled fragment beginning 'There is no doubt about it . . .'

The vagueness of the leadership about the future to which we were committing ourselves, about the future constitution of the move-ment, about the tactics to be employed was not only a product of the rush and tumble, the always eleventh-hour rush, the lack of money and time, it was a cleverly foreseen method of carrying us on into action before we had begun to reach personal decisions, before we had made a choice, before we had been admitted to any share in decisions. One of the younger married women in the group said to me before a meeting interruption to which we were both commit-ted, 'I could do this with much better heart if we had all discussed this policy and decided for it.'

To which I replied, 'You wait a while. These are early days. When we have a constitution we'll get properly organised.'

We were both thrown out and breveted home to Manchester from Liverpool bruised and shaken, still cherishing one illusory hope.

With Annie [Kenney] there was no illusion. The principle of the greatest of Jesuits had been indoctrinated and accepted. Between my departure to Staffordshire as ILP woman organiser in April to my return to Manchester in October, the fiery little democrat had become the practical politician in Christabel's pattern. 'The excluded must use whatever weapons they can seize,' she had said; and 'Do a little that is technically evil in order to accomplish a great good.' She knew her world. By the means of short term judgment, multitudes will say she was right. It was not a road I could follow with self-approval.

I accepted the [WSPU's] anti-Government policy,[27] the questioning of its representatives, to the point of meeting interruptions; I accepted the petitions to Parliament and the processions to present them; I was a convinced and effective by-election orator and I organised such political campaigns. I broke by-laws and protested in Magistrates' Courts; I led a procession of working women to interview in May Mr Asquith, Chancellor of the Exchequer; with Annie and Irene Miller and the three chief East London stalwarts Mrs Sparborough, Mrs B and Mrs Knight. I was the first Suffragette prisoner in Holloway. Alone I took a momentary chance and rushed into the H[ouse] of C[ommons] then with Annie, and Irene Miller, I was led before the Speaker of the House, who, permitting us to say nothing, informed us that he had decreed that we should never again be admitted to the precincts of the House – a silly gesture, which we just ignored.

## From 'Suffragette Chat'

'Do you suppose,' asked one girl when the train was halfway up England, 'that Mrs Despard[28] ever commited a sin?'

There was an angry protest from one end of the carriage and then a shout of laughter.

'You are a very dear infant,' said I. (I felt so much more mature than any of them that it pleased me to ignore that two or three or more years were of no great moment. It was even seven in one case! But older women than I often seemed to be crudely young to me.)

What followed now was an earnest discussion of the amazing goodness of this newly-met associate of ours, known to me and to Annie for some months [but] a name to most of them until this October of 1906. Stumbling words of admiration and sudden words of insight. Questions. Why in the midst of the turmoils we created she seemed placidly at peace, how with police thrusting and East London worshippers pulling, she was a picture of placid dignity? How her very clothing refused to be deranged – that uniform which called to mind a unity of a great Spanish Lady and a devout Catholic nun.

'She was born saintly,' declared Annie Kenney.

'Then,' suggested Adela, 'she would never be tempted to do anything evil.'

'But how easy that would make life,' murmured another Kenney voice.

And my little devil lifted its voice. 'And how dull,' said I.

A cold water drench. TB again, bringing the sentimentalists back to earth.

Mary Gawthorpe struck for harmony. 'Did you ever ask yourself,' she said, 'whether it was better to be born good or to struggle into goodness?'

'Well, to be born good would make life easy. There would be no temptations. You could go right ahead doing the right things. The world would not have to wait until your conscience wakened up. All the time you would be making life better all around you.'

I poured cold water again. 'That does not follow,' I said. 'You cannot assume that judgment and sound knowledge always go with saintliness. Saints in the past have done queer things to the world of their day and to other people and have often allowed dreadful things to go on without protest. They don't all have a social conscience. You are assuming that they do.'

'Then which,' asked Mary, 'is the best type in itself? And which the best type for its value to others?'

'This calls for philosophy, Mary's favourite concern. Go to it!' I said. They did.

To be born a saint made it easier for you, the saint, they decided. But the value to the world depended on what you did with your saintliness.

'And upon the accident of place and time,' I interjected. 'A thwarted missioner isolated in a desert, a great healer working in a chain-gang, a Christabel born in a slum . . .'

'Don't run away from the point,' snapped an elder. 'A slum child could be a natural saint even in a workhouse, but a Slum Christabel couldn't.'

There was a hush, an awed hush.

'That's neither here nor there,' said the Irish voice. 'What you are considering is whether Mrs Despard or Christabel is the greater saint.'

'No, it isn't,' came a chorus. Comparisons absurd. Two entirely different elements.

'Not entirely different,' I suggested. 'Incongruous personalities, yes, but both fighters, brave, daring – which is a special kind of bravery – both committed to service, both gallant.'

# The Birth of the Women's Freedom League[29]

This WFL Jubilee awakens many and varied memories in one who was in the thick of the Suffragette Movement from the beginning until 1911. When the WSPU was formed in Manchester in October 1903, I was already in touch with Mrs P[ankhurst], and I must have joined it in December, or possibly in the January following.

When I attended my first or second meeting, I was asked to draw up a draft constitution which would serve as a basis for shaping into whatever form the movement desired. It followed the usual democratic pattern of governing executive [committee] and annual conference, all controlled by the voting members in their branches. Meanwhile, we were gathered together for one immediate and compelling object; time was urgent, the political atmosphere was electric, a General Election of unusal intensity was pending, and we had to seize the moment to put Votes for Women on the map.

Hence, although we knew that a constitution was a necessary guarantee for the future, we left it aside and concentrated on action. From time to time, the formal shaping of the draft into an agreed constitution came up in discussion but was always postponed. So far as I know there was never any distress on this account, for there was never any doubt but that ultimately it would be shaped and passed.

This confident attitude may be taken for granted because the original WSPU members were all from the political Left. Dr and Mrs Pankhurst had joined Keir Hardie's Independent Labour Party when they had given up hope of getting women's suffrage through the Liberal Party, and she had remained there, when left a widow, doing general humanist and public work and giving herself in service to that young idealist movement, from the great majority of whose members she won admiration and affection. She had a great emotional appeal and she was a clear and quick thinker. I have known her bring a badly managed meeting back to order with a few words and to reduce an audience to tears.

Also, of course, she had her critics, for she could be passionately resentful and she was fully proficient in the under-cover arts of the politician. But the over-riding attitude towards her was real affection and admiration.

As her henchmen and supporters, all doors in the progressive movements were open to us in our campaign for an early equal suffrage bill. We won a hearing in them all from Fabian groups and Labour Churches to trade union branch meetings and odd groups meeting in odd corners such as basements and barns where they devised the making of a new world.

Our converts therefore were naturally of the kind that take a constitution and the member's right of voting for granted.

Among them were women and men of national reputation – poets and preachers, artists and writers, stage celebrities and medical women – and just plain ordinary folk, women and men from every grade in the community, but mainly from the intelligent middle class who have always been the chief campaigners for female emancipation, as they have for social service.

But all the time our task was a hand-to-mouth rush . . .

To give a glimpse of the feeling in those days, I record the 'wild scheme' I based on Mrs Pankhurst's personal popularity. I suggested that as a dramatic challenge to the law excluding us, we should get her nominated for Parliament. I was of course taking the Bradlaugh fight as a prototype, when a constituency elected and re-elected a member again and again in despite of the law of the time, and finally won a victory. Loved and admired as she was, I felt sure through working with them that friends in the ILP could carry through the preliminary electoral steps necessary and the enthusiasts of the WSPU could turn the plan into an effective gesture likely to fix the attention of the world.

But on the question of tactics there was an invisible wall between the ordinary member and the Pankhurst family. Suggestions were made and heard of no more. Things happened as the urge or the opportunity occurred, and so long as they fitted in with the spirit of the plan of action, we tacitly or actively agreed to share in them or to justify them in our speeches. Some of us, of course, were just carried along in the tide of feeling and did little thinking.

I have always been prolific of suggestions, and I had argued that there were four ways of action open to the half-nation of excluded citizens: protest and petition, which covered the Pankhurst policy, and the two methods of assertion and rejection which I would have liked to add. Raiding a polling booth and voting, despite the law, and standing for Parliament, are examples under the first head 'Assertion'; and tax resistance with the refusal to obey laws come under the 'Rejection' heading. They have neither of them been fully used in our movement.

Mrs Dora Montefiore made the first tax resistance move in 1906 and was supported by Annie Kenney and myself,[30] but Manchester cold-shouldered this co-operation, and so far as I know, no effort was ever made to organise the refusal by women to accept laws made for women without their consent. Only three or four women followed my lead in refusing to acknowledge the right of the Magistrates' Courts to try them.[31] Edith How-Martyn and I tried Police Court protests in the early WFL days and had a few imitators, while the Tax Resistance Movement received its greatest impetus from Freedom League activity. But otherwise the whole policy of agitation was channelled through protest and petition in different forms.

In the spring of 1905 I gave up my teaching, my Equal Pay [League] work[32] and my activity at the Manchester University Settlement and sacrificed my chance of a science degree to forward the women's cause through the ILP. This was at Mrs Pankhurst's request and by her arrangement. My task was to combine the ordinary organising work in the district to which I was appointed with the enrolling and education of the women so that they would form a supporting body for action in favour of the Women's Suffrage Bill, and the Party itself would become more aware of their value.

About Easter 1906, again at Mrs Pankhurst's request, I transferred to organising in the WSPU itself, and with Annie Kenney began the work of creating a national headquarters in London. Previously Sylvia Pankhurst (committed to discretion as a scholarship arts student) had managed to form in London only two loosely linked groups in Bow and Bromley. They were earnest and kindly women, vaguely anxious to improve the world, who were quite happy to join in with us when called upon because we were 'against the Government' and 'for' Keir Hardie and Mrs Pankhurst, who had assured them that they ought to demand the right to vote. For the rest we had to knock on a closed door and to build from the foundation.

It seemed a long period then and looms large even now, but the strenuous and picturesque effort continued only until mid-summer. Yet it was so highly successful that we ourselves could scarcely credit our own progress. From our unending meetings, interviews and protests, our appearances as interrupters at political meetings and in the House of Commons and later on the door-steps of Cabinet Ministers – with a resultant visit to Holloway – we had built up a membership we could not keep pace with and a Headquarters

Committee which included such women as Mrs Despard, Marion Holmes, Maud Fitzherbert and Edith How-Martyn, our first Honorary Secretary.

At this date I cannot even begin to give lists of names, but somewhere, at some time, this should be done, for there were women who enlisted then who served the movement heroically and gave us immediately hope and status and women who were handmaids in our service expecting no recognition, and men whose staunch support lasted through the years until the fight ended – and after.

The change that came in mid-summer [1906] was a matter of wonder and delight. By introduction through Keir Hardie, the movement secured the cooperation of the Pethick-Lawrences, who, once enlisted, created a revolution. They were prepared to make us financially safe and to devote their great abilities to providing an efficient organisation with a headquarters capable of carrying on the militant policy and coping with the crowding membership which the pioneer efforts had collected.

We rejoiced greatly and, almost dazed, watched the transformation scene. Within weeks the whole scene was changed almost beyond recognition, and we were proudly installed at Clements' Inn with a staff of organisers, clerks and secretaries that appeared to grow daily.

To complete the change-over, Mrs Pankhurst who had made only flying visits to us during the earlier months now gave up her Manchester home to work wholly from the new centre, and Christabel, having taken her Law degree, also emerged upon the London scene.

These sweeping changes were not accomplished without arousing some anxiety among the London membership. The sudden improvements delighted them but they began to feel confusion and a sense of loss. The close compact centre group was broken up by the disappearance of the three who had pioneered the London work. Sylvia Pankhurst was sent into a form of retirement to write a Suffragette history, five great cases of her father's and mother's accumulated papers as her material. Annie Kenney was despatched to organise the West of England, and I myself given the like job in Scotland. We were soon unmentioned in the London Press, whose cuttings Annie had collected and preserved for us so assiduously, and in which we had figured at first as 'females', 'hooligans' and 'viragoes' and at last as 'the indomitables' and the 'redoubtables.' We were heard no more in the London halls, parks and at street corners; we appeared no more in the London Courts for carrying sandwich-boards and obstructing traffic or selling pamphlets and picture postcards in the Strand. We rang up no more the reporters' rooms of the newspapers. We led no more little groups to lobby Cabinet Ministers down in St Stephens.

I remember particularly two items which disturbed the London members – the first, the issue of *Votes for Women* to which neither Annie nor I had been asked even to send a message of welcome; and the consigning of Annie to a role of silence on the platform when she brought up her first contingent from Bristol. This the meeting would not endure, and it thundered its demand to hear her. I was never included in the London platform party after October 1906, just before my second imprisonment.

Much of this was probably unavoidable in the rush of work and the changing conditions at the centre. The 'provinces' now had to be organised. The leaders must be centred in London. But it naturally took some time for the ordinary members to realise this, and meantime they were rebuffed by being received as strangers by a strange staff and finding their new leaders had become high and hidden personalities in inner sanctums instead of fellows working on the same level.

I do not think that these failures in taste or decisions of policy did much to foment discontent, but, of course, they had some disheartening effects. They were accompanied, however, by the feeling of the Committee . . . that they were being increasingly ignored. From this stage, the postponement of the consideration of the constitution began to look sinister, and the old members asked that the date of [the Annual General] Conference should be fixed. After delay, a date in September 1907 was chosen and Edith How-Martyn, still Honorary Secretary, sent out the necessary document. With Scottish work and by-election campaigns, I was now seldom in London, but was kept in touch with events by an unsought for but welcome and copious correspondence mainly from members but also from some Committee members who were unsettled in their minds or seeking advice or information as to how branches should prepare for this second Conference.

When the Conference day came it was attended by delegates and individual members indiscriminately who assembled ready for discussion on constructive lines. But, instead of discussion, there was an announcement of dictatorship put forward with all the eloquence, skill and feeling of which Mrs Pankhurst was capable. The draft Constitution was dramatically torn up and thrown to the ground. The assembled members were informed that they were in the ranks in an army of which she was the permanent Commander-in-Chief. (Mostly the reaction to this challenge was the silence of stunned surprise.) The metaphor of the army eased the situation for some, especially the newer members, enlisted in a mood of emotional admiration for the charm, ability and assurance of the combined leadership that had turned what had been a new agitation into something impressive and endowed with a new horizon of hope.

But the poor document that had been interred and resurrected so many times since 1903 was not yet done with. The abortive Conference was scarcely over before the original democratic spirit became vocal. The majority of these members believed in the democratic principle in all avenues of life, in the home and in private associations as well as in politics. The vote must be granted in the movement as well as in the country. How else could women of such spirit work? How else could they face the world? The Conference must be held and the constitution created.

It came, as you know, in a short few weeks on October 11, 1907, and the gathering then assembled created the Women's Freedom League and made possible the long record of worthy and productive work which has been associated with its name during fifty years. This actual name was not chosen at that first delegate meeting, for some members claimed that, as the constitution had been promised and prepared for the WSPU and they had joined it on that basis, we were the rightful heirs to that name; but after a short interval, we were all united in ending what was a confusing rivalry. At the next general gathering the title we know and love was adopted and we set out without rancour to do in our own way our share of the work both sections of the movement were pledged to accomplish.

I presided at both the conferences of the WFL which decided its future and at those that followed annually until 1911. This was by the express wish of Mrs Despard, who felt that the conduct of big business meetings was not the job for her. Also for the same reason I became Chairman of the WFL Executive Committee, although my actual working job was that of National Honorary Organising Secretary. The queen-pin of our movement was of course Edith How-Martyn, who, as Honorary Secretary, carried the heaviest burden with a spirit which never faltered and won admiration from us all.

The case for democratic control has been made throughout this statement, but the case of the other side must not be ignored. Mrs Pankhurst and Christabel had a knowledge of suffrage history and of the political dances that had defeated earlier efforts which was unique, for Dr Pankhurst had done drafting and pioneer work right back in the days of John Stuart Mill. Therefore they had felt and thought deeply on the methods necessary to win victory. They had formed a policy and were prepared to take the risks of carrying it out. Now, having announced their policy and displayed their methods, they held that those who enrolled knew that they did so to co-operate in carrying on the work under their personal direction.

A case can be made for such a claim with one proviso: that it is made clear from the beginning that the direction is autocratic. This was not done in the early years, so the earlier members could claim to have been deceived and a cleavage became inevitable. The later enrolling supporters knew the position and can therefore be regarded as willingly consenting to a dictatorship with which they agreed.

It always seemed to me, however, that it was a pity that these two – Christabel and her mother, outstanding women – could not trust their adherents. I believe that they could have obtained from them a wide range of directive power and a reasoned acceptance of a status above that of the ordinary elected official. Democrats can afford to cherish and endow with power those who bring to it inspiration for the redressing of wrongs, and I believe in this case they would have done it.

# Part II
# *Theory in the Midst of Battle*
## *Essays of a Suffragette*

# 'The Militant Policy of Women Suffragists'*

A little over a year ago – on October 13th 1905 – two women suffragists were imprisoned in Manchester. Technically, they were guilty of obstruction, having tried to hold a meeting outside the Free Trade Hall in defiance of the orders of the police. But the fundamental cause of their imprisonment was the determination of the two women, and of the society to which they belonged, to force the question of women's enfranchisement to the front, and to get a declaration from Sir Edward Grey who was speaking that night in Manchester as a future Liberal Minister. These two, Miss Christabel Pankhurst and Miss Annie Kenney, were the first, but during the year that has intervened 173 [TBG has scratched the word 'eighteen'] other women have willingly suffered imprisonment. They have all been declared guilty of some technical breach of the law, some of them have been guilty, but all of them have deliberately chosen the method of vigorous protest, and welcomed the suffering which it entailed, in order to expose the outlawry to which women were subjected and to awaken the public conscience, so that the bar to their citizenship might be removed.

The Press, the politicians, the older suffrage societies, united at first in scornful or angry denunciation, and ridicule. A clamour of abuse and misrepresentation rose in every part of the country, which for a time served the purpose of entirely discrediting the agitation. Some part of this was due to the strong feeling of the General Election, more to the mere fact that the agitators were women, and a great deal to ignorance of the issue, or to an over-developed sense of decorum.

The insurgent women continued steadily upon their predetermined line. The meetings addressed by prominent members of the new Government were consistently visited, and a declaration of

* Manuscript signed 'Teresa Billington, His Majesty's Prison Holloway. Nov. 12. 06.' Box 404, File 3, TBG Collection, Fawcett Library.

Liberal policy on women's suffrage demanded. The opening of Parliament brought the agitators to London, where processions and demonstrations of women were organised, deputations were forced on Cabinet Ministers, and protests were made in the House of Commons. Before the rising of the House the question of women's suffrage was a living question, mainly because nine women had been imprisoned, a suffrage siege had taken place at Hammersmith, and the campaign against Mr Asquith had commenced. During the vacation the country was covered from Aberdeen to Portsmouth, the fiery cross was carried from end to end of East Fife – the constituency of the Chancellor of the Exchequer – and a policy of opposition to the Government nominee was followed in three by-elections.

Meanwhile great changes have taken place in the public appreciation of the agitators and their work, which have been particularly marked in the case of the Press. This is no doubt due greatly to the sounder judgment based on longer experience of the agitators. The more carefully weighed utterances of politicians and older suffragists, and the steady growth of public support, have also contributed greatly to this end. As a result the advance of the London Press towards fair treatment of the agitators has been remarkable. Nor is the London Press alone affected by the change. It has been forced upon the provincial Press by the coming of the fighting suffragists into their districts. To those in the movement the experience of the summer has been highly amusing in this respect. The naïve surprise of the provincial pressman when he discovered that the 'notorious suffragette' was a mild mannered and ladylike woman of parts is a thing to be remembered.

The older suffragists were naturally at first inclined to condemn the new departure. They had been climbing up and down a step ladder for years, sometimes near the top, sometimes near the bottom, but always believing that ultimately they would reach the topmost rung. They had evolved a theory that only the politest requests, only the mildest persuasion, only the highest appeal to the best instincts of men, were worthy of their cause, or could carry it to success. They assumed that argument, right, and reason, would finally triumph. They were prepared to wait until the time arrived.

To the younger and no less earnest suffragists this position appeared to be fundamentally unsound. The history of the women's suffrage movement was a history of a scandalous series of betrayals, of despicable tactics and broken pledges. Such a list of contemptuous refusals to enfranchise women as is to be found in the annals of the House of Commons during the last forty years, could never have existed had the women suffragists made the members of the House fear their influence. Bills talked out, blocked, and killed in Committee, while a 'friendly' majority of legislators revelled in the annual or bi-annual amusement of woman-baiting, do not form a record creditable either to the House of Commons or to the non-protesting suffrage societies. The great Liberal betrayal of 1885, when more than 100 Liberal Members of the House deliberately broke their pledges to the women at the bidding of Mr Gladstone, reflects little credit upon the men of the party, or upon the women who remained members of it after their cause had been betrayed. Such methods as were employed by the societies advocating the suffrage may have had their virtues. At one time – the beginning – they were essential and satisfied the wants of the day. But they have been outgrown by circumstances. They are condemned by results. Neither enthusiasm nor growth resulted from them. The most self-sacrificing suffragists were always ahead of, and doubted by, the organised societies. The want of vigour in the movement, its utter incapacity for protest, rendered possible the constantly recurring insult that was poured upon it. The younger women saw these things and writhed under them. They determined on new methods, condemning the old ones by their record. Such a record, they said, of which failure and discredit are the outstanding features, is not a record which can be quoted in recommendation of the methods which have allowed it, step by step, to be built up. We will try to establish a new and better one.

Women's need of the vote, the justice of their claim, the many logical arguments by which they supported it, have not proved sufficient to move Parliament. Such things may be sufficient when they accompany the demand of an enfranchised class. The power of the voter turns theoretical acceptance of a principle into an Act of Parliament. But when argument and justice and need are on the side of those who have no votes, the support they win alone remains merely sympathetic. The voteless have no votes and therefore no power to get. Their work is sterile of practical result unless they show in a perfectly unmistakable way their determination to have the reform they seek. The power of the voter must be replaced by the persistence and immovable determination of the voteless. This is the only road to success.

Not only is this the one practicable way, it is the one logical way also. Upon those who are makers of law, laws are naturally binding. Upon those who are not, there can be no bond. The authority of law over them rests, not upon consent, but upon brute force. Legislation is made for them, not by them, and is thrust upon them by a government which is a tyranny. By it they are taxed and restricted but over it they have no control. To be so shut out from the rights

113

and privileges of law is to be an outlaw. An outlaw must be either a rebel or a willing serf. Anyone who believes in human liberty and self-government is forced to rebel. There is no other way. It is either servile submission to tyranny or rebellion against it.

Woman is denied the rights of citizenship. She is an outlaw. Thus logically and justly she ought to be a rebel. For her, as for every race and sect that has won liberty, it is the only way to freedom. The fact that the government, which is a representative one for men, is an autocratic tyranny to women, makes an essential difference to the relations between men and the government and women and the government. The House of Commons is responsible to men. It is a great half-national assembly fulfilling their will and securing their interests. The parties in that House depend upon the support of men for their existence, and win that support by concession. Therefore Parliament acquires meaning and value, almost sanctity, to men, in that it embodies their liberties and carries out their behests. But to women it only bears the relation that the Czar bears to his people. The House of Commons, its legislators, its Law Courts, and its laws, embody no freedom for women, and can have no sanctity for women. It is well to remember this essential difference, which must remain until the sex-bar is removed and women are enfranchised.

Woman has tried while still submitting to the law to achieve her freedom. She has tried to act as though she were a citizen. She has pulled all the strings of what is called legitimate agitation – but the machine has not worked. She has fitted together all the usual and constitutional elements of political machinery – but the motive power has been wanting. She has achieved a certain point in education, a certain point in theoretical support – and there has been a dead-lock. She can carry her cause no further with the weapons she has used. She must employ some new force. The appreciation of this fact has been slowly filtering through the women's movement for years. But the logical justification for the adoption of unusual and uncon-stitutional methods has not been realised until the very recent past. It has needed the object lessons of a year to get it recognised at all by the older suffrage leaders. But it is slowly being accepted today. It will be accepted more generously still within a very short time.

Such a lesson cannot be hard to learn. For all history is full of examples of the fact that liberty is only won by revolt. The political liberty of men, religious liberty, liberty of speech, have all been finally obtained by conflict with existing authority. The heroes and martyrs of the conflicts are extolled and venerated in every part of the world. Without them liberty had not been. Without them slavery and tyranny had divided the world. Government authority and law represent at any given time not the progressive ideals of liberty of which the people are capable, but the amount of liberty the forerunners of the people have been able to wrest from earlier and equally unwilling governments. Government is essentially opposed to new liberties, it rests upon and acts in accordance with the limited foundations of liberty which have already been laid. These foundations have been laid by the rebel outlaws of the past. The wider foundations of greater liberty must be laid by the rebels of the present.

This is true for all outlaws but especially for women. In obtaining the enfranchisement of women there is not only the prejudice which every unenfranchised class seeking liberty has to meet, but the prejudice of sex as well. As a result women have to face more of the prejudice and passion of selfish and ignorant opposition than would have to be met by any class of men. The reasons advanced by opponents of the citizenship of women show this conclusively. There are nine reasons based on sex prejudice advanced for every one based on any other foundation. There is no consciousness in the minds of many men that women are human beings. They are regarded as merely sex-beings, segregated wholly, and not always honourably, for sex uses. The great mass of men who consider women only in this light are not conscious of their prejudice. The minority of them are bitterly and violently conscious of what they consider their opposing sex interests.

The old quiet methods are absolutely useless with either the majority of the minority of this large class of men. The first is not reached by them, the second is not ruffled by them. And strange as it may sound we want the bitter, prejudiced and unreasoning opponents to be ruffled into speech and action. He is a strong if unknowing ally who allows his bigotry and abuse to escape him. The dramatic protests which occasion his outspoken opposition startle the unconscious opponent into thought. In this newly awakened condition of mind he is eager for argument and inform-ation. Then it is that the irrational masculine bigot quickens or completes his conversion. Thus the man in the street is reached and popular support gained. Only by methods which break through the indifference and carelessness of the public which set the opponents condemning, and the ignorant questioning, can apathy be turned into sympathy and a popular demand be created. This element has been long wanting for the woman's movement. The protests of the last year have created a phenomenal advance in the right direction.

Not only in the case of men has this been so, the awakening has been even more wonderful in the case of women. To rouse women must always be a harder task than to rouse men so long as women are restricted by custom and law. Women have been shut out from

115

political life, restricted in social life, and robbed and degraded in industrial life. In every department of life additional burdens have been placed on their shoulders because of their sex. They are poorer than men, have less leisure and less freedom than men, and have been bound by stricter conventions than men. Poverty, custom, creed, dependence, keep many women silent. The age of chivalry may be dead; certainly the age of tyranny over wives is not. Yet in spite of these things a great rising of new thought, a great seeking after freedom, has manifested itself around the suffrage agitators wherever they have worked. Hundreds, nay thousands, of converts have been drawn into the movement, a new spirit of enthusiasm has been kindled in the hearts of those who were already suffragists. 'We have been born anew' said one such to me – a suffragist of thirty years' standing – 'It has been a revolution.' She is only one of many.

There are many other arguments which could be presented to show that the vigorous tactics, the rebellion and protest against the Government, which have marked the suffrage movement of the last year, are justified by experience, by reason and by result. They have made the movement live again. They have arrested the attention of the country, broken the boycott of the daily Press, and shamed the pledged politicians into speech and action. It is claimed by the women who have initiated the policy and so far carried it out, that it is necessary, justifiable, and deserving of support. They make these claims because

1 No liberty has ever been won without revolt.
2 Those who are outlaws must be either rebels or serfs; self-respecting women prefer rebellion to serfdom.
3 It is the duty of believers in equality and liberty to rebel against inequality and tyranny.
4 The industrial and social condition of women is so grievous that women cannot wait longer for political power.
5 The politicians had to be convinced that women were in earnest.
6 The great mass of the people were unconscious of the urgent need for the reform and had to be awakened.
7 Nothing but a dramatic and unusual agitation could have broken the conspiracy of silence and inaction.
8 Every other possible policy had been tried and had failed.

There are only left now to consider those constantly repeated objections to the fighting policy which are based on antagonism to the principle of women's suffrage, on party feeling, or on expediency.

Those people who oppose the enfranchisement of women will naturally be opposed to all methods of advancing that reform. The advocacy is condemned because of the cause. But as the militant tactics of today are calling general attention to the question they are attacked with increased violence by suffrage opponents. It is enlightening to discover the unanimity of opinion as to the wickedness of these tactics amongst our opponents. The enemies of their cause give the women who want the vote a gift of good advice. They advise women to revert to the old policy. But 'Timeo Danaos dona ferentes.' Their advice is indeed the best recommendation of the insurgent policy that I have met. When one's opponent does not like one's methods it is a sign that those methods are likely to succeed.

But it is said the methods are likely to anger and irritate the enemy into active agitation against women's suffrage. If this be so it is well. The marshalling of the opponents' forces is a recognition of the growing power of women's demand for freedom. Women should rejoice when their cause is seriously opposed, because their case is so irrefutable that every opportunity of displaying its strength hastens the victory. Then an angry opponent is better than a contemptuously indifferent one. The portion of the suffragist has been for a long time open indifference and ill-disguised ridicule and scorn. The change of quality in the opposition is an advance. There is respect often with anger, there is none with contempt.

The party arguments at present come chiefly from those who are Liberals. Many women who are members of the Women's Liberal Federation or Association desire strongly the enfranchisement of their sex. Some few of them sacrifice principle and self-respect to party and feel the insult of the sex-bar too little. These latter have found party ties too strong for a clear appreciation of the position. Had a Conservative Government been in power when first the rebel tactics were adopted their vision might not have been so much impeded. Any government that refuses to give to women a pledge that it will enfranchise them, must be regarded as an enemy. The hand of every woman should be against the government which has the power to free her and refuses to use it. The Liberal Government occupies this position today. No one can make it move from that position more quickly than the Liberal women. So far, as a body, they have refused to try. It is to be hoped that they will not delay so long as to make it appear when they act that they act only to save the reputation of their party. The Liberal women have moved very slowly, but they are moving, one must admit. They are beginning to understand that overmuch trust is a vice, that the continued postponement of their enfranchisement is insulting to them and unwise for their party, and that since that party is in possession and has power to do it must be made to do. This is the only attitude that a woman who respects herself or her sex can take up. This is the only attitude that will bring her to freedom.

At the beginning of the new movement many objections were brought forward on the score of expediency. Some friend had recanted, some donor had withdrawn, some Member of Parliament had declined to again support a Women's Suffrage Bill. Because of these things the fainthearted sisters pleaded for a cessation of the methods which 'were putting back the movement.' But in truth the movement is stronger for the recantation of 'friends' who are too illogical or too artificially conventional to understand its principles or its needs. Part of the necessary work of all reform movements is to rid themselves of the hypocritical friends who profess a mild support in order to retard progress. Those who are so incapable of reasoning as to withdraw support from a cause because of what they consider wrong advocacy are also better gone. They are best described as of the school which supports the principle of women's suffrage so long as all women are good little girls. The support which has been obtained because women were useful to the politicians at election times is of the same class. Women are better without it. The 'honourable' Members of Parliament have been guilty of this dishonest practice very generally. 'It keeps the women satisfied,' one young M.P. is reported to have said to another, 'if you say you're in favour of women's suffrage. They work for you, and it keeps them quiet.'

But for one false or fainthearted friend that is lost fifty new friends are found, and fifty old ones enthused. Even the man who calls the methods employed 'disgusting and disgraceful,' has to admit after a few days, 'These women are galvanising a corpse, and making thousands of followers.' Indeed this is proved by the fighting society's forces. New branches spring to life of themselves, the funds come with the need, the workers at the call, friends send support and sympathy from every class and every nation. The working women – the most heavily burdened, the most deeply wronged, the most in need of political power – have seen a new hope before them. Even in this prison convicts have whispered in passing, 'We know you are fighting for women. It is a shame you are here.' The sense of bitter need, the sense of shameful wrong, which lie deep in the hearts of these women are spurs to them when awakened. They are gathering round the rebel suffragists as they never gathered in this movement before. But it is not merely working women, nor leisured women, nor Conservative women, nor Liberal women, nor Socialist women, it is *women* who are uniting at last. The movement has been re-born, and it is palpitating with life.

So we gather the gains and the glories and weigh against them

118

the loss, and we are not ashamed of our work. Proudly, deliberately and gladly we follow our rebel path, knowing that we are right, and that as the present has given, so will the future give more than justification.

# 'Woman's Liberty and Man's Fear'*

Man is afraid of woman. He proves it every day. History proves it for him – the history of politics, the history of industry, the history of social life. An examination of woman's present position and of man's attitude towards the woman's movement shows evidence of fear at every turn. Yes, it is quite true. Man is afraid of woman because he has oppressed her.

It is only to be expected after all. Why should one be surprised to discover the plain truth? The Czar is afraid of his people; the master is afraid of his subject workers; the government is afraid of the mis-governed masses; and man is afraid of woman. It is ever so. Injustice and wrong thrust upon our fellows rest on so unstable a foundation that the dread of rebellion is always upon the oppressor. There is always for him the fear that the end may come, and rebellion carries with it not merely the throwing off of the yoke but alongside of it the dread of such vengeful retaliation as corresponds to the oppressor's tyranny.

So, because man has oppressed woman, he is afraid of her; because he has denied her liberty and bought her and sold her, he is afraid to face her free; because he has forced her to marriage with iron bonds of poverty, and driven her to sell her body for bread, he stands as a coward before the ages: it is a fitting curse.

There are some superficial men who are blinded by their own prejudices so far as to deny this fact. 'Afraid!' they cry – 'afraid of *women*!' and they laugh. But their laugh is still the laugh of fear. The bully and the coward always laugh bravely when the gates are barred and the keys turned upon their victims. So these men laugh believing in their ignorance that the bonds by which woman has been fettered

* Manuscript signed 'Teresa Billington,' pre-February 1907, Box 404, File 6, TBG Collection, Fawcett Library.

120

hand and foot are too strong to be broken. But the bonds are breaking under their blinded eyes.

I do not believe that any thinking man today accepts the old dogma of masculine superiority. Those who do not think of course are many. They still believe it fondly and foolishly. It is a comfortable and pleasant doctrine for a fool. But the growing capacity of women today, their startling development, the progress they are making in every department of life, are too obvious to be mistaken. The theory is dead.

But it is amusing and enlightening to note how these very believers in the incapacity of women are the ones who most strenuously oppose the loosening of their bonds. There is such delightful masculinity in the logic! Yet these are the folk who tell women that the male sex has the monopoly of reason and of rational action.

Two children are about to run a race. Says one to the other, 'You cannot run so well as I can so I will bind your legs with a cord.' Then as the race proceeds he cries, 'You can't run – you can't run. I am cleverer and stronger than you are.' 'Unbind my legs' is the answer, 'that I may have a chance.' But the free-limbed child capers about and says, 'Unbind you? No, indeed. You have not come as far as I have. You do not know how to run. But when you catch me I will unbind your legs.'

In all essentials this little fable is analogous with the facts in the life of woman. On the ground that she is less able than man she is penalised in the struggle, and denied the opportunity which she most needs. Her demand for liberty is met by the reply that when she, with her additional burdens, has shown herself man's equal according to his standard of judgment, her claim will be considered. On the injustice and immorality of the position I will not comment. But I feel compelled to emphasise the depth of muddle-headed absurdity to which the masculine mind has fallen in its effort to justify the subjection of women.

In the industrial world man is afraid of woman. All the best-paid work is in the hands of men, and women are rigidly shut out. From all the higher posts in the lesser trades, and from all the chief trades and their subsidiary industries, women are rigorously excluded. When I was quite young I desired to be an engineer. I was almost as happy among the wonders of machinery as among flowers. The theories of impact, of momentum, of tension – the arrangements of levers, pulleys, planes and screws to make machines, were things to conjure with, with me. But as I was a woman such mechanical talent as I possessed had to be wasted. No department of engineering, theoretical or practical, was open to me. As the desire of women to practise as doctors was opposed, as the would-be woman lawyer today is thwarted, so is the would-be woman engineer, surveyor, or architect, so is the woman who desires to enter any of the better organised departments of industry.

Men shut women out of these industrial avenues, not because women are proved incapable of entering them, but because of their fear of women's entrance into what they have regarded as their preserves. All that chatter about women being incapable of doing this that or the other is so much balderdash. I apologise for using the word, but I know no other that so aptly expresses the truth. Men can never prove that women are incapable of following any given trade or profession, until women have had equal opportunity with men to follow it, and have failed. If women really were incapable the arbitrary and artificial ring-fence which men have erected, and which they so carefully preserve, would not be needed. The fact of its erection and preservation is an acknowledgement by men that they fear women's equal competition.

In such departments of economic production and exchange as women have won admittance the same coward policy is pursued. When the work is specialised women are generally given the worst work, and for this they are underpaid. Where they do the same work as men they are paid at a lower rate. It matters not what the work itself is, the principle is applied right through – from tailors to university lecturers, from prison warders to matrons of hospitals, women are robbed of a certain part of their earnings because they are women.

One can understand the employer doing this. Woman is voteless, and of the lowest social and industrial status. She is the more easily sweated and she can be used to level down the earnings of men. All this is quite satisfactory to the employer. But one cannot understand the workman giving his support to the employer's injustice. Yet this is precisely what he has done. Men teachers, men in the potting trades, in the hosiery trade, in tailoring, in printing, and in a thousand other trades, draw a jealous line between women's wages and their own. This is a grievous injustice and a lamentable mistake on the part of the male-worker. He supports a system of robbery of women-workers which by keeping their wages beneath his own immediately makes them dangerous to himself. Woman entering the labour market for wages artificially depressed because of her sex, reduces the general level of wages, undersells man, and ousts him from employment. Man has been afraid of woman's fair competition in the working world, has shut her out from the best work, and underpaid her work in all departments. He reaps the harvest he has sown.

Not only has the subjection of woman to men been harmful

directly and indirectly in the economic world, but it has produced far-reaching evil effects in our social and sex-relations. There is a vital connection between woman's outlawry in industry and her pitiable position of dependence in marriage. Because man desired to keep woman under his control he has denied her the chance of economic independence, he has forced her to feed herself through him. He has done this because he was afraid that if she were free he might lose her. The cloak of marriage has been used to cover unspeakable horrors which women have suffered. Men have known this, and seen the rebellion in women's hearts, and in effect they have said, 'Unless women have no other way of livelihood we shall lose them.' The other alternative – that of removing the evil conditions against which women rebelled, and of making marriage such that they would willingly have entered it, either never occurred to men's minds or was rejected by them because of the restraint which it entailed for themselves.

Although it has been demonstrated that the economic dependence of women is harmful to motherhood, and therefore to the race, although it has produced a class of serf women who have enslaved their children, men still cry out against all efforts at reform on the frank ground that women who had an open world at their feet would not marry. 'What would become of the race?' asks many a man when one demands full economic opportunity for women. Which translated into his true thought becomes, 'What would become of my chances for the satisfaction of my desires?'

This attitude is due to fear. The fear is bred of the knowledge that women are in a state of more or less repressed revolt. It is a bitter commentary on what men have made of marriage that it should be so. But it is true. I do not believe in their doleful prognostications. Women who are economically free will not refuse to marry. But they will refuse to marry on the present terms. They will be the equals of the men they marry – neither serfs, nor chattels, but equals. It is perhaps this that the men who oppose the woman's movement fear. They are so far commercialised as to prefer to bargain – even in the matter of marriage – with someone who is at their mercy. They would lose so much if they were not able to dictate terms. So the fear of the self-indulgent tyrant, of the coward, goads men on to oppose the emancipation of women. They prefer the continued degradation of marriage, they prefer the continued public sale of sex upon our streets, they prefer the nameless diseases and shames that today corrupt the souls and bodies of the people, to that freeing of women which is the only foundation on which the reform of these evils can be based. They must be hard driven by fear to prefer such things to the welfare of the race.

123

The political disabilities forced upon women are continued for a similar reason. Men know that women are entitled to the vote and need its protection, but they are afraid of the reforms which women will institute. This is constantly and frankly admitted though not always consciously. Men say, 'It is the thin end of the wedge. Beware of it.' Or 'We must protect politics from the introduction of sex questions,' or again 'Women would ruin politics by enquiring too minutely into the private life of candidates.' Behind every one of these arguments lurks fear – craven, pitiable fear – the fear of those who know that redress and reform is needed, but who are not willing to sacrifice their share of the gain or pleasure which results from the evil.

It is this fear of the woman freed that lies behind the greater part of the present secret or open opposition to the enfranchisement of women. The demand for the immediate carrying into law of a measure removing the artificial disability of sex in politics is growing louder and more insistent every day. It is a vital question now. It will have to be dealt with. The awakened conscience of the people is behind the insurgent women who will not cease their protests until they are free. They are certain of victory. But meanwhile the men who are of the earth earthy oppose their demand with violence and guile, and many who are better than they contemplate the coming change with fear. They are afraid of woman. How can they know the heights to which free woman can lead humanity?

# 'The Woman with the Whip'*

I possess a small dog-whip which I shall always treasure as a memento of this present struggle. I shall not treasure it vaingloriously, nor from a personal egotism because I was the woman who used it. I shall treasure it rather as a sign and symbol of much that remains unspoken.

The plaited brown leather of this whip looks quite new. It is an everyday-looking article, such as one sees constantly in shop windows and in the hands of the owners of pet dogs. It does not seem to be a terrible or a wonderful instrument, and yet I become grave and sad and bitter of heart when I look upon it. It has a history, this small dog-whip. It is significant of much more than its appearance would imply. There lie whole realms of wrong in the world it opens to one who knows – realms peopled with the accumulated wrongs of centuries. Not only this, but in our present suffrage struggle it marks the one occasion upon which we have been deliberately aggressive.

## Facing Personal Dangers

The spirit of all other protests that have been made during the active campaign has been the spirit of self-sacrifice. The object of our organisation has been to awaken public interest in the suffrage question by submitting ourselves to such violence, ridicule, and punishment as followed from our justifiable demonstrations and protests. Propaganda, demonstration, and protest were essential. Women had to be roused to action, public sympathy had to be awakened; the dead body of the suffrage movement had to be revived. If, in doing this work effectively, we have had to face

* From *Towards Woman's Liberty* (Letchworth, Herts: Garden City Press, n.d.)

personal dangers, we have faced them. The danger has not deterred us; it has been rather an added argument for the deed.

Thus we knew that by forcing a deputation upon a Cabinet Minister we rendered ourselves liable to violence, and ultimately to imprisonment. In the interests of women the deputation was necessary. Therefore we sought it until it was obtained, willingly suffering the consequences. Similarly, in holding meetings within and without the Houses of Parliament we incurred similar dangers. Again we deliberately sought these dangers, and paid the price demanded by outraged red-tape officialism with all willingness. In like manner we faced the blows and bruises, the insults, the vile language, the affronts, which were the price of asking questions of Liberal leaders in public meetings. But there are some insults not to be borne meekly. And because of these, one woman, at one of these public questionings, carried an offensive weapon – the dog-whip I preserve.

## When the Whip was Carried

The general election, with its continuous round of meetings, was over when the whip was carried. The incident occurred at Northampton on June 14th 1906. It was naturally seized upon by the yellow press with immense satisfaction. The figure of the woman with the whip was hailed as typical of those unsexed creatures who demand the right of voting. The scorn and cheap condemnation of the press were poured forth with very joy upon the whole suffrage movement, and especially upon those who dared defend the use of the whip. Harpy, Amazon, and hooligan, were the epithets most frequently employed by the young journalist in his explosive comments and his inaccurate if highly-coloured news communications dealing with the event.

This continued for three or four days. Then at a public meeting the user of the whip made a defiant statement of defence. It appeared but in a few papers – garbled and cut down. But a great calm fell upon the tumult of newspaper abuse at once. Here and there, in insignificant corners, one noted references to the dog-whip. But these were few and far between. The great storm had been stayed by a few plain words. What were they? They were few and simple, but they embodied the statement that at several previous meetings the treatment meted out to the women who questioned the speakers had been not only brutal, but criminal also. Insult of this kind could come only from curs, and for them the dog-whip was the fitting punishment.

## Man Still a Semi-Savage

It seems as though the blind prejudiced brute is but hidden in some men by an artificial garment of culture. Touch his primal passions and the great unreasoning prejudices built upon them, and he stands revealed as still a semi-savage. Party passion is itself a strong, unreasoning force. But when alongside it is roused the blind and brutal resentment which wakes in the deeps of some men's natures against women's claims for liberty, you have a force to destroy gods and shatter morality. This force we had aroused.

Many strongly partisan Liberal men were wrought into a state of frenzy during our questioning campaign. The treatment of the women by the stewards of the meetings grew steadily worse. In districts where meetings were repeatedly visited, or where for any other reason specially bad feeling had awakened, the treatment to which the questioners were subjected ceased to be merely the rough usage that would be given under provocation to men, and became an affront specially turned against their sex. Women came away from meetings in Manchester and in London in a state of nervous humiliation, shocked, weeping, and shuddering.

## The Floodgates of Revolt

The floodgates of revolt were opened wider in our women's hearts when these things became known among us. It was felt that such insults called for retaliation and punishment. Such things were too infamous to be borne meekly. Therefore at the historic Northampton meeting I carried my dog-whip. On that night I was to occupy the most dangerous post. I was to question Mr Asquith when the anger of the stewards had already been raised to white heat by four other questioners. The last woman to be ejected had suffered the insult complained of on other occasions. I faced it on this night – but I went armed. How many self-respecting women would have done otherwise?

These incidents opened the eyes of many women to the evil that was bred in the race by our present sex oppression. Women who were lukewarm became as flames of fire. The revelation showed the deeps to which poor humanity was trodden down by the degradation of women, by the sex outlook it created in men, by the sex barter it fostered. The unfair marriage laws, the divorce and separation laws, the laws of parentage, the criminal offences laws, were

127

seen in a new light. Not only were they immoral and unjust in themselves, but they formed an evil environment in which men and women were besmudged and degraded. They set up a code of immoral license for men and of equally immoral subjection for women, by which women were regarded as merely sex things to be used for men's pleasure. Public opinion, through the novel, the music hall, the drama, the press, expressed and fostered this idea by the presentment of sordid intrigues, divorce stories, and high-life scandals, in which women were always and only concerned as sex beings. Women's human needs, rights, and nature, were hidden away, neglected, forgotten.

## The Standard of Right

Public opinion and morality are influenced directly by the standard of right set up in the nation. The standard in sex matters is unjust. A man may freely commit deeds which are punishable as crimes in a woman. A man is lightly pardoned for that for which a woman is eternally condemned. By our divorce laws an unfaithful wife can be cast off at once, but against an unfaithful husband there is no law. No wife can obtain release from her marriage because of her husband's infidelity. She has also to prove desertion or physical cruelty before the law considers that her husband has wronged her. But this is not the worst. A wronged husband can claim money damages from the male offender. A wronged wife can make no such claim. So that the law regards a wife as the property of her husband, while the husband is not regarded in any way as the property of the wife.

The parentage laws are equally prejudiced. The children of a marriage belong to the father in the eye of the law. The mother is not their legal guardian. She may bring them into the world. She is even graciously permitted to toil and strive and suffer for them. But the law does not permit her to have any authority over their young lives. The fact that most fathers are better than this law does not make the law less unjust. It is an insult to women. It is also absurd, and often works out very unpleasantly for men. For instance, a man is liable to prosecution and punishment when through his wife's neglect their children are unvaccinated or stay away from school.

## The Injustice of Laws

The criminal offences laws are also unjust. There are even some laws among them specially framed to punish women without punishing their men fellow-criminals. There is no law of solicitation where men are concerned. There is one for women. A woman being approached insultingly by a man can only charge him with annoyance, and the charge is not made easy to sustain, as in the opposite case. Day after day at a single Police Court in London scores of wretched women appear charged with solicitation, but it is a rare thing for one man to appear for annoying women. Yet so constantly is this offence committed in that district that women avoid it in the evening as a plague spot.

Not only do our laws deal heavily with the woman and lightly with the man, but our customs and usage are similarly unfair. Upon the bowed head of the immoral woman we visit the scorn and condemnation of the world. The man, who is at least equally guilty, faces the world brazenly and is smiled upon and forgiven. And in the hands of men only rest the making and administering of all laws by which women are judged and punished for such offences.

## Driven to the Street

There is a vital difference which men overlook between the position of the woman and of the man in this market of vice. The man is not driven by poverty, by the denial of the right to work, to this traffic. The woman often is. The sweated woman worker who cannot earn a sufficient pittance on which to exist is driven into the army of the street. The seasonal worker, whose wage when work can be got is too low to permit of saving, finds the same degradation. Thousands of other working women – the domestic servant turned suddenly out of place, the shop assistant dismissed without a character, the pretty girl tempted once and then eternally banned by society – fall a ready prey to the sharks that prowl ever on the outlook for victims.

The stream can only be stayed by legislation dealing with the evil itself, by legislation ensuring women a fair chance of employment and of living wages, by the gradual raising of the status of women in the eyes of men, and by the inculcation of a standard of equal morality. But this legislation will never come, this change of outlook will never come, until women hold the power of lawmaking in their own hands. So, for the sake of uplifting the men and women of our race from this cesspool of vice, for the sake of purifying our human and sex relations, for the sake of bringing salvation to the soiled and tainted children of humanity born with poisoned life-blood and an inheritance of evil, women must win and use those powers of citizenship which the vote alone can bring. For men and women together can solve those terrible problems which man alone can never hope to solve. Then the dog-whip can be burned, and the memories it wakens be forgotten.

# 'Socialism and Sex-Equality'*

Socialists are divided into two great camps on the question of Women's Suffrage. Some of them agitate for the immediate removal of sex-disability, regardless of everything but principle. Others oppose or are indifferent to its removal, because of the class of the women who would first benefit under the change. In the first case it is a matter of principle; in the second of persons. The Socialist of the first type looks beyond the mere matter of votes and all other non-essentials, and says it is not good for man to class woman as his inferior, and it is not good for woman to be so classed. Such a one recognises that women suffer under two oppressions, one sexual, and one economic. He sees clearly that every hampering bond of sex-oppression impedes and frustrates economic reform. He sees more. The exploitation of women by men unfits and incapacitates humanity for Socialist thought and organisation, and this under-lying wrong of male monopoly is the greatest bulwark the monopoly of capital possesses. The men who, without protest or effort towards reform, allow to continue such evils as the unpaid life-indentured, servile labour of married women, forced motherhood, the social banning and police-hunting of the horde of despised street women, whose partners in vice are uncondemned, the underpayment, because of sex, of women workers of all grades, and the exclusion of women from the majority of well-paid employments, are not capable of instituting a state of social justice. Arbitrary sex-inequalities have tainted their life-blood, and produced in them an unhappy condition of partial mental blindness. These things being so, the immediate establishment of sex-equality is essential to human progress, to economic reconstruction, and to racial health and morals.

The Socialist of the second type, though fired with the enthusiasm

* *The New Age, June 20, 1907.*

131

of the reformer, is at heart an autocrat still. It is not principle by which he judges, but expediency. Like the land-owner and commercial man in past times he demands that measures of liberty shall be drafted so as to suit his personal party interests. His belief in democracy is very much more a matter of expediency than a matter of principle. If it was proved to him that universal enfranchisement would endanger his industrial panaceas he would have none of it. Only those who by conviction or social position stand in agreement with him are entitled to liberty. This, of course, is the extreme case, and is not voiced by many. But a large section of men Socialists arrogate to themselves the right of saying on what terms women shall vote. Are they incapable of seeing that women have an indisputable right to vote on precisely the same terms as men, whether those terms are good or bad, and that only by carrying this principle into law can women be secure in the future from the danger of exclusion or special limitations? Women are entitled to equal recognition now, not only when the millennium is reached. They are not entitled to the greater or less measure of freedom which men may be willing to give, they are entitled to equal freedom with men. Only by putting this principle on the Statute Book are they secure. Once there it will stand for all time as a basis for the future. But a special measure instituting a new basis of suffrage for women can only stand alone. Every further step will have to be won by a further fight. Such a course would establish no principle, and would only establish the precedent of voting, not of equal voting rights. It would be a case of men allowing certain women to be voters, and would therefore continue in men's minds the evil of sex-prerogative.

I am fully convinced that the establishment of sex-equality is the first issue with which women should concern themselves. Moreover I feel justified in claiming the support of Socialists and Democrats for this course, for sex-equality is an absolutely indispensable preliminary to the reorganisation of society which they seek. I hold that Sex-Equality – not Women's Suffrage, as the Editors imagine – is more important to women than Socialism or Democracy, for without it they cannot benefit by either. I believe that as the road to full democracy is barred by two obstacles, one of which is the barrier of sex, the final aim cannot be endangered by the removal of one or other of them. I see no other way of attaining the end in this generation than that of first equalising the franchise between men and women, and then simplifying and broadening the anomalous basis of representation.

But the Adult Suffrage opponents, and those who approach their position, are apparently not concerned with the security of women's future, but only with the immediate result of establishing political sex-equality. This to me is non-essential and immaterial. If the course the Women's Social and Political Union approves establishes sex-equality, and thus secures the final full enfranchisement of all women, the status of the women first enfranchised is of no great moment. It must be regarded as an accidental circumstance, all the dangers arising from which can be obviated by the agitation of the democrats themselves for a simplified franchise basis.

But what are the facts with regard to the women who would be entitled to vote if the sex-bar were now removed? The chief franchises under which men vote are the property, house-occupier, lodger, service, and university franchise. The first is the one which is regarded as the greatest bug-bear. The outcry against propertied women voting has been long and bitter. But surely they have as much right to vote as the propertied men? Yet there is little danger of these women swamping the new voters' roll. The male monopoly of commercial opportunities and the laws of inheritance have made this impossible. There are not many women who are rich in their own right. Most so-called rich women are merely the dependants of rich men, and would not be qualified as voters in their own right. The household franchise, as judged by the municipal registers, would be an overwhelmingly working class one. The I.L.P. inquiry undertaken in 1904 gave 49,000 working women out of a total of 59,000 on the registers examined. Thus for the widely scattered districts investigated the percentage of working women householders was 82.4 of the whole. The new latchkey decision has since extended the household qualification downwards – and a very large number of the poorer working women would be able to qualify under it. The lodger vote, with its rental of 4s weekly as a basis, is not low enough to admit all women living in lodgings. But teachers, clerks, and many other fairly-paid classes of women would be able to qualify. The fear that the rich man would enfranchise his wife and daughters is groundless. He has not enfranchised his sons to any great extent, and he could long ago have secured the enfranchisement of the women of his own class if he had so desired. The service franchise would bring on to the register caretakers, nurses, matrons, and residents in institutions, all of whom must be classed as workers. The university franchise would apply to all women university graduates, of whom 75 per cent are self-supporting. These facts satisfy the working women to whom we appeal in our work all over the country. They have satisfied one of the Socialist bodies for years. The application of the principle of sex-equality to the right of voting will not result even in temporary class enfranchisement, and it will give to women by one measure what men only obtained by three different efforts. The problem of the married woman is a separate one, and requires separate treatment. But, judged only from the standpoint of expediency, the course adopted by the united Suffrage Societies should recommend itself to the real democrat.

# Part III
# *The Militant Suffrage Movement:*
## *Emancipation in a Hurry*

# The Militant Suffrage Movement*

## CHAPTER I

## PERSONAL FOREWORD

I write this book in criticism of the militant suffrage movement because I am impelled to do so by forces as strong as those which kept me five years within its ranks. I write because I am convinced that speech is necessary, because I know that no one else so well acquainted with the facts is prepared to speak, because I cannot keep silent longer without self-contempt.

I would be clearly understood from the first, and so I set down here at the beginning my confession of faith and the articles of my unbelief. I am a feminist, a rebel, and a suffragist – a believer, therefore, in sex-equality and militant action. I desire to see woman free and human; I seek her complete emancipation from all shackles of law and custom, from all chains of sentiment and superstition, from all outer imposed disabilities and cherished inner bondages which unite to shut off liberty from the human soul borne in her body. I believe that woman is in freedom the equal of man, and that any disabilities imposed by man upon woman or by woman upon man are evil. Against all such evils I believe in the sacred duty of insurrection. Women, along with every other unjustly restricted class, are not only entitled to revolt but have revolt imposed upon them; it is their gateway to liberty. This, and all that it implies, I believe.

I do not believe in the modern militant suffrage movement. I have

* Frank Palmer, London, 1911.

137

believed in it, worked in it, suffered in it, and rejoiced in it, and I have been disillusioned. I do not believe in votes for women as a panacea of all evils. I do not believe that any and every interest and consideration and principle should be sacrificed to the immediate getting of any measure of suffrage legislation. Votes for women we must have, and many other things for women; but votes for women over-hurried and at any price may cost us too dear. I do not believe that woman is the superior of man any more than I believe that she is his inferior. Pretensions of sex-superiority are like bad coins; they are just as bad whichever face is turned up. I do not believe that the best avenue for the emancipation of women is through emotionalism, personal tyranny, and fanaticism. To none of these things do I subscribe.

I am setting out to condemn the militant suffrage movement, but not to condemn militancy, for I shall be a militant rebel to the end of my days. I am setting out to expose the tone and tactics of the Women's Social and Political Union and the suicidal weakness of the Women's Freedom League. I have served in both these societies, have shared the burdens of the early days in both, have had my part in their successes and in their failures, and now I find both inadequate, fallen from a high estate full of promise to narrowness and incapacity. I do not condemn the present day militancy because it has gone too far. I fear that it has not gone far enough, and that it will never rise to the heights to which it originally showed potential claim. What I condemn in militant tactics is the small pettiness, the crooked course, the double shuffle between revolution and injured innocence, the playing for effects and not for results – in short, the exploitation of revolutionary forces and enthusiastic women for the purposes of advertisement. These are the things by which militancy has been degraded from revolution into political chicanery these are the means by which it has been led to perjure its soul: it is against these evils that I mean to use the whole strength of my power of protest. I am not at all concerned that the militant movement has outraged convention, that it has shocked self-satisfied and blind benevolence, that it has made the exquisite and dainty suffer pangs of revulsion against sordid realities; it is not for convention that I plead. The crime of the militant suffrage movement in my eyes is that it is not real, that it is itself dangerously and determinedly conventional, that its militancy claims to be but is not revolution, that it has given itself over to the demon of hurry and has abused the great cleansing forces by means of which the world is carried into purgatorial fires and brought out purified. Other movements have failed in rebellion, but it has been left to this woman's movement to ape rebellion while belittling and abusing it. Other rebellions have failed; this movement has failed rebellion.

I undertake the task of critic very unwillingly, for I have the common desire shared by all healthy people to escape martyrdom and to spend my days in peace. But no one so well qualified to deal with the movement frankly and mercilessly from the broader feminist standpoint has shown any intention of making the effort. I can sympathise fully with this reluctance, for I have not overcome it easily. No one desires to be suddenly cast down from a seat so raised as to bear a close resemblance to a pedestal, and having been cast down, to be condemned as a traitor and a criminal. All suffragists are aware that to those in the militant ranks there can be imagined no worse crime than this I am now committing – to go over to the anti-suffragists would be a venial offence by comparison. So strong is this feeling that I believe that I shall write in vain for seven out of every ten of the women with whom I have worked during the last six or seven years. Two forces will make it impossible for the majority of them to meet my attack in a fair spirit: in the first place there has been no serious public criticism until now – there has been abuse, misrepresentation, party condemnation, sux prejudice in more or less violent explosion, but no serious criticism based upon a knowledge of the facts and forces; in the second place the emotional atmosphere and the strain of hurry have tended to produce an attitude of fanatical loyalty at all costs, and the resulting conspiracy of silence has introduced the strongest forces of intolerance. All outer criticism is abuse; all inner criticism is treachery. These conditions will suffice to close the doors against my appeal for a hearing and to cast what I write into the flames. The yellow Press will aid this end by confusing the issues and striving according to its usual policy to bring the whole matter down to the level of a petty personal squabble. The militant women having had no experience of meeting criticism but with angry repudiation or contemptuous silence will greet with hot anger or the laughter of ridicule my serious claim that militancy has failed, that it has brought over-much evil with it into the suffrage movement. But none the less the charge must be uttered. For while its truth will not be generally acknowledged there is a minority to consider. Within the ranks there are women who are ready for better things, who have suppressed their higher aspirations and their deeper beliefs with difficulty, who are craving for release from the evils of their present condition. To these women I appeal. I believe that strength and spirit and capacity will die out of the woman's movement unless the clean outer air is let in upon its ways. I wish to break down the subtle barriers which have been raised between women and their spiritual and mental freedom by the emotionalism and dominance of the militant directorate. I wish to see reason substituted for hurry, growth for eruption, cool courage for hot frenzy.

In setting out to seek these things I intend to show little mercy, and I ask for none. I stand prepared for expulsion from among those who are merely suffragists, for condemnation varying in degree from mild to vindictive, from the great majority of women in the movement. But I believe that the women who are out to fight for fundamental things – some of whom I hope still to number among my friends – whatever their first feelings may be, will finally recognise with me that the ultimate emancipation of women cannot be achieved upon present lines.

I do not willingly make this book a personal document, and it shall be as impersonal as it is in my power to make it under the circumstances which obtain. This preliminary word I must speak; and I must show clearly what were the forces of reason and feeling which drew me into the militant suffrage movement, kept me a willing and earnest worker within its ranks, and made me accept official position and responsibility for five years; I must also show from what events came the growth of that slow disillusionment which gave me my personal freedom again and a shrine full of broken idols, and which has determined my present action. Unless I make these things clear, the purpose and value of what I write will be seriously endangered. My personal experience and effort alone entitle me to speak with any authority, and I can only say all that is necessary to be said by dealing frankly and personally with the things that I know. I have to strive to interpret them to others who have not had my opportunities; I have to show them as I think they are; I have to be the glass through which others may see them. And if my readers are to reach a fair judgment and to know what weight to give to my opinions and my deductions, they must have some material from which to ascertain my personal equation, temperament, and convictions, for only with the aid of this knowledge can they strike a just balance of decision upon the matter with which I deal.

But while I recognise that I must make this criticism a personal document and speak out frankly and clearly, I do not intend to devote any space to the personal relations between myself and other suffragist leaders. Some of them are totally unknown to me except as they are known to the public, some of them are personally very dear to me, close and valued friends, some of them I marvel at and condemn unceasingly; but towards none of them do I cherish ill-will, and none of them do I despise. I can honestly subscribe to much of the admiration that is daily meted out to them. I have probably seen more of the finer and more intimate of their virtues than the ordinary suffragist who is their unending adorer. But I shall judge of them by the work they have done, by the forces and influences they have employed, by the effects they have produced in the movement of woman's revolt. I write from the inside, and I intend to write what I believe is the truth. I intend to speak strongly, to shoulder my own burden of responsibility, and to make clear the responsibility of others.

This task would be very much easier if an ordinary system of management prevailed in the larger militant society. One of the difficulties in the way of frank criticism is created by the personal government which obtains in the Women's Social and Political Union, and which makes it impossible for the critic to avoid the introduction of individual names. But this condition can supply no excuse for silence. Those who claim in person the power of leadership and the credit of success cannot expect exemption from criticism and responsibility. The names of Mrs Pankhurst, Miss Pankhurst and Mrs Pethick Lawrence recur again and again in every panegyric and favourable review of militancy. Their names cannot be excluded from a serious criticism of the movement. And I shall not shrink from the task to which I have committed myself because the enemy and the uninitiated will allow themselves the privilege of misrepresenting what I write.

The need for speech is much too great for any of these considerations to affect my decision, and those who wish to understand, those who are willing to give their ears, will not fail to recognise that only an earnest conviction of the need for speech would have brought me among the shoals and pitfalls with which the way of the critic of this movement is set.

I do not want to give the impression that I deny the good forces in the militant movement and refuse to acknowledge its achievements. I do not. I have no desire to belittle the work to which I have devoted five years of my life. I know what we have done, as one who has been in the movement from before the beginning must know. I see evidences of our work on every side: I mark them in the faces of the women I meet, in the voices of the men, and in a hundred little recurring experiences of every-day life. I have seen the wonderful awakening which the movement brought with it, the stimulation of courage and co-operation which it may count among its effects. I have clung as long as I could to the militant movement because of the great promise of its beginning and because I have cherished almost to the end the belief that the evils could be rooted out and the weaknesses overcome.

But the movement has not realised its promise. The emancipation-in-a-hurry spirit has eaten up the spirit of emancipation. Daring to advertise in an unconventional way, the movement has dared nothing more. It has cut down its demand from one of sex equality to one of votes on a limited basis. It has suppressed free speech on fundamental issues. It has gradually edged the working-class element out of the ranks. It has become socially exclusive, punctiliously correct, gracefully fashionable, ultra-respectable, and narrowly religious. It pays for its one breach of decorum with additional circumspection in all other directions. 'I do interrupt meetings, but I am a perfect lady,' expresses the present poverty of spirit. 'I knocked off a policeman's helmet, but I only want a little thing, a quite respectable little thing – a vote.' This is banal. One loathes to hear it. One loathes to write it. But it is true.

I know that the outward and visible effects of the militant campaign have been such as to impress the man in the street, the ordinary Pressman in search of racy 'copy' and the politician who deceives himself and the multitude by playing a similar game. I know that it has impressed and enchained man and woman of better calibre. The money results have been great; the list of names and titles is impressive; the energy and alertness shown is not to be equalled in the political world; there are great meetings, great demonstrations, and much sacrifice and enthusiasm. In its own way the movement has become as effective in its methods of revivalism, advertisement, and management as the Salvation Army, to which it bears more than a superficial resemblance. Nothing done is allowed to go unchronicled; there is constant Press notice and much personal advertisement; everything is big in a spectacular, noisy way. The public, the Press, and even the politicians say that the vote is nearly won, that some hastening of the first suffrage measure has been achieved. This little feather of success the movement can wear in its cap, unless now when it should wear it proudly through the days of truce it chooses to throw it into the dust.

I admit this gladly, even while reminding my sister suffragists that emancipation is not wholly a matter of politics and votes, and that as subtle slaveries can be imposed upon woman by over-zeal as have been imposed by prejudice. For plainly as I see what has been done, I see as plainly what we have failed to achieve, and I can compare the achievement with our original hopes and intentions. I see how far we are fallen, how far we have sold and debased ourselves, how far the legitimate urgency of the rebel has been transformed into the politician's greed for early and personal victory. And seeing these things, I cannot do otherwise than point them out to others, asking them to pause in the headlong rush, to take a new grip of the problems of woman's liberty, and to seek a wider and straighter way to the goal.

# CHAPTER II:

# THE GENESIS OF THE MOVEMENT

Rebellion is the necessary result of injustice. It may not always achieve its purpose, or be intended to do so, but a conviction of injustice endured must precede articulate rebellion. Nor is it always certain that injustice will be followed by rebellion – it would be very much better for the world if such were the case. But where the victims of aggression or custom are ignorant and disunited the opportunities for reasoned and effective revolt are practically reduced to nothing. For many centuries women must have been rebels, but they have had to rebel singly and instinctively and under the spur of sudden feeling. Their discontent and unrest has been inarticulate and undetermined in direction. The rebels in spirit have not known why they desired to rebel; they have struck out blindly and stupidly and unscientifically, like children harried to sudden defiance, and they have rued their outbreaks as bitterly.

But with the coming of educational opportunities these things were changed. The education of women during the latter half of the nineteenth century diffused at once the knowledge and the independence of spirit that are required to turn resentment against arbitrary sex discrimination into organised rebellion. A struggle for equality of opportunity, for a higher social status, for wider personal liberty, for admission to public life, accompanied the educational advance; and the partial success of these demands, while satisfying the older and more conservative women, only whetted the appetite of the younger. What had been an unjust restriction to their mothers and grandmothers became an unjustifiable tyranny to them; what had been recognised as a slow advance became a burdensome succession of delays. The younger women, who had enjoyed the wider educational facilities, were at once more eager, more capable, and more rebellious.

For these feelings of revolt there was little outlet in the latter part of the nineteenth century. Women whose work was chiefly confined to private and domestic channels were honeycombed with unrest, vague, spasmodic, and entirely unorganised. Women who had proved their powers in science, art, and letters were incapable of tamely submitting to the archaic survivals of a condition of subjection in social and political life, but they scattered their energies over a hundred separate issues and accepted no central principle as interpreter or guide. The spirit was willing; but there seemed no way of action clearly defined. Into some avenues of effort only the bravest dare descend, and when meetings and other means of propaganda were of the rarest it was only very slowly that recruits could be won to take the plunge. For women who were interested in political affairs and for those who devoted themselves to the betterment of social and industrial conditions – an eager army – the need for change found an easier and more practical expression. The burden of political impotence which resulted from the surviving disabilities imposed upon them by law turned their attention chiefly to the winning of the Parliamentary vote. They believed that the want of political power barred and bolted against them the avenue of reform by legislation. They resented the constraint which forced them to stand helpless in the midst of evils they desired to remedy. The trend of legislation towards industrial affairs and its interference with the woman worker inadequately organised, unable to express herself, and exploited and neglected by the men of her own class, set the current of desire flowing more strongly in the same direction. The men's Labour Representation movement[1] aroused further feelings of rebellion; it showed that the working man had come to regard not only the possession of the vote, but the organisation of its use, as necessary for his own protection; and the woman's need for political power stood out the more glaringly by contrast.

All these varied causes contributed to the strength and direction of the rebellion which found expression in the first militant outbreak in 1905. The outbreak came at a time when women were seeking eagerly for some vigorous mode of expression for their discontent, and when outside the woman's movement there was a concentration of general attention upon politics. Without these external forces the woman's rebellion could not have been so easily restricted to the political channel at the beginning of the phase of militancy. But the looming large of politics in the industrial and social worlds, the extension of political activities into areas previously untouched, gave an extraordinary impetus to the purely political aspects of sex disability. Like so many other movements organised for the extension of liberty, the woman's movement was drawn into the whirl. More and more women came to realise the great possibilities of electoral power and to magnify, as was the contemporary habit, the dignity and value of the suffrage. Above other disabilities, that which debarred them from citizenship assumed paramount importance until all the various resentments and grievances which operated in the minds of women were able to be concentrated upon the removal of the barrier which excluded them from the right of voting.

The treatment of suffrage motions and measures in the House of

Commons has always served as valid excuse for resentment, and when under the new conditions it could be contrasted with the access of respect accorded to legislation demanded by the working classes it became a source of much bitter feeling. It began to be urged that women deserved contempt so long as they tamely submitted to it, and there was talk of deeds which could not be treated contemptuously. Men seeking the right of voting had had to employ rebellion as a final manifestation of their determination to have political power, and this began to loom before us as an imminent development. For years it was commonly admitted among suffragist enthusiasts that the women's agitation, like all other agitations for liberty, would have to end in violence. This feeling was not confined to Manchester, where the first militant action took place; there was the same strong passion at work in many units all over the country.

The growing urgency of the demand for the franchise was expressed for some considerable time in futile attempts to move existing organisations to immediate and effective action, and every occasion of failure in this work generated stronger discontent. Efforts were made to stir up the older suffrage society;[2] but it had long been without energy or new ideas, was kept alive by the faith of a few leaders and force of habit, and was easily immune to the awakening that was attempted within its ranks. The organisations of party women, which had contained a large proportion of suffragists in their early days, were now composed almost entirely of women who worked in their party in the interests of some male relative or under such relative's influence. It was impossible to win them to sudden revolt. The attempts to permeate certain industrial organisations met with the same ill-success. Along this line it was clearly seen that there was no possibility of rapid progress.

When in 1903 I met Mrs Pankhurst and became a member of the recently formed Women's Social and Political Union activity was still mainly directed towards the permeation of other organisations. Membership of the Union was then and for some time after practically confined to women who belonged to the Labour movement, and our ostensible object was to work through the various Labour societies to secure that the new Parliamentary party, then in process of formation, should be sound on questions affecting women and active in securing their early enfranchisement. During the whole of 1904 and 1905 this task kept us busily employed. We secured invitations to address meetings of every type that the Labour movement comprised – meetings of Independent Labour Party branches, of Trade Unions, Trade Councils, Ethical Societies, Labour Churches, Clarion Clubs, and other groups. On every occasion we urged the immediate need for votes for women, and appealed for such practical support as would help us to carry the woman's suffrage resolution at Labour conferences and party meetings. To this work we added the addressing of outdoor meetings, chiefly in or near Lancashire, and we employed our position as members of the different Labour and Socialist societies to keep the suffrage issue persistently before all the branches we could reach. The greatest part of our effort was concentrated upon the Independent Labour Party, to which the members of the Pankhurst family had long belonged, and in which Mrs Pankhurst at this time occupied an official position as member of the National Administrative Council.

But as the General Election approached our work became depressingly difficult. All effort and attention within the Labour ranks were concentrated upon the using of the votes already in the possession of men, and the necessity for the winning of votes for women was deliberately ignored. To the Labour leaders this issue offered to complicate seriously the lines of their appeal to the electorate, and with one or two exceptions they manifested an unfriendly spirit. The rank and file workers, even when of a favourable disposition, became careless and indifferent during the excitement of preparing for electoral contests. To make our struggle the more difficult, we had to fight the adult suffrage demand,[3] to which most of us were not in principle opposed, but which was obviously raised to postpone our equality measure. Such experiences bred suspicion and unrest in our minds, and from these feelings there finally resulted a declaration of independence on our part, though it was still some considerable time before this was fully admitted or fully achieved. But there was another result which followed directly from our loss of faith in the new parliamentary candidates, who proclaimed themselves as the new leaven of the political world. They were our last hope; and we had found them wanting. From the older political parties, tried by their record of forty years of suffragist effort, we had no hope of any success other than that which could be won by protest and pressure. When the Labour Party failed us, when we were thrown back upon ourselves, when we found ourselves re-committed to such methods of work and agitation as were possible to a voteless sex, methods which had already been proved ineffectual by forty years of futile agitation, militancy became inevitable. The only problems were when and how it should be supplied.

The militant suffrage revolt drew its strength from many varied causes, of which only a few were political. The great human rebellion of woman against subjection was thrust into a political avenue; but as its spirit sprung from roots deeper than the political, so its purpose aimed at things beyond. To those who read history with more than the cursory attention of schoolboys and politicians it is clear that there has never been a franchise agitation which has attained any success in which the spirit of revolt has not been called forth by ultra-political wrongs. The vote has few of the characteristics or associations which stir the mob to uprising; our political system does not tend to the ennobling of the voter; alone the right to vote could not inspire more than a few to deeds of defiance and disorder. This was the position in the woman's movement. The women who from the beginning grasped the wonderful potentialities of the militant policy were not merely suffragists seeking the right to cast their votes at a parliamentary election, they were feminists athirst for complete sex-equality, women who were out for fundamental things. The vote had for them two values: it was one of the means to the greater end; and it would create indirectly a higher appreciation of women and an atmosphere more favourable to their freedom and development.

The world stood shocked and dismayed before the first outbreaks; but the feminist rebels rallied to them and dreamed high dreams of them, and heard in them the call to a work of great liberation. To the mob mind woman, being woman, is ever required to seek even her soul's salvation decorously, and it was a thing of shame that she should cast off her immemorial chains of correct behaviour for any right on the face of the earth or any star out of the heavens. The feminists found in this abandonment of the worship of propriety the great cause of rejoicing. Militancy interpreted itself to them not as the mere expression of an urgent desire for political rights, but as an aggressive proclamation of a deeper right – the right of insurrection. It was woman crying to the masculine sovereignty: 'You do not only deny me the right of self-government, you deny me the right of rebellion against bondage, against the worst servitudes, against every manifestation of your control. This first right I take. I disavow your authority. I put aside your cobweb conventions of law and government. I rebel. I claim my inalienable right to cast off servitude. I emancipate myself. And the liberty that I have claimed and taken you shall register in the writings of your law.'

I stood with these women, attracted by the fact of rebellion and viewing with initial disfavour the narrowing down of the woman's demand to the parliamentary vote. But we were led to accept it as being but a preliminary concentration against the most important of the political disabilities. From this point of view it did not appear to matter vitally whether the first assertion of right took place in the political or some other department. The initial demand was not the whole, and we believed that all the way to the first victory would be paved with words and deeds which would undermine the servitude of women in all other human relations. It was the revolution for which we gathered. We were suffragists as a matter of course, as all who believe in the greater sex-equality must be; but we knew that our revolt itself was of very much greater value than the vote we demanded. Women might have the one and still be slaves; to share in the other they would have to free themselves from at least some of their shackles and come nearer to personal emancipation.

There were other women attracted by our initial protests, women who were mere suffragists, women who had worked long and vainly for the parliamentary vote, but whose further desires were confined to a few narrow legislative enactments. These women were driven rather than attracted into the new movement. They came trembling at their own daring, and fearful of the methods which had opened new doors of hope to them. They came because the hopelessness of their old outlook drove them to accept any means of hastening the pace. Everything else had been tried; everything else had failed. They realised that the vote itself would never awaken and enchain women in great numbers, and the absence of numbers was threatening worse neglects and delays; they realised that suffragist effort has so far been conducted upon a plane ethically too high to reach the politician and socially too high to reach the people. The suffrage movement had been a ladies' movement, restricted almost entirely to the middle and upper classes, conventional, and punctiliously observant of a high and narrow code of honour. The new movement promised to cast away these chains. Where the feminist saw in its initiators the high courage needed to turn the malcontent into the rebel, the suffragist saw the political capacity required to turn the lady into the politician. The one hailed militancy as a revolution, and has reaped disappointment; the other accepted it under constraint and accepted it fearfully, and has found it harmless.

# CHAPTER III:

## THE CHOSEN GATEWAY

There is a popular notion that all revolution is spontaneous, that it is impossible to decide either the time or the direction of any rising, and that, as in so many human affairs, we must be content with the moment and the avenue of revolt afforded us by the gods. But this is not strictly true. Where great warrant for discontent exists and the discontent is conscious and acknowledged, any sudden happening may precipitate a revolt. But in most cases it is only to the mob that the choice of avenue is denied. Nine out of every ten rebellions are determined in their initial aspects by the preliminary deliberations of their leaders; and it was so with the militant suffrage movement. The first imprisonment was deliberately determined upon, pre-arranged. It was planned to take place in a particular way and at a particular time; the method, the direction, and the ostensible excuse of action, the atmosphere and the basis – all these were decided upon. Like every other body of rebels, the militant suffragists had the choice of their own gateway to liberty.

Such choice always lies between the big human way, the way of the revolutionist, and the little political way. The latter was the choice of the suffragists. They chose the small deed, and boomed it to make it big. There has been some justification for the gibes of the enemy about 'a policy of pin-pricks,' for self-imposed narrow limits have marked the movement from the beginning. The forces of the revolt are big, but they have been confined in a straight channel and have been degraded by a doubtful and partisan use.

The first militant protest was decided upon by Miss Pankhurst, and announced by mother or daughter to a small number of the more active members of the Union. The body of members knew nothing of the plans until they heard with the public that it had been carried out. No resolution, general or particular, concerning militant action had ever been submitted to them. The Union had devoted some time and attention to bringing the women's suffrage demand before any prominent politicians who visited Manchester, and had generally received anything but satisfactory replies from them. It was decided to hinge the protest upon this practice, and to carry out in the Free Trade Hall meeting of October 13th, 1905, a persistent questioning of Sir Edward Grey calculated to end in forcible ejection from the meeting, arrest, and imprisonment. This line of action was admit-tedly narrow and partisan, but it was urged in justification that it was necessary to fix from the outset the responsibility of those who were about to become the Government[4] of the country, and that no broadly human line of revolt would have so easily served this end. Similar vindication was advanced against objections to the doubtful morality of making the Liberals the scapegoats for an imprisonment which we had pre-determined and set out to make inevitable.

It was at this point that the sense of difference of outlook, of which I had always been conscious in my association with Mrs Pankhurst and her daughter, became acute. I did not approve the line of protest determined upon. It seemed to me to provide a very inadequate outlet for the expression of our rebellion. It was reckless, small, and unfair. I did not even believe that it would prove effectual in achieving the immediate object. To my initial dislike of the course suggested was added the fear that the effort would be extinguished in laughter tempered with that pose of benevolent chivalry which rebel women feel is often the worst insult. I did not believe that it was possible to bluff the British Government. I approved rather a policy of doing something so big that it could not be minimised into insignificance, while at the same time I sought for lines of protest that should be capable of steady evolution from stage to stage until a grand climax was reached. For these reasons, and because I did not consider myself a free agent, I refrained from participation in the protest. I refrained reluctantly and against my own feeling, but I could not undertake important action of such a nature without faith in myself and the deed that was to be done.

The plan was carried through. The authorities were bluffed. They allowed themselves to be made use of; they took the little thing and made it sound big. The Government allowed itself to be made use of with a Simple Simon air that was very diverting. I was proved wrong in this point of judgment. I arrived at the Free Trade Hall from a meeting I had addressed in another part of the city just in time to see the two questioners arrested, and all my conscientious objections went down before the flood of mixed feelings which the sight aroused. The thing achieved swept everything else before it, the challenge loomed larger than the manner of its utterance, the great fact that showed in the amazement of the following crowd clamouring for information was that the woman's revolt had been made vocal, that the insurrection had commenced. Outside the police station in which the women were detained I addressed the crowd in protest, and while Miss Pankhurst and Miss Kenney lay in Strangeways Gaol I took up the work of explanation and justification in the Press and on public platforms, and I shared the responsibility of organising the series of meetings addressed by the prisoners upon their release.

This first protest was conceived in the same spirit that is found manifesting itself in ordinary party warfare; it was planned to hit the enemy and to make a good political beginning for the new movement; it was on the level of the ordinary double-dealing party move. I was on the level of the ordinary party apologist in my defence of it.

I do not offer any apology for this public vindication of particular lines of protest to which I could not give convinced personal support. I had to compromise. I could not reject the revolt, I had to accept it because of all that it implied, and accepting it, it was impossible for me to criticise the details of its first application. While these details of the protest were obnoxious to me the rebellion itself gave me great joy. Between them I made the only choice I could. It did not occur to me at that time that these methods indicated a settled and permanent policy and would determine the tone and direction of all our future work. The channel of revolt did not seem essential; the revolt itself did. I did not realise until long afterwards that the first protest had not only been the beginning of the revolt but also the inauguration of a policy; that the little way of action was always to be preferred to the big way. The phrases of revolution have been employed, but in their employment they have been rendered ridiculous by exaggeration and incongruity. They have been used as bustling business men use 'attractive lines' – catch-women phrases instead of catch-penny advertisements – and as the politicians use their election red herrings. Such militancy is not revolution – it is the exploitation of revolution.

I am announcing no new discovery, I have made no new discovery. In the early days that succeeded the first protest many women felt these things dimly or fearfully. But they chose to be silent, blinded by admiration in the face of action and loyalty in the face of abuse. I believe some of them see with me now that we did wrong to suppress our doubts. The conviction of the need for rebellion warred all the time in us with the conviction that this was not the right method of rebellion, but since this way was launched and launched by those who had no doubts, it seemed best to be silent. Perhaps the history of the militant movement might have been very different if at this early stage we had insisted upon full discussion of a militant programme, so far as general lines of action and the principles to be observed were concerned.

The General Election of 1906 followed close upon this militant beginning, and it was characterised by a continuance of the questioning campaign, which did not, however, again lead to imprisonment. It was felt that a sufficient beginning had been made, and our numbers being all too few for the work in hand, no further imprisonments were arranged for this period. At the early meetings the questions were asked at the usual question time, but this policy was soon abandoned. I cannot fix the date more exactly than by my own experiences. In December Miss Kenney and I were responsible for interrupting Sir Henry Campbell-Bannerman[5] at the Albert Hall, and in the same month there were interruptions at a Glasgow meeting and at one in Liverpool. Thereafter the interruption policy was regularly followed. There were divided counsels upon this point as upon that of the first imprisonment, but all objections were swept aside. It was necessary to keep the revolt in evidence; there were but few workers, and funds were almost wanting, and the anxiety and strain involved in these conditions left little time or energy for the deliberation of any question of methods. We were absorbed in keeping things going; we did the thing that was first put forward; we kept up a day-to-day struggle, a sort of hand-to-mouth fight. It was not until the Election was over that the differences of opinion as to our attacks upon Ministerial meetings became evident.

Gradually thereafter three schools of thought expressed themselves upon this matter: the one claimed that all bodies of discontented men interrupted speakers, and that women should take the same liberty; the second declared for questions at question time, urging the sacrifice of some part of the dramatic effect in order to gain the sympathy of the audience; and the third school advocated the complete holding up of Ministerial speakers until a Government pledge was forthcoming. The first policy may be called the policy of advertisement; the second the policy of practical and political expediency; and the third the policy of revolution. The course of action which recommended itself to me was that we should follow the second policy until we were strong, with the third in reserve, if necessary, for a final defiance. But the first course has been the one applied; and it has achieved no more than could have been achieved by the second, while it has entailed all the drawbacks and payments and losses of the third.

Attempts have been made to justify it by the statement that questions asked at question time have been ignored by chairmen and speakers, and that Ministers have sometimes deliberately left the platform before the questions could be asked. But it would surely always be better to let such an evasion occur, and then to make a protest which would appeal to the audience assembled, than to assume that it will happen and lose the audience by interruption. If the questions interpolated in the Ministerial speeches brought any replies the case for interruption would be arguable, but they only achieve publicity, and that a later protest could be made to secure in equal measure and under better conditions. The one thing that interrupture provides for, and that the questioning policy fails to supply, is the irritation and annoyance of the speaker – a policy much believed in by the Social and Political Union – and of which the results have so far only been reckoned on one side and greatly magnified.

But the questioning policy offers greater opportunities of real personal pressure. A persistent and skilful application of the policy would finally have secured a hearing, and a series of carefully drafted questions would have sufficed to drive the Minister into a corner and to estrange from him the sympathies of some members of the audience. The doors of meetings would not have been shut against women, and when an occasion arose which justified the complete destruction of a meeting by the holding up of a Ministerial speaker it would have been possible to apply this policy. If we had respected the rights of the audience during our general campaign we should have found it possible to rely upon some measure of support from the public when such a time of crisis arrived. Whatever hopes may have been cherished of it, the use of the weapon of interruption has only resulted in weakening the militant movement; it has estranged thousands of possible sympathisers; it has kept many women who were both suffragists and Liberals out of the fighting ranks and has prevented the awakening of many more; it has promoted the growth of a passionate irritation among Liberal men, and this has led, in the case of stewards of meetings, to retaliation and brutality; it has tended to reduce the effectiveness of the anti-Government Election policy; and most important of all, it has protected Cabinet Ministers from the worst exposure and has created for them a feeling of sympathy which has confirmed them in their evil ways.

Perhaps the worst possible example of the folly of this practice was that provided by the interruption of Mr Lloyd George when he addressed the meeting of the Women's Liberal Federation in the Albert Hall.[6] This was an occasion on which every possible preliminary provision had been made for the answering of questions, and where the turning of the vast audience of women against the militant movement was an obvious act of madness. If the interruption policy had been justified on every other occasion, it should have been suspended upon this. No excuse can avail in defence of its application.

But I want it to be understood that I do not condemn the interruption of meetings because I think it an evil policy in itself, a course that is not justified. I am fully convinced that when the political and social interests of any class have been abused as those of women have been that class is morally justified in any act of rebellion which it has the power to perform. But I am also convinced that only a minority of rebels are capable of distinguishing between their desire for retaliation and their desire for reform. The moral justification of every possible means of revolt must not be interpreted to mean that free rein can be rightly given to the desire to strike back. The policy of striking back if it comes to be preferred to the policy of striking to win spells suicide. Many methods of revolt to which the position of outlawry in which women find themselves gives sanction would, if applied, seriously endanger the prospects of reform, and tend to increase rather than remove the disabilities of women. To apply these methods is to prove that the longing for retaliation is stronger than the judgment, stronger than the desire for reform, and of this error the Social and Political Union has been persistently guilty. I do not desire to escape my personal responsibility in this matter: I have interrupted some half a dozen meetings, all in the early days of the struggle; but I have questioned at perhaps a score, and I have thus realised the possibilities of both policies. For the last three years the society with which I have worked, the Freedom League, of whose militant policy I have been officially in charge, has followed exclusively the questioning course, with one exception, though the opportunities for its development have been seriously reduced by the interruption policy carried on by Mrs Pankhurst's society.

I could forgive this interruption policy, with all its blocking of a better way, if it really achieved anything. But it was never really effective, and now it is become a ghastly failure. The temporary irritation and excitement caused by the 'usual voice from the roof' crying 'Votes for Women!' followed by the scuffle among the rafters, does not even spoil the speaker's temper, while it leaves the audience perfectly comfortable and only a little more convinced of the partisan spitefulness of the organisation responsible for the intervention.

# CHAPTER IV:

# AGAINST THE GOVERNMENT

The militant movement began only after the older suffrage society had failed to win for itself any political standing and had shown a complete incapacity to change its tactics with the changes of condition brought by time. Chief among its weaknesses were its failure to realise the necessity for pressure and the diffusion of its political effort along lines that were vague and antiquated. It took no notice of the change that had come over the position of the private Member of the Commons, and continued to devote much of its attention to winning pledges of support, although a sufficient majority of pledged members had been in existence for quite twenty years and their inability to carry a Suffrage Bill proved that the problem had shifted to that of providing an adequate opportunity for voting,[7] it failed to realise that the old practice of petitioning was played out; it continued to keep its advocacy in the academic and drawing-room stage, although the great forces of politics had passed to the street corner and the industrial world. The suffrage movement stood in great need of the revivification which militancy brought with it, a change of policy had been long over-due, and nowhere was the need more strongly shown than in the sphere of its parliamentary direction.

During the half-century of suffrage effort a great change has come over the parliamentary world. Under the influence of party considerations and the pressure of public business the Commoner has been steadily reduced in dignity and limited in opportunity, while the Ministerial body has attained paramount importance. This change had passed unmarked by the suffragists of the old school, and the Cabinet, while exerting almost sovereign power, and demonstrating its direct responsibility by the blocking of several suffrage Bills, was allowed to escape all direct pressure. This error the militants set out to remedy, and our political policy shaped itself upon quite other lines. Where the old suffragists had been content with a policy of appeal, the new developed as aggressive a plan as the circumstances permitted – a policy of antagonism to the Government in power.

This anti-Government course was first fully stated at the Cockermouth By-election[8] in July, 1906, in which Miss Pankhurst, Mrs Coates Hansen, and I toured the constituency against the Government. The policy had shaped itself upon the recognition of the

155

predominance of the Government in power at any given time, upon the need for a central point on which to focus attack, and upon the example of the policy of Parnell.[9] We claimed that under any system of political control the Government in possession of power is ultimately responsible for the condition of the people, and therefore for the votelessness of women, while under the British system at the present time the responsiblity is direct and immediate. From this we deduced that we were logically committed to opposition to the Government in power until we were enfranchised, and at the same time our personal and political independence forbade us to support any party. In theory there is no contradiction between the two positions, but the attempt to define a line of action in accordance with both discovered an array of difficulties. A clear way was cut through the tangle by the decision that we should appeal to electors to refrain from supporting the Government nominee, leaving to themselves the further problem as to the use or non-use of the vote.

But the line of demarcation which we defined for ourselves between the necessary opposition to the Government and the undesirable support of some other party has long ceased to be observed. The 'Do not vote for the Government nominee' has been translated by force of circumstances into 'Vote against the Government,' and our original rigid independence has been thereby undermined. The basis of the anti-Government policy is sound; but the machinery of politics and the defective education of the electorate in this country combine to make a negative attitude and absolutely independent action almost impossible. As a result in election contests the anti-Government suffrage forces, however unwilling, cannot escape the position of unofficial assistants of the opposition candidate or candidates. This must be frankly admitted. Furthermore, the policy when confined wholly to opposition to Government nominees is prone to lead to the entire neglect of the individual Member's convictions and his powers within the House. But after giving due weight to both these limitations I believe that the anti-Government policy must be admitted to be the best possible policy for by-elections, as soundly based in theory and as perfect in practice as circumstances allow. But as with every political policy, there are strict limits to its value, and its development into an anti-late-Government policy for use at General Elections is neither wise nor sound. Against this development I used all my powers of argument and analysis in the Freedom League, and I succeeded only in delaying the adoption of the policy from January to December of last year. The phrases of the by-election fights have become as shibboleths to the women in both militant societies, and to question the application of the same policy at a General Election is to be suspected of party leanings and cowardice.

Quite early in the struggle it was recognised that the coming of a General Election would be a test of our political independence. When angry Liberals interjected at our meetings queries about 'Tory gold'[10] we always referred them to the General Election, either airily, as those who had complete security in the sense of their own honesty, or with weighty asseveration, that the seriousness of our political independence might be understood by the members of the audience, to whom we promised a triumphant demonstration when the appeal to the country finally came. I know that these statements were made in all good faith by the women with whom I was most in touch during the early days of the struggle, for we realised from the beginning of our application of the anti-Government policy that it would be put to the test, and that our statesmanship would be tested along with it, when the existing Government came to an end. The problem of what we were then to do to secure the best results for the Suffrage Cause had deeply concerned us.

The General Election situation is essentially different from that which obtains when any government holds the reins of office, and this difference is not seriously affected whether the election is the result of a dissolution or of a resignation. In either case both parties are competitors for power; both parties are possible governments; both parties are to be considered as defining the attitude that will be observed in office. Under these circumstances any attitude of antagonism specially directed against either of the competitors is an anti-party attitude, for there is no effective government in control to be attacked. The electors are holding the balance between two possible governments; this position is the essence of a general election. An anti-party attitude on the part of suffragists cannot be justified except by reasons conclusive enough to over-ride the most serious of permanent considerations, those of independence and the advantage to the Suffrage Cause. A weighty public pledge given under such circumstances as to render it fully satisfactory, or a definite antagonistic proclamation which makes it necessary to defeat one of the two parties at all hazards, would warrant the strongest pro-party or anti-party campaign. But nothing less than public declaration accompanied by guarantees or as clear and un-equivocal an announcement of opposition could justify a party attitude.

In January of last year neither of these conditions prevailed, and tactics of a non-partisan character were absolutely essential. Yet when the General Election came, the Women's Social and Political Union concentrated its opposition against the Liberal Party, attacking the Liberal nominee in those seats in which the majority was small. This action gave immediate and sufficient sanction to the charge of anti-Liberal bias. It is impossible for anyone but the leaders concerned to say whether such an attitude has always been intended or whether the strong feelings engendered during the five years' struggle were responsible for the abandonment of the old independent position. The Freedom League decided upon the policy of attacking those anti-suffragist enemies who were prominent members of either party, ex-Ministers, or men in the circle from which Cabinet Ministers are chosen. This policy we justified by the argument that when the anti-government policy was impossible suffragists should concentrate upon enemies among the men who form governments, either keeping them out or bringing pressure to bear upon them in the direction of conversion. As the result of such a policy the prospects of suffrage legislation would be improved whatever government happened to be returned by the electors.

But this attitude on the part of the Freedom League was not of long standing, and at the December election the two militant societies followed the extraordinary course of applying anti-Liberal tactics, although the Liberal Ministry had just given the only serious woman suffrage pledge that has ever been drawn from any party or government.[11] It is quite true that the pledge was a pre-election one and therefore to be suspiciously regarded; it is also true that it left open ways of evasion and delay. Was there ever a political pledge that did not? But it stood to the credit of the Liberal Cabinet as the best pledge ever given, was accepted by leading Conservative papers as a final commitment, and was enhanced in value by the utterances of several individual Cabinet Ministers who publicly advocated an early settlement. The full folly of this antagonistic attitude can only be realised when it is remembered that the Conservative Party went to the country in stony silence upon this issue, entirely and completely unpledged, and with prominent anti-suffragists among those who would be in the Ministerial circle should they be returned to power. Opposition to the Liberals under these circumstances was not only partisan, it was suicidal. Had the suffragist efforts been of sufficient weight to decide the result we should have had to watch the pretty spectacle of women eager for votes turning out of power the Government that offered facilities for early suffrage legislation in order to gratify their feelings of resentment – the spectacle of the suffrage cause being sacrificed to anti-Liberal feeling. The pledge was not good enough to command support of the Liberal Party; far from it. But it was quite good enough to relieve Liberalism from differentiation and special attack.

I want to make myself quite clear about this matter. I recognise the strong grounds of feeling upon which the inclination to attack the Liberals is based. The Liberal Ministerial record contains many instances of evasion and double dealing on this suffrage question, and it is marked with deeds of unnecessary violence and unjustifiable brutality to militant women and their supporters. But while I remember this I am constrained to remember also that the Liberal Ministry were the victims of our tactics as much as we were the victims of their brutality, and that under the existing leadership we had from the beginning chosen to take courses specially designed to provoke retaliation and bad feeling. Our attack came like a storm from a clear sky; no mental preparation for it was possible, no planning, no trimming of sails to meet the new wind. It was scarcely to be wondered at if the Government stumbled into folly, failed to realise the quality of our resistance, and struck back. It could scarcely have been otherwise at the beginning. Furthermore, I think we ought to admit that we should have got no better treatment from the Conservative Party had the attack been conducted upon the same lines. These considerations should have sufficed to combat any inclination to endanger the work for which we were organised by yielding to partisan and revengeful feeling.

Women suffragists, militant and non-militant, are out to win the parliamentary vote, not to harry the Liberal Party. Like every other possible policy the harrying of the Liberal Party must be judged on its merits; if it is a good method to use when the Liberals happen to be the party in power, then let it be used; when it is obviously wrong in principle and inexpedient to take this course it should be abandoned. However good the anti-government horse may be it is not necessary to ride it to the devil. I quite approve of the opposition to Mr Winston Churchill and Mr Lloyd George: they did not only deserve to be opposed, but it was sound politics to oppose them. With the chance of the return to power of a Conservative majority, however, such attack should have been balanced by opposition to anti-suffragists of that party like Mr Austen Chamberlain and Mr F.E. Smith. In this way considerations of policy, principle, and sentiment would have been satisfied at the same time. The Fates seemed to conspire to make the December election an unhappy one for suffragists. As if the folly of the militant suffragists were not enough, the National Union of Suffrage Societies indulged in the pastime of running Suffrage candidates, with the minimum of preparation and organisation, and under circumstances which might have been specially designed to produce the worst possible results.

As the position now stands the militant suffragists have opposed the Liberal Party at three General Elections, and thus conclusively disposed of their claim to political independence. I do not mean to suggest that the rank and file members of the two militant societies are conscious of an anti-Liberal bias. They are not. They believe in their own asseverations of party independence and would concentrate upon opposition to the Conservatives once that party was securely established in power. But they are not governed as a body by reason: in the Social and Political Union they are controlled by the arbitrary dictates of their leaders, and in the Freedom League by the force of a vicious example. This reduces the problem to that of defining the attitude of the leaders, of discovering whether the trinitarian group[12] which controls the election policy of both societies is itself anti-Liberal in sentiment; and some little show of argument can be marshalled in support of such a contention. Dr Pankhurst was a Liberal and a Liberal Parliamentary candidate before he and his wife joined the Labour movement. It is known that their severance was dictated by a loss of faith in official Liberalism and disappointment with the Liberal attitude on certain issues, and that the Manchester Liberal Party showed some resentment against an action which necessarily cast reflections upon it. That the experiences of suffrage advocates within any political organisation tend to produce strong feelings of discontent and suspicion I can give personal evidence, and in all probability similar experiences had produced their effect upon the Pankhurst family.

The record of official Liberalism in the matter of woman suffrage is very black. From 1867 until the present day the reports of Parliamentary proceedings show a continuous application by Liberal leaders of all the weapons of opposition and delay, and the officials of the party outside Parliament have displayed considerable antagonistic leanings. Mr Gladstone's record is particularly bad; whether in office or out of it he used his voice and vote and influence against the enfranchisement of women. He killed the first Woman Suffrage Bill in 1867; he was solely responsible for keeping women out of the Reform Bill of 1884; and he displayed his antagonism against the measures of 1891 and 1892. These facts will go far to explain an anti-Liberal bias in women who have worked long and vainly in the Liberal Party, and who have seen the honest intentions of the majority of its members translated into dishonest subterfuge and opposition in official circles. But no indignation against past betrayal can be justified or extenuated when it leads to the endangering of the present and the future of the Woman Suffrage Cause. One cannot pass easily over the repeated evidence that resentment and the desire for retaliation, partisan bias and the frenzy for martyrdom, are constantly blocking the way to the very goal that suffragists are out to seek. I have every sympathy with the angry feelings, but I cannot excuse their practical expression in such a manner as to endanger suffrage legislation: and this is the result that has now been attained.

# CHAPTER V:

# SUCCESS THAT BROUGHT DEFEAT

After the General Election of 1906 we conducted a special campaign in London for which Miss Kenney and I were made specially responsible. Our chief work consisted of organising deputations to Sir Henry Campbell-Bannerman and Mr Asquith,[13] then Chancellor of the Exchequer, and to this we added hundreds of public meetings, the forming of branches and visiting of all men and women likely to be sympathetic with our work with whom we could get in touch. During this period we played a part at Mrs Montefiore's siege against taxation at Hammersmith,[14] spent a week organising a mob demonstration against Mr Asquith at Northampton, and made flying visits to Huddersfield, Birmingham, Manchester, Oldham, Cumberland, Staffordshire, and Suffolk. In April, during these same early days in the capital, we raised the ire of all politicians by our protest from the Gallery of the House on the occasion of the usual talking-out of the Woman's Suffrage Bill, for which protest Miss Irene Miller, Miss Kenney, and I were placed under a ban by the Speaker and forbidden admission to the House for a period of one year. In June the second arrests took place in Cavendish Square, on the occasion of a deputation to Mr Asquith. I was first arrested, and being committed at once to Holloway, was the first of the long series of protestant suffragists to enter its gates. Miss Kenney and two other London members were arrested a little later on the same day, but they reached Holloway only after a fortnight's legal struggling with the police prosecutor. Meanwhile, my sentence of two months had been reduced to one by the Home Secretary, and a few days later I was released through the interference of a London morning paper which purchased a cheap boom by the payment of my fine. The House having risen we turned our attention to the provinces and occupied the summer months with meetings, chiefly in the open air, in most of the large towns and cities in the North and in Scotland.

Our vigorous tactics and the second imprisonments produced everywhere interest and excitement in the public and attention from the Press. The public flocked to see and hear us, chiefly from curiosity, and often, indeed, to manifest its complete disapproval of our policy. The standard of Press comment was commonly pitched at the lowest level. Every possible device of misrepresentation was employed against us, and personal abuse and scurrility were our daily newspaper fare. Anonymous letters of the vilest description used to reach us. When we travelled about for meetings hotel keepers and land-ladies were loth to take us in, and on one occasion we were compelled to seek the hospitality of a kind-hearted and disapproving acquaintance in the early hours of the morning. We were faced daily with a hundred petty indignities and insults. I do not think that any of the few women who bore the brunt of those early days will ever forget them.

But more than compensation was given to us by the adhesion of numbers of women of character and principle who recognised the spirit of emancipation, the great hunger for human progress and liberty which was seeking utterance through the channel of militancy. We knew that the channel was narrow and ill-chosen, though as yet we had scarcely dared to admit this even to ourselves, for it seemed to us that so long as it served to give outlet to the great forces of feminine revolt against injustice it was uplifted and vindicated by its purpose. This was the doctrine we preached and believed; this was the doctrine we won other women to accept. For although always from the beginning we have disliked the methods we have had to employ, disliked them as no angry Mrs Grundy could ever dislike them, disliked them when we were most passionately applying or defending them, disliked them in spite of the bitter provocation which gave them excuse, we have forced ourselves to believe that they were inevitable and that they were glorified by the great purpose of revolution. As well as these woman rebels we gathered about us also a great number of working women, earnest, unlettered, and poor, having nothing to give but personal service and sacrifice, and giving of these willingly. Women of progressive environment and of a higher social grade mustered more slowly under the militant standard, and more slowly still came a few women of the upper classes. With representatives of these different grades in social life around us we began to cherish great hopes of a union of women of all classes to serve the common cause; this was one more of the dreams that were to end in sudden disillusionment.

Up to October 1906, the movement had been regarded by the Press and the public generally as a kind of hysterical hooliganism finding an outlet by variety show methods. It had been systematically written down. Its exponents had been given Press notice on the same plane as that given to smart criminals and self-boomed variety performers. The provincial tours of the summer months had done something to prepare the way for a change, and in London the appeal of the movement to the multitude had begun to gather large weekly crowds in Hyde Park and in other such centres. But we were still an ostracised few, a band of 'branded female hooligans' to the gentlemen of the Press and the public who were guided by them. The greater number of those who were curious about us were curious only as they would have been about a new comedy dancer to whose name a breath of scandal attached, or to a recent murderer who had evolved a new thrill in his methods of butchery. But in October the arrest of ten suffragettes at the House of Commons was followed by a storm of protest which entirely changed the situation. The first phase of the movement came suddenly to an end, and we who had struggled and foundered in shifting sand found ourselves on firm ground.

The Government had gone too far and its foolish severity caused a revulsion of feeling. Among the imprisoned suffragists were women of family and position and one of great historic name,[15] while it was obvious that three of them had been arrested without good cause. The attention and sympathy of the public were won by the publication of these facts, and attempts to secure our release came from most unexpected quarters. While we lay in Holloway we were conscious of the changed atmosphere, for we were removed from the Second to the First Division,[16] were permitted many privileges and relaxations, and ultimately were released when our sentences were but half expired. We came out of prison to find ourselves heroes. On every side there was laudation and approval. We were invited into 'respectable' social circles, the constitutional suffragists made a great banquet in our honour at the Savoy, a group of well-known writers and sociologists endorsed our claims and poured ridicule upon the Government, a prominent artist presented us with a memorial sketch of our triumphal progress towards the House of Commons: the rebound from contempt and obloquy carried us to sudden heights of dizziness.

It is a commonplace that many people who rise to the heights in adversity and live lives of simple usefulness and dignity under ordinary conditions cannot stand the strain of success. It is the same with movements. I had set out in the militant struggle sure of the great work we should do for the ultimate emancipation of women, but doubtful to the last degree of any early acknowledgment or success. I looked forward to a pilgrimage of protest in which we should prepare the way for the women who came after us, and should see but little of the harvest ourselves. I felt that our work would not be understood or valued until, like other rebel pioneers, we had been dead a few hundred years. The parliamentary vote would, of course, be granted much earlier because of our efforts, but it would appear to the world to be granted in spite of us rather than by means of us. We must be prepared to be execrated, misrepresented, condemned, to the end. But beyond this question of

163

immediate results we should, by our revolt, be awakening women to see, rousing them to rebel, undermining the superstructure of servitude by sapping at the roots of woman's acquiescence in her own subjection. The sudden rehabilitation of October changed this outlook at once. It began to appear as though women and the world were riper for advance than we had dreamed. We held out our hands to the acknowledgment we had never counted upon, and felt the sudden promise of the dawn. And almost before we uttered our thanks for the unexpected lifting of our burden we knew that it was a false promise, a mistaken acceptance, not a dawn but a mirage. We had won a new position indeed, but one full of dangers.

We were now met with unhealthy hero-worship and exaggerated devotion. New members tended to worship us rather than to understand and co-operate with us. The Press found sudden explanations for, and extenuations of, our unruly conduct. The pose of propriety was made almost inevitable by the obvious shock of surprise which showed itself when we were beheld in the social circles that had been barred against us. 'These militant suffragettes are actually ladies!' was the gasping cry; and straightway most of us became ladies again, and the rebel woman was veneered over or given hasty burial.

The chorus of approval and excuse brought out another weakness: it confirmed in us the pose of martyrdom of which we had been rather ashamed until then, and it strengthened that curious mental and moral duplicity which allowed us to engineer an outbreak and then lay the burden of its results upon the authorities. The final responsibility of the Government for women continuing unenfranchised is quite another thing from that special and detailed responsibility which had been placed upon the shoulders of the Ministry after the first protest and which had come to follow each successive one. The Government holds the key of legislation; but it is expected also to administer the laws, and those who deliberately set out to break laws, even for the good reason that they are urgent to share in making them, cannot expect immunity. Women who are out to fight organised authority are rebels, and they should never forget the fact; they should stand frankly forth as rebels; they should confine their attacks upon the enemy to the primary cause of revolt and should not belittle their final object and descend to prevarication by making a grievance of every response to their disorder. This is a particularly pernicious course when at the same time it is frankly admitted that the movement lives and grows by its outbreaks. Under these circumstances the only course consonant with self-respect is for the rebels to admit their own responsibility for the disorder and to take the consequences.

The feeling within the Union against this double shuffle, this game of quick change from the garments of the rebel to those of the innocent martyr, was swamped by the public approval and extenuation of our protests. We were too speedily rehabilitated; we were exonerated before we had declared ourselves. We were accepted into respectable circles not as rebels but as innocent victims, and as innocent victims we were led to pose. If we had frankly and strongly stated that we had set out to make the Government imprison us, that we had deliberately chosen just those lines of protest and disorder that would irritate those in authority into foolish retaliation, if we had told the truth, the very proper persons who became our champions would have spent many weary months and years in condemning us before they had finally realised the value and intention of our efforts.

Under these influences of rehabilitation the movement became conventionalised and narrowed and hypocritical. We were accepted for what we were not, and immediately began to live up – or down – to the standard expected of us. There came to be one speech for the council chamber and another for the platform; the propaganda of the society suffered a sudden loss of breadth; the industrial evils which had formed the basis of much of our appeal were gradually pushed aside for the consideration of technical, legal, and political grievances; the advocacy of reformed sex-relations was reduced to the vaguest generalities, and even these were discouraged; the working-class women were dropped without hesitation and the propaganda of the organisation confined to the middle and upper classes; the 'advanced' women, an eminently undesirable class in a socially superior society, were even more speedily driven out or silenced.

The new conditions brought out other weaknesses – weaknesses in principle and internal government and further weaknesses of methods – which we were loth to recognise or admit, but which became grave enough to force admission from the most unwilling during the next few months. The forces which began to show themselves did not find sudden birth at this particular time – they had been in existence from the beginning, but the early glamour of the movement had blinded us to the real nature of them. I had believed in the leaders in spite of warnings and personal experiences which ought to have shown me the true circumstances. And the undermining of my belief in the aims of the present leaders and the movement as moulded by their ideas would have been a very much slower process had it not been for their attitude towards internal management.

The government of the society had always been very loosely carried out; there had been strong opposition to any constitution at

165

all during the first two years, but by a sort of mutual consent members exercised voting rights over such business as was allowed to come before them. It was understood in an indefinite way that some form of democratic management would be secured to the members as soon as the size of the society made the original free and easy method impossible, but when action towards this end was suggested it was put off again and again. I had given this pledge of a constitution to the branches that I had formed in various places, and the continued delay rendered me a little restive. At last in the early summer of 1906, before I left London for a propaganda tour in Scotland, and while Mrs and Miss Pankhurst still remained in Manchester, it was decided that the arrangements for the drafting and passing of a constitution for the society should be carried out, chiefly, I believe, because of my attitude within the society and the friendly pressure of a Labour politician outside. October of that year was fixed for a conference of delegates, and I was instructed to return from Scotland in time to make all the preliminary arrangements for the event. A formal notice of the Conference was sent out before my departure; but by an arrangement made later my responsibility for this and other matters was handed over to Miss Pankhurst while I outstayed my term in Scotland to work up a demonstration and deputation to Mr Asquith in East Fife. This kept me away from London until two or three days before the date for which the delegates were summoned.

I returned to find that absolutely no arrangements had been made for the Conference, that no resolutions had been asked for or received, that no skeleton draft for submission to the branches or the delegates had been prepared, and that no instructions, no rules of procedure, and no order of business had been even considered. The Conference apparently was to be turned into a meeting for arranging a deputation to the House of Commons. I made immediate protest, which was so received as to remove my feelings of suspicion and led me to regard the neglect as due to carelessness rather than design. Then I spent a couple of hours the night before the gathering in drafting a constitution, an agenda, and a series of suggestions on policy and the conduct of business, and these, having been approved by the other officials with but slight alteration, formed the basis of our proceedings on the morrow, and of the famous Constitution. This Constitution was adopted by the delegate meeting just prior to that October protest which wrought such a change in the public estimation of our movement.

Under the new influences and in spite of the Constitution – perhaps indeed because of it – the methods of personal control which had always been employed began now to be emphasised. The real decisions of the society had rarely been made by the society, but from the formation of the London branches and Committee I had made every effort to carry forward the business on ordinary orderly lines. But now the society came to be governed by decisions made at little private conferences in a private apartment, and these were then submitted to a farce of approval or announced as settled policy to the other officials. Quiet insistent methods were employed to get the complete control of affairs into the hands of the present trinitarian group; and the members of this group were singled out and elevated to a position of preeminence in a peculiarly unblushing and undesirable way. An organised effort was made to turn the whole stream of public laudation – at this time flowing about us in fulsome and lavish fashion – into one channel in order to effect the booming of these same two or three names. The arts of skilled social intrigue were employed and personal devotion was sedulously cultivated.

Alongside of these evidences of intention to confine the leadership and control of the society to a self-chosen group, there was manifested also a tendency towards the employment of the political methods of evasion, manipulation, and exaggeration. There grew up an admitted policy of playing purely for effect, to excite the public curiosity, to fill the treasury. Tactics were adopted which seemed to indicate that militancy would be degraded to the purposes of advertisement and the movement reduced to the level of a spectacular suffrage show. Women who were taking part in the movement because of rational conviction and not as the mere slaves of feeling saw cause for fear in the excessive growth of emotion and excitement. Under the cover of this emotional condition the will of the leaders rapidly came to be substituted for the will of the members; free choice and personal liberty dwindled into insignificance; the subtle tyranny of affectional appeal showed itself as a serious danger. Women were being carried into protests and positions of danger by the misuse of their emotions; and the steady setting up of agencies of influence showed that this was becoming a deliberate plan of action.

These threatenings of danger from within brought about a sense of active unrest among women of earlier membership, and after a period of suppression from mistaken ideas of loyalty several independent legitimate attempts were made to bring about a general consideration of these matters at the Annual Conference of October, 1907. When knowledge of these things reached headquarters in the ordinary course they were met by direct attacks upon the women supposed to be responsible. One of these women was censured by the Committee under Mrs Pankhurst's direction without being granted a hearing or being notified that she was to be tried, and the meeting was packed with paid organisers who, rarely appearing at Committee meetings, had on this occasion been called up in force. These proceedings awakened feelings of resentment, and branches and members until that time entirely unaffected were seriously shaken, with the result that the preparations for seeking a remedy at the Conference were redoubled. But the Conference was never held. In September, about a month before the date arranged for the gathering, Mrs Pankhurst, ignoring the Honorary Secretary,[17] called a Committee meeting, declared the Conference annulled, the Constitution cancelled, and the rights of the members abolished, and proclaimed herself as sole dictator of the movement. She appointed herself secretary, Mrs Pethick Lawrence treasurer, and Miss Pankhurst organising secretary. She chose for herself a committee consisting of paid organisers and two or three women who were willing to lend their names for this purpose. This body was practically only a committee on paper, and judging from my earlier experiences it would seldom, if ever, be summoned to a regular meeting.

The malcontents rallied under this blow and showed a bold front, circulated statements to the branches affirming that the Conference could only be annulled and the Constitution abrogated by the will of the members, and summoned the delegates to attend at the place and time fixed. Fully half the original membership of the Union answered the call and declared by a series of resolutions their claim to internal suffrage in the affairs of the society, further re-affirming the doctrine of political independence and militancy as the basis of suffrage work. For some months there were two societies in the field, both claiming to be the Women's Social and Political Union, though Mrs Pankhurst's society added the word 'National' to its title. But in January, 1908, the self-governing section changed its name, to put an end to the public confusion and the appearance of bad feeling between two groups of women working for the same end, and thenceforth called itself the Women's Freedom League.

There was no defence of Mrs Pankhurst's *coup d'état* issued either in the Press or to the members; the deed was excused, extenuated, admitted as technically incorrect, but justified by a regrettable necessity. By this pose the aggressors cloaked themselves in the mantles of saviours who had boldly nipped an insidious conspiracy in the bud and had saved the Union at the price of their most cherished principles, while the rebel section came to be regarded as renegades who had plotted to sell the movement to the Labour Party. This statement was repeated in the Press and upon platforms until it was really believed by people who ought to have been better informed. The charge was challenged at once, and never substantiated, and it has now been completely disproved by the three years' political independence of the Women's Freedom League. But it did not bear the most superficial examination. Had such a conspiracy existed it would have been met in open fashion at the Conference, exposed and destroyed; and such exposure would have strengthened the position of Mrs Pankhurst and her followers.

That the *coup d'état* was considered necessary is an acknowledgement that open criticism and discussion could not be met. The only shadow of evidence brought forward to support the charge was that Mrs Despard remained a member of a Labour society. In comment upon this statement it is only necessary to point out that Mrs Pankhurst herself, for many years and until only a few months earlier, had been a prominent member of the same society, that Mrs Pethick Lawrence was or had recently been a member, as had all the younger members of the Pankhurst family, and that I, though preferring a freelance position, had joined this society at Mrs Pankhurst's request, but had resigned before she did. To these facts it must be added that a large section of the original Manchester members, who remained with the dictator when the cleavage occurred, continued to regard the Union as a branch of the Labour movement, and to speak and act accordingly for some time after that event, and indeed until a special pledge was devised to make them toe the independent line. The cry of Labour leanings was the first plausible excuse on which the autocrats could seize. It was as true and as false as such plausible excuses usually are. But it was seized upon, not because of its truth but because of its plausibility, because Mrs Pankhurst with that quick instinct for effect and that political unscrupulousness which mark her out, knew that it was just the kind of excuse that would confuse the issue and leave the burden of justification, with its long explanations and repudiations, upon the new rebel group that had refused to submit to her authority.

But the final condemnation of the *coup d'état* is that it was a stupid and unnecessary mistake. From every point of view it was a mistake. It was unprincipled, inconsistent, and unnecessary. It reduced the right which the movement was organised to obtain to a mere matter of expediency. If it lay in the power of a leader of a society to decide that for the good of the society its members could be deprived of self-government, the same claim must be allowed on behalf of the chief of a State. If Mr Asquith excludes woman from the suffrage on the grounds of expediency, Mrs Pankhurst has supplied his justification – she has done the same. From the point of view of policy also the move was bad. By denying votes to her followers Mrs Pankhurst belittled the very function which it was her desire and intention to magnify above all other rights. Besides, the *coup d'état* was unnecessary. The members of the Union would have willingly created an autocracy, for internal independence had already been undermined by the subtle use of personal influence. The clumsy declaration of autocracy broke the spell for many who would willingly have voted away their rights. Numbers of those who stuck to the Constitution and formed the Freedom League were moved by resentment against the method of the attack, rather than by the attack, upon their independence. This reversion to autocracy, this denial of suffrage in their own society to women seeking suffrage in the State, with the methods by which it was attained, brought to a sudden close the second chapter of the progress of militancy. Our great hopes in the movement, the very foundations of our belief in it, had been undermined. But we refused to realise this, and entered into a futile struggle to make the militant movement what it ought to have been – a movement of reasoned revolt, aggressive, and, however small in numbers, large in methods, working with clean hands, and without the employment of hustle and advertisement, employing no aids of artifice and emotion to carry women beyond their depths, and seeking ever to apply the principles that we proclaimed.

# CHAPTER VI:

# THE FREEDOM LEAGUE FAILURE

We had broken up the original militant body because such action was forced upon us. The wrecking came from the other side. It was not possible for a few women chiefly responsible for the rally to the Constitution which secured the members' rights to have engineered such a movement out of destructive desires. The work we did was constructive. We took upon ourselves the burden of making a new start. We paid for our principles the price of shouldering a burden which was in some respects heavier than that which had had to be shouldered in the beginning. We started out with eyes open, stronger in some ways because of our disillusionment, to make the militant movement what it ought to be. No more potent explanation of what we hoped our rebellion might lead to can be quoted than this: when the name of the society came to be changed this little central group gave unanimous support to the title of 'The Emancipators,' and the dreams we dreamed were as big as the title to which we aspired.

I have to admit frankly that we have failed. There are some half a hundred good reasons that can be urged in excuse of this fact, but none in denial of it. 'The Emancipators' were laughed out of court by the rank and file of the society who rose to the height of 'The Women's Freedom League' only by a small majority; and this rejection of the flag under which we could have gathered women of big ideas for the doing of big deeds was more ominous than we knew. At first brave efforts were made to grapple with the almost insuperable difficulties, and some sturdy fighting has been kept up to this time, but the original hope of the seceders has long vanished, and the Freedom League has dropped steadily to a position of mediocrity. Capable and promising women began to drop away from it almost from the beginning. I have been called the first traitor; but this is folly. I can afford to wait my time as to the term of abuse; but the adjective is ridiculous. I am not the first to leave the movement discouraged. I am but the last of a long line of women who have had to do the same, women who have had to go out and put their hands to some other task, women who could not go back to the old militancy, women who were not permitted to develop the new, and for whom therefore there was nothing but individual action. The Freedom League had its opportunity, and lost it. It tied its own hands and committed political suicide. It was not strong enough to cast off the obsession of the earlier movement, and at the same time it exhausted itself in excessive recoil from the earlier excesses.

This failure has been due to many causes: from one point of view the League may be said to have succumbed to its inherent virtues, for with some rare exceptional occasions, for which I have been chiefly responsible, it has sacrificed itself continuously to mistaken ideas of loyalty and generosity; from another point of view the failure may be traced to the equally inherent difficulties and limitations which all rebels have to overcome when they reach the work of construction. We carried with us in our refusal to submit to arbitrary authority the great body of democrats within the original society, and by the very conditions of the secession their attention became unduly confined to matters of machinery and management; we carried with us a body of women whose distaste of cheap and petty militancy had made them question militant tactics altogether; we carried with us women who were in a condition of protest against the pose of propriety, the shoulddering out of the working women and the worship of wealth and class, but who brought with them the love of excitement and emotional appeal; we carried with us also a number of women suffering from personal grievances whose only difference with Mrs Pankhurst's society was that they had been allowed no prominent place in it; and the number of rebel feminists willing for service in the widest campaign of emancipation, were but as a little leaven in the great lump.

There was some justification for the women of parts who resented the suppression of their individuality and the denial of opportunity and liberty, for it was obvious that during the course of time all the women who had shared the burden and publicity of the early days were being gradually edged out of the public eye, silenced, exiled, from the centre of the movement, and excluded from the positions in the society to which their work entitled them. 'Where is Annie Kenney?' people had begun to ask. 'Where is Mary Gawthorpe?' And the same question might have been asked about others, and might as justly be asked now.

But the wrong done to the women themselves was not of much account by comparison with the wrong done to the movement. It lost in losing their service; it lost in losing their names; it lost its breadth of appeal which the varied personalities and capacities supplied. It is not upon exaggeration or supposition that these statements are made; they are based upon facts. A policy of assiduous self-seeking of the centre of the platform and equally assiduous pushing of all other women to the sides or over the edge cannot be continued long without leaving evidence. And there is evidence in plenty in the hands of those who are familiar with the working of the society from within. These policies of suppressing and edging out

172

were supplemented by a policy of keeping out. When women of ability who were already sufficiently prominent to ensure that they would occupy positions in the front rank in any society to which they gave their services offered themselves to the trinity of leaders, they were systematically discouraged, except where they were regarded as amenable to influence or where special reasons existed for giving them temporary prominence. Many suffragists relying upon these circumstances stated their firm conviction that the *coup d'état* itself was deliberately undertaken to rid the movement of women of prominence and character who had proved themselves difficult to manage – women who, like Mrs Despard and myself, could not be relied upon to subjugate their principles and understanding, upon request, and who, if edged out in the ordinary way, could not be trusted to drop into insignificance.

Under these circumstances it was not possible to look slightingly or with special disfavour upon the women with a grievance. Many of their grievances were quite real, and some were weighty. But the effect of the influx of this body of women was that the old type of militancy was desired, and it was expected that we would apply the same methods of action as those which had caused the unrest in the original society and given excuse for the declaration of autocracy. Had we been able to analyse these forces from the beginning we should have realised that our hopes that the militancy of revolution, as contrasted with the militancy of effect, would find a re-birth through the Freedom League, were doomed to disappointment.

At the very earliest stage, weaknesses manifested themselves which were to reduce the democratic movement to impotence. There was little to be expected from a society that commenced its separate existence by making a free gift of the funds, name, prestige, and achievements, which had been acquired by the efforts of all combined, to the section from which it has had to secede on a matter of principle. This impractical generosity hampered the League financially from the beginning, reduced its status, and supplied a precedent for further sacrifice of a like kind. The movement next committed itself to a course that meant general impotence. Its incapacity to set itself free from the obsession exercised by the dictators of the other society showed itself, within a few months of the split, in the passing of a self-denying ordinance which forbade its members to make any defence under attack or to utter any criticism of the sister militant society. This meant the suppression of its new-found individuality, the sacrifice of all its potentialities, a reduction of the League to a position of futility.

It was not possible for the new society to initiate a policy of bold attack, to defend its action or inaction at a particular juncture, while its speakers and writers were debarred from any utterance that might be construed as a reflection upon Mrs Pankhurst's organisation. Under such restraint the League lost its distinctive character almost before it acquired it, and became a mere echo of the larger group. One example of the conditions which prevail will suffice. The Tax-Resistance Campaign,[18] organised first by the Freedom League, was regarded with scant respect by its members, and in the course of over three years only about one hundred women took this line of protest against disenfranchisement. But when some months ago the Social and Political Union declared that 'the time has now come for women to refuse to pay taxes' the policy was hailed with acclamation as a new and brilliant stroke of genius. A few words of gentle reminder that the policy had been applied for three years by the Freedom League, while individual women had resisted taxation since the early seventies, and that a special Tax-Resistance League formed with Freedom League assistance now existed, was commented upon as ungenerous by our own members.

No advance, especially no militant advance, was possible under such conditions. It was not possible for us to explain our general position to the public. It was not possible for us to defend our own course of action or to contrast it favourably with that of the other militant society. No original action stood a ghost of a chance of general acceptance among us, for we could not defend or explain it without appearing to cast aspersions upon the fellow-militants. When the errors of judgment of which we were guilty were pointed out by our members we could not retort by indicating the worse errors of the sister society from which we were trying to escape. We were committed to submit to all criticism and to utter none. We were condemned to seek after such applications of militant tactics as would neither excite the fear nor the contempt of those whose minds were wholly absorbed by the policy enunciated from Clements' Inn.[19] The only vigorous lines of action permitted us were lines of imitation, and since our strength and membership were of an essentially different nature than those of the Political Union we could only appear as bad seconds in the game. It is astonishing to me now that we managed to make any militant changes at all. But of all of those upon which Freedom League advocates pride themselves, I believe, the only one which escaped all condemnation from within our own society is the Grille protest[20] in the House in which Miss Matters played the chief part.

Where the self-denying ordinance was not in operation the older policy itself blocked the way. The case of questioning at meetings has been referred to. If the interruption policy had not been continuously applied the Freedom League might have carried out successfully its attempt to do some serious political work by carefully planned and conducted questioning. But this was rendered impossible. Similar impediments blocked other valuable lines of protest. Ultimately the result has so worked out that nothing can go uncondemned within the self-governing militant society which has not already been endorsed by the Political Union.

On the one side we were limited by this obsession of the Freedom League by the Pankhurst influence: on the other side we were as strictly limited by the recoil from the excesses of the original society. The first limitation was due to the weakness of the mass: the second must be placed in a particular degree on the shoulders of the leaders. I frankly admit my personal responsibility, acknowledging that I can offer no adequate excuse. The elected leaders of the League had been nauseated by the campaign of publicity, and rushing to the opposite extreme we neglected the most elementary rules of Press notification; the turning of the limelight upon individuals made us afraid of the slightest personal advertisement, such as is required to secure the attention of the public. As a result legitimate advertisement was sacrificed along with illegitimate. This affected the financial position, for modern subscribers to reform movements like to see a return for their money; in Mrs Pankhurst's society every possible arrangement is made to gratify this natural craving, nothing, however sacred, being allowed to interfere with its satisfaction; in the Freedom League the subscriber is almost ignored.

Women who in the one society had been bred to give in the midst of public plaudits, to receive the warmest thanks of the leaders, and to feel a sense of well-expended gold in the big advertisements and the exaggeration, could not be expected to give generously when all these circumstances were withdrawn. The atmosphere of the rebel society was too cool. The Freedom League officials were not capable of carrying out such methods of financial appeal; this is shown as clearly by their one ghastly failure as by their otherwise consistent refusals to stoop to the attempt.

A similar recoil manifested itself in the tendency to shun platform boom; but for my share in this work, though I believe it was carried to excess, I can never apologise. We suffered from a necessary reaction towards truth-telling, and on some glorious occasions almost achieved it. But the egotistic exaggeration of language and a confident over-estimation of the effects of our words and works had become almost as the breath of life to a large proportion of women in the movement. The absence of hyperbole and clamour took the heart and courage out of them. They stood shivering and naked in an atmosphere in which an attempt was made to use reason and fact as the basis of speech and propaganda. They sought such shelter as they could with the more emotional of the speakers in the new society, and if this proved insufficient they fled back to the warm corners of self-satisfaction provided by the Social and Political Union.

For another bad aspect of the rebound the members were more responsible than the leaders. This was the development of red-tape democracy, which caused the concentration of over-much attention upon matters of machinery and management, and tended to develop the worship of the letter rather than the spirit of democratic control. If no other experiences had tended to show me this truth my experiences within the Freedom League would have proved to me that a mob with a machine can be the worst kind of tyrant. With this knowledge I could have forgiven Mrs Pankhurst her repudiation of democracy if it had really culminated in the assertion of her own liberty and not in an aggression upon that of others. In earlier days the denunciation of government by anarchists had always left me adhering to the practical possibilities of working the governmental machine, and in spite of much sympathy with the anarchist ideal I held firmly to political democracy. But now I can understand what the anarchist means when he says that the machinery of democratic government if successfully employed merely serves to impose a mob tyranny, and if unsuccessfully employed only draws the attention of the people from realities to the machine itself. Both these evils have been exemplified in the Freedom League.

While the cleavage was fresh in the public mind the Freedom League was recognised as having potentialities, but in the further practice of militancy it has naturally failed to win from the Press or the public any special recognition. No essential difference between it and the Social and Political Union has been established; the tone and direction of militant tactics has continued unchanged to the outsider. He did not mark these small differences upon which the Freedom League prided itself; he did not know that this society refrained from using militancy for advertisement and frankly admitted that its deeds of disorder were upon its own head; for the League made those changes in its attitude but failed to make them public. As a natural result it has come to be rightly regarded as a smaller militant group, sometimes milder than the larger, sometimes more aggressive, but always imitative.

It is suggested that much more good for the suffrage movement and for the Freedom League would have followed if I had done my work as a critic within the ranks, and used the advantages of my position to bring about redress. It is argued quite plausibly that I could rely upon a following of earnest women who, while possibly differing from me in details, would have energetically backed the efforts I had made to redress the chief evils I point out. But I know my Freedom League, and I know my own strength; this course was not possible. It would have ended in disruption of the Freedom League; it would have turned the whole energies of the society into a mighty wrangle; it would have produced none of those benefits which I believe will follow from my going out into the wilderness alone, there to say my say.

The members of the Freedom League who urge this course are not honest with themselves nor with me. They know that no sufficient exposure of the evils to be redressed could be made without attacking the Women's Social and Political Union. They are aware of the existence of the no-criticism self-denying ordinance. Even if this could be repealed, and it could not be without loss of many members of the League, the eradication of the evils would necessitate constant attack upon the autocratic society for some considerable time. Would they prefer this course to the one I have chosen? They are aware, too, that in the matter of the future of militancy I have very strong views, and that those views are not shared by other prominent individuals among my late colleagues.

Briefly, I do not believe that the slur cast upon the work of the Conciliation Committee[21] by the Social and Political Union has been deserved. I believe that militancy is not justifiable at the present juncture. I believe that if the big constitutional issue[22] had not arisen the Conciliation Committee would have carried some measure of woman suffrage during 1911, and that neither the Government nor the Conciliation Committee can be accused of such neglect or betrayal of our interests as justified the breaking of the truce. The Government did not arrange the dissolution in order to postpone the Suffrage Bill, and we are guilty of silly hyperbole if we say so. We have been temporarily swamped by the constitutional issue, but that is no reason why we should seek to rush to Holloway *via* Westminster. I believe that militancy *alone* would never get the vote, and that only by conciliation can the difficulties of the last stage be bridged. If the Conciliation Committee is given its opportunity I believe that it may yet bring things to an early finish, and until its incapacity is clear it is a matter of honour and common sense for suffragists to observe the conditions of peace. This also I believe: that the Government should be given every chance of keeping its pledge to the Conciliation Committee within a reasonable time. There should be no foolish haste, no hurry, no acting under the impulse to be revenged, at this stage. But if the Government should refuse to redeem its pledge, and militancy be again resorted to, it should be real militancy, the militancy of violence and revolution. This or nothing. This is my position: the Freedom League position is very different; it is prepared to continue the feeble imitative policy; to follow the

Political Union; to act because Mrs Pankhurst has acted; to strike with little effect when it ought to stand silent; to strike with equally little effect when it ought to strike hard.

Even this is not all. The Freedom League members who ask why my severance should have preceded my criticism might by reflection have found still other reasons why it must be so. I do not any longer believe in the potentialities of the Freedom League. I think that it has not the power to fulfil the task that it set out to do, to secure the general freedom of women. I know that it carried over-much emotion with it from the original society, and that robbed by the cleavage of idols that erred in seizing power and position for themselves, it has set itself up a new idol. I do not believe in the worshipping of idols, even the better ones that are human. I believe that it leads to loss of independence, courage and conviction. I believe that in propaganda and in spirit the Freedom League has show a growing tendency to narrowness during the last two years. I believe that it wants to put the whole burden of thought and action upon its officers, while retaining all responsibility for itself, to place upon them all the limits of democracy and all the burdens of dictatorship. And these facts rob me of any shreds of confidence that my general discontent has left me. I do not believe in a commercial weighing of the gifts one gives to a reform movement; but neither do I believe in waste. Such power and capacities as I possess I must use to the best advantage, and I do not believe that they were being so used within the Freedom League. I can do better work for the emancipation of women from the outside.

# CHAPTER VII:

# THE DOMINATION ESTABLISHED

The effect of the cleavage upon the Clement's Inn section was such as to intensify its weaknesses and to reduce it to a lower level. The evils that had remained of small dimensions in the face of the little criticism that was allowed grew to greater proportion when they were entirely unchecked. The hostages given to win the fashionable and wealthy section of women increased in number and degree. The pose of convention became universal; the movement became honeycombed with snobbery. The door was shut upon the real revolutionary spirit and purpose, and at the same time the functions of politics were glorified and exaggerated in order to make sacrifice and subscription worth while. Extravagant expectations were deliberately awakened on the one side to stir the rebel women to take part in protests, while on the other side no definite or concrete ground for fear was allowed to disturb the most intolerant conventionalists.

It is noticeable that the simplest development from the claim of voting rights for women has been slurred over and evaded. The militant advocate cannot be brought to admit in public even that she desires to see women in Parliament; she evades the issue, lest the mere suffragist should be alarmed – lest the conservative and moneyed element should be alienated. Under the action of this same influence the suffrage demand, based upon the principle of sex-equality in every other suffrage society, in this case to be based upon consideration of expediency.

Until the Women's Social and Political Union had been transformed into a trinitarian dictatorship, all women's suffrage societies were pledged to sex-equality. They asked for equal sex rights in voting. But the Women's Social and Political Union abandoned this claim. It flung away the basis of principle. It declared on its official publication, and in its official utterances, that it demanded the Parliamentary vote for women tax-payers. I do not refer to the device of printing in heavy type, the statement beginning, 'We are not asking for votes for all women,' under the declaration that the object of the Union is to obtain votes for women on the same terms as they are or may be granted to men. This, a piece of political jugglery, from which the dictators could find several plausible ways of escape. But printed letter paper was issued soon after the split on which the old claim, 'We demand the Parliamentary vote for women on the same terms as it is or may be granted to men,'[23] was replaced by 'Tax-paying women are entitled to the Parliamentary vote.' This cutting down of the demand was perhaps sound, political sense; but it was undoubtedly hastened by the presence within the society of an increasing number of women of the wealthier classes, whose conservative tendencies could not safely be opposed. The women of the old school would never of themselves have reduced their primary demand. If less had been offered them they would probably have accepted it – as in the case of the Conciliation Bill – but they would not have gone out of the way to show that they were willing to take less than a measure of principle. The suffragists of the new school made the sacrifice quite calmly. They were out to win, not sex-equality, but any measure of votes for women – any obtainable measure. It was one of the prices they paid to hurry.

All the way along the line similar sacrifices have been made, and gradually the movement has lost status as a serious rebellion and become a mere emotional obsession, a conventional campaign for a limited measure of legislation, with militancy as its instrument of publicity and the expression of its hurry.

The leaders of the militant movement do not want a revolution; we were mistaken who believed that they did: they would be afraid of one. They want a measure of woman suffrage on the statute book, and they have engineered an advertising campaign to secure this end with the least possible delay. They are prepared to rush and raid and advertise untl they get what they want. The Suffrage Bill is long overdue, and some measures of hurry are requisite and commendable. But hurry at any price is suicide. It is not the Suffrage Bill that has to be saved; it is the women. And when women are being sacrificed for votes; when the personal liberty of women, the integrity of women, the self-respect of women, the mind and spirit of women, their warm hearts and their rebel souls – when these are being sacrificed for a piece of machinery, a mere tool of government, it is time for an examination of the forces at work, for exposure and criticism. I believe that the movement of militancy has exploited and betrayed many women; I believe that it has abused the name and spirit of revolution, and waved a red flag from the seclusion of a select drawing-room; I believe that it has given itself to a thousand servitudes to win one small symbol of liberty. It has sacrificed its principles in its internal management. It has cut down its legislative demand. It has imposed upon women the very evils of subjection from which it sets itself to deliver them. It has given women chains that it may win for them a weapon that it has taught them not to use. The success that it will bring to women will 'leave them crushed as no defeat had done.'

The Women's Social and Political Union now depends upon

personal dominance for its existence. The leaders impose a yoke of emotional control by which the very virtues of the members are exploited; they produce a system of mental and spiritual slavery. The women who succumb to it exhibit a type of self-subjection, not less objectionable than the more ordinary self-subjection of women to men, to which it bears a close relation. The yoke is imposed by a mingling of elements of deliberately worked up emotion, by the exercise of affectional and personal charm, by an all-pervading system of mutual glorification in which each of the three leaders by turn sounds the praises of the others, by the deliberate exclusion of other women from all positions of prominence, by a policy of shameless boasting and booming, by an ingenious system of clever special pleading through which everything the Political Union does is chronicled and magnified, and everything that other suffragists do is belittled or ignored, and by that undoubted financial and political stage management which caters for all the elements of snobbery and narrowness and intolerance, while employing the language of outlaws in revolt. This obsession is one of the most remarkable manifestations to be seen in the political life of to-day. As with all emotional degradations, its victims glory in it. Every woman snared ensnares her fellow and adds the weight of her obsession to the burden upon the minds of the rest. Under this direction the militant movement is a movement of political revivalism – that, and nothing more.

The individual members of this society are not the only suffragists affected. The bad influence is strong enough to affect all. Though the Political Union at the worst is insolently and brutally indifferent to the rights of other societies, and at the best scornfully tolerant of them, these other societies yield to its pretensions at the cost of their own progress. The National Union of Suffrage Societies at first made a practice of repudiation after every militant demonstration, but this has died down. To quote a well-known suffragist politician, it has been found that it does not pay. The amazing protest of November last,[24] prior to the Dissolution – which appeared to have nothing to recommend it, and seriously hampered progress along the only avenue of advance open at that time – was merely commented upon adversely in the editorial notes of *The Common Cause*. The necessary public exposure of the folly of militant action at that juncture was not forthcoming. The Freedom League officials dared to defend their abstention – and the most assertive section of their members rose in arms.

In this particular society the obsession has acted in three ways: It has limited and restricted militant action to the lines approved in practice by the W.S.P.U. – every deviation from the political lines of protest employed by Mrs Pankhurst having been criticised or boycotted to death; it has applied the same rule of weak imitation to the general election policy; and it has insisted upon the suppression of any murmur of dissent from the decrees of Clement's Inn. The attitude of its members towards the Police Court protests,[25] the Bermondsey protest,[26] and the Tax-Resistance movement, as well as the inconsistency in the olicies applied by the League in the January and December elections, can all be quoted in support of the statement that the Freedom League has neglected the first law of self-preservation, and has destroyed its own potentialities by a policy of weak imitation and weaker adulation.

In part the suffrage societies that have suffered from this disease have been impressed by the smart methods and the noise and rush and the poses of omnipotence and revolution; in part they have yielded because they have found that protest not only failed to secure redress of grievances, but rather intensified the loss to be endured; and in part they have submitted because of the fear of harming the suffrage cause in the public eye by exposing the disunion that existed. A show of peace has thus been preserved in the suffrage world, but it has been the sort of peace preserved in many households where one member of the family is a bully and the rest for the sake of name and blood are constrained to hide their injuries, and to put a fair face upon an unhappy condition.

The cultivation of personal dominance by the leaders of the Political Union is not an unconscious or accidental happening. It is deliberate. It finds its origin in a determination to win early results, in egotism, and in an experience that has bred distrust in the majority of other women. Before the militant movement began Mrs Pankhurst laboured long among women who could be, and had been, deceived by party leaders or cajoled by husband, brother, or son; and she has come to believe that the only honest and independent feminism is the feminism that agrees with her, accepts her leadership, and is prepared to submit conscience and principles to her dictation. Only those women are to be trusted who can be dominated and controlled. She and her co-adjutors are convinced that they are capable of carrying the suffrage movement to victory; they believe that other women admitted to the inner councils will only interfere with the carrying out of their plans; they believe that the spirit of unquestioning submission in the mass of members is preferable to voting rights and free discussion because it is the only condition which will give them complete and continuous control of the machine by which their desires can be realised. They do not believe that any other women in the world are to be trusted with a share of the power and direction of the movement, and they are determined to take no risks with colleagues, with constitutions, or with loyalty. They believe in themselves – a most commendable thing to do in reason – but they believe in themselves in a way which destroys their belief in other women, and this is neither admirable nor wise. I do not want to magnify the evil of this distrust. I have not a great deal of trust in either men or women in the mass myself, but I have less trust in the leaders of the mass. There is far more danger of corruption and one-sidedness, of narrowness and final shipwreck in absolutely unlimited autocracy than in the stupidest forms of democracy. And the choice in this movement was not between the one and the other; there were middle ways open for use, which would have provided a wide discretion for the leaders and the right of some share of control for the members; but these were rejected. The clean sweep of machinery was the only thing which would give the trinitarian group unlimited power, and the clean sweep of machinery it had to be.

If the intention of the women concerned was to bring the movement through just those stages and conditions which have manifested themselves, it was perhaps a wise thing from the point of view of the autocrats that autocracy was declared. For there would certainly have been rebellions against some of the sacrifices paid to the spirit of hurry. The purchasing of the support of the respectables and the fashionables by limited speech and the pose of propriety, by the censoring of persons and subjects, and by the dropping of working-class women and industrial propaganda, aroused strong feeling in many quarters, and would certainly have been met with protest had an avenue for such protest been available. I believe that some limits to the extravagance of speech which persistently magnified the results of the militant action undertaken would also have had to be made. 'I strongly object to this absurd use of superlatives,' said a staunch militant of the autocratic society to me very soon after the split. 'It makes us look silly to those who know.' She spoke for many others beside herself. The effects of both militant and anti-government election activity have been absurdly exaggerated, on the usual commercial principles that he who shouts loudest gets the most customers, and if you keep shouting long enough people will believe that what you say is true. The hyperbole has been so patent as to become blatant and the nerves of many willing servitors have been put on edge by persistence in this practice. Undoubtedly some system of representative control would have secured the moderation of this evil.

I think also that there is no doubt but that the wishes of the members if given opportunity for expression, would have interfered with the system by which the regular London meetings, at Queen's

Hall and Albert Hall, were retained as the private preserves of the directorate. Even the most earnest supporters get tired of the same oratorical fare when it is set forth week after week, in season and out of season. And if no reasons of justice, good taste, and the advantage of the movement, would have moved the mass of members to demand a system of fairer play, the study of their own comfort undoubtedly would have produced some slight improvement. This theory of mine is borne out by the fact that on one historic occasion at the Albert Hall a speaker of early prominence who had been edged into the background, and who was present on the platform though not upon the programme of speakers, was called for so vigorously from the audience that she had to be allowed to speak.

This distrust in the body of women, this fear of other women of capacity, is a petty thing. There were some who admired the bold defiance of the declaration of autocracy. It was a brave and necessary deed, masculine in vigour, I was once informed. But when one examines why it was necessary it begins to lose its noble proportions and to become not only an aggression upon the rights of the members but an insult to their intelligence. When we find some suffragists who, in spite of this insult, are prepared to admire the deed still, we are driven to believe that there must be something in that pitiful proverb that states that a woman always loves the creature that masters her.

Steadily before the cleavage, more rapidly since, the firm rule of personal authority has been built up. Under its shadow the members have been enslaved, and the leaders have given themselves to seal the bondage. Under democracy there is admitted control of the leaders by the mass, and this is often found to be irksome by the men and women of initiative and capacity who submit to it; but under autocracy the leaders who have to rely upon personal loyalty are under obligations that are much more degrading. In the one case the leaders are governed by the will of the majority; in the other they are forced to use the weapons of finesse, strategy, influence, sentiment, and personal appeal – they have to give *themselves* in order to keep their hold upon their creatures. To this the leaders of the Social and Political Union have been reduced; where they would not employ reason and argument they have had to employ emotion, personal charm, affectional appeal; and the flood of extravagance to which this has led has brought further dangers and degradations in its train.

# CHAPTER VIII:

# A CRITICISM OF MILITANCY

It is indubitably true that militancy has brought new life to the suffrage movement in Great Britain, but it brought that new life upon a lower plane. The movement has posed as a revolution; but those who hoped from it a great human emancipation as well as a small political one were doomed from the beginning to disappointment. Militancy as designed and carried out by Miss Pankhurst and her mother has not tended to work a revolution by the enslaved woman, much less to work a revolution in her. It has not been designed to clear away the accumulated barbarities of ages in order to prepare the way for a gospel of free womanhood.

The experience of the last five years goes to prove that militancy is the exploitation of the natural forces of sex revolt for the purposes of advertisement. Militant machinery is put into action purely for its advertising values. It is a bold method of advertising what is now quite a common-place and conventional movement – a movement as conventional as Liberalism and Conservatism, and every other 'ism which to-day goes uncensored. In these days of great hurry even the old and strong and wealthy conventional things find themselves in need of the fillip of occasional new attractions, and the organisers of the Social and Political Union recognised from the beginning this modern need. They knew that there were forces of rebellion seething in the women around them. They knew that these forces could be directed in any chosen channel by those who were courageous enough to make a beginning. They made the beginning; but they dared not make the movement the mouthpiece of revolt. They chose to indulge only in so much militancy as would attract attention and keep the public and the politician aware of them. They coquetted with rebellion. They made revolution into a political red herring. They started in the political world a gigantic game of bluff to which every other consideration has been sacrificed.

They knew that twenty years of regular rebellion against servitude would fail to attract these people to whom the Press and the politician and the public gave fictitious value, and by whose co-operation alone they could hope for the early legislative results they sought. They knew these things and they fought on lines in accordance with their knowledge. They fought to win. They demonstrated to attract the attention and adherence of the type of people they wanted, just as a business firm advertises to bring the class of

185

customers with whom it is most profitable to deal.

I need only give four facts for those who hesitate to accept this conclusion. It is the regular practice in Mrs Pankhurst's society for all militant demonstrations to be publicly announced beforehand by the agency of the Press, by posters, by handbills widely distributed, and by various other attractive devices. The preliminary notices of the next show with a new attraction in the bill, are already tickling the palate of the public. Is this the method of revolution or stage management? If these means were employed for the summoning of scattered supporters at a moment of crisis, such as the declaration of war, they would deserve every commendation. But this is not the case. All the soldiers required in action can be reached without publicity at all. Furthermore, every chance of stealing a march upon the enemy is thrown away by this method, and the authorities are always given sufficient notice to enable them to reduce the protest to the level of a stereotyped Palace Yard performance. This preliminary announcement in itself is sufficient proof that militancy is not intended to achieve anything more serious than advertisement. Then militancy is always so arranged as to produce the maximum of effect for the minimum of work done. A revolutionary movement would consider the work to be achieved and leave the effect to take care of itself. It would not hinge its chief demonstrations of discontent upon some technical legal point, some political usage or custom; it would hinge them upon its great basic right. It would fling its defiance into any direction in which it could do the most damage upon the barriers set up against it. It would strike to destroy, and not to advertise. The big human revolt would be the real thing, the advertisement a non-essential effect.

I give as my third fact of my indictment that all militant demonstrations, with perhaps a solitary exception, have failed as *revolution* – they have only been successful as advertisement. It is only necessary to ask the question, Would revolutionists have been prepared to continue tactics which always failed? The deputations never get into the House, the meeting-smashers never smash the meetings. If they progressed in that direction one would willingly wait. But they do not. The militant leaders make extravagant estimates of the success of these tactics. They proclaim every new failure as a success. This is an acknowledgment that they regard effective advertising and the failure to perform as success itself, that they are satisfied with it, that it is all they are out for.

The fourth fact to be noted is that the burden of disorder deliberately planned is always publicly transferred after its occurrence to the shoulders of the police and the Government. I hold no brief for the Government. I know too well how it has abused its power, and retaliated against the militancy of irritation with equally petty and objectionable brutality. But I strongly affirm that the policy of planning outbreaks and then using the resulting imprisonments as a stick with which to beat the Government is an unworthy political game. It is neither revolution nor consistency, nor does it show a high standard of honour. Revolution should never be ashamed of itself. It should never evade its responsibility. It should stand frankly upon the human right of insurrection against any imposed injustice. It should glory in its deeds of revolt. If the object for which militancy is undertaken does not justify these methods of revolution then it should not be honoured and magnified by the use of the name. It is farcical for the phrases of revolution to be grandiloquently employed upon every possible occasion while the resulting deeds are explained away or wriggled out of. One cannot at the same time be the aggressor and the innocent victim. I do not condemn advertisement; I regard it as a necessary evil in our modern large communities. I do not condemn revolution: I approve of it with all my mind and all my strength. But I do condemn the exploitation of the revolutionary spirit and the revolutionary idea for mere advertising purposes, and I do condemn the policy of claiming the revolutionary glory while repudiating the revolutionary responsibility.

It is only fair to say that the Freedom League must be absolved from both these reproaches; it has never used militancy for advertisement – and has, indeed, lost both money and popularity by this abstention; and it has never pretended that its protests were anything but protests. Militancy in this society has failed to do its work and to rise to the height of revolution, because of divided counsels, red-tape democracy, and an incapacity to emancipate itself from the emotional influences of the Social and Political Union, but it has not been cloaked under the respectable guise of deputations, or used as the beating of the big drum.

There is something further to be said about the promotion of militancy as a policy of irritation. From this point of view the double shuffle referred to above, by which all the responsibility for militant demonstrations is placed on the shoulders of the Government while all the glory accruing is claimed by the demonstrators, becomes even more distasteful. From the beginning the tactics have been deliberately intentioned to produce retaliation in order to work up the martyr cry and the martyr spirit. As in all other franchise movements the vote itself is recognised as insufficient to arouse women to unremitting struggle. Without the spur of the martyr cry the modern re-birth of the suffrage movement would have been less a phenomenal rocket rise to the sky – and down again – and more a steady growth. But the steady growth would have doubled the time required for the winning of success and was not, therefore, in the running. The retaliation of the Government was angled for, and the passionate impulse it awakened has supplied the place of conviction. The policy, in brief, was to irritate the Government until it should strike back and then to exploit the forces of feeling aroused; and the Government lent itself to the game.

No observer of the militant movement can deny certain outstanding qualities in its dictators. They have the power to turn converts into followers, and followers into worshippers. They refuse to know when they are beaten or when they have made mistakes. They can live up to amazing pretensions, which would subdue greater and more sensitive women, without a quiver or a blush. They have shouldered a huge responsibility with cool courage. They have demonstrated the woman's capacity to play the political game, and have outshone the male politician in the capacity for hustle and advertisement. They are as adept in the use of flattery and sentiment and suggestion as any ministers of the most effete government or superstition. But, in spite of all these qualities, militant tactics, as they have directed them, these tactics of advertisement and irritation, would not have survived the first year of application if it had not been for the co-operation of the Government, and especially of the Home Office. Lord Gladstone[27] must be credited with much of this responsibility. Without his assistance the militancy of effect rather than execution would have been played out long ago, even for the purposes of publicity. He magnified technical offences into crimes. He exalted demonstrators into martyrs. He made the Government look silly and sheepish and vindictive, and the women greater than their deeds. He played the part of a big school bully, by contrast with whom the women, like ordinary schoolboys, became heroes. He supplied to the movement the needed stimulus of passionate enthusiasm, the spirit that always rises under oppression, and he contributed to supply the second need of advertisement.

From one point of view the late Home Secretary may be given a large share of the blame for the restriction of militancy to its original narrow channel. I believe the forces of revolt at first at the disposal of the movement were strong and stern enough to have found bigger and better ways of protest, if these early partisan efforts had been allowed to remain in their natural insignificance. The whole area of administration, supplying dozens of cases daily of unfair laws and laws unfairly administered, was open before us. A system of protest against these administrative evils could have been devised. The obstruction of legislation and interference with its administration might have been developed. The great natural forces of emotion could have been more legitimately aroused by protests against the real victimisation of women in our law courts than by the creation of artificial victims. Industrial evils were open to the same legitimate use. These would have been wider ways and they would have wakened bigger forces. Not enfranchisement alone, but the awakening which must precede emancipation would have resulted from such a crusade, and it would have improved incidentally the administration of law, prepared the way for a purified Statute Book, and instilled and vindicated in its advance every principle of individual liberty while it was winning for women political liberty. It was towards the development of some such policy that the Police Court Protests were originated by the Freedom League, but these were contemptuously committed to death during the first few weeks of their application by women who, being obsessed by the purely political advertising methods originating at Clement's Inn, could neither understand them nor believe in the possibility of a wider way of revolt.

In spite of the pain and suffering it entails, militancy is more popular than suffrage. If militancy should come to be abandoned, because considered no longer necessary, a large number of present adherents would drop away from the movement. The means has come to be elevated above the end. The condition is unconscious, of course, but it is plainly shown in the speech and action of the average militant woman. It is the only conclusion that can be drawn from the occurrence of militant demonstrations at moments when no adequate advantage can be obtained from them. It is demonstrated by the exceeding bitterness with which anti-militant suffragists are treated. You may have given all but your life for the Suffrage Cause, but if you declare against any militant action you are at once judged, condemned, and executed. Your status with the militants is gone; your courage is questioned. You are enveloped in an atmosphere of suspicion. 'Do you think she is sound?' is asked mistrustfully; 'Is he honest?' This, accompanied with shrugged shoulders and lifted brows, as a final condemnation. Nobody believes in the critic after that.

It is not extraordinary to find such an atmosphere about a militant movement. Emotional revivalism sufficiently strong to impel its votaries to sacrifice is always intolerant. A necessary accompaniment of such exaltation is persecution. This is partly due to the state of nervous tension which necessarily exists, and partly to the contrivance of the priesthood. Militant action, which has become a fetish, must be protected like every other fetish, from the light of reason and the breath of criticism. Every superstition employs the same means; while criticism from without can be interpreted as vulgar abuse, and criticism from within subtly made to appear as treachery, the most irrational fetish can be preserved from injury.

The popularity of militancy within the movement does not only lend itself to intolerance, it threatens another danger. Manifestations of the revival spirit are not always as easily checked as they are started. The incantations of anointed priests and the use of symbols and mysteries have always produced undue influence upon the human mind; and once the mind is completely mastered by emotional excess the discretion of the most wise and humane leaders cannot always provide a sufficient curb. The danger is great in itself, and it is only too strongly accentuated by the popularity of militancy with the Press and the public. Both welcome militant demonstrations. The modern lust for excitement in the masses is catered for by newspapers, by promoters of sport, and by political parties. The public loves a drama with lust and blood in it. The details of gory fights and fearful calamities are read with insatiable appetite and gloomy enjoyment in every corner of the land. Militancy invests the suffrage movement with the same unholy charm. The only drawback it has for the mob is that it is not bloody enough. At aviation meetings the men must fly – even if they fly to death. The suffrage demonstrations would be more popular if a few people could be killed in them, but they cater successfully for the craving for thrills when there is no greater excitement going. Militancy has one advantage over murders and accidents in that one is always informed beforehand when and where to come and see it.

It does not matter whether the young barbarians come from the East End or the West End. They gather for the row. By choosing the method of advertisement and dramatic display the militants bring numbers to share the excitement provided. But the numbers are not with them as a mass. And the folly of the advertising short-cut is shown when one remembers that had the materials at the command of the early movement been fully used, this weakness would have vanished long ago. The London mob could have been won in two years; but it could have only been won through the working classes. The working-class women, and those having the nearest power to appeal to them, were either edged out of the movement or stifled long ago. They brought the danger of big demands with them, and it was not realised that they also brought great strength.

The lines of protest first used have been somewhat monotonously repeated. There has not been any evolution, any evidence of progressive design. Public meetings are still roused to momentary excitement by the ejection of a few interrupters, as they were five years ago. Deputations are still beaten back from St Stephen's entrance to the House of Commons, though they are now big enough to get in if they did not themselves bar the door. The only real advance has been the hunger-striking, which came with its mad bravery from Russia. Nothing else has changed, except the number of women involved; the only growth has been a growth of numbers. Stone-throwing and such expressions of violence are not new developments. Militant suffragists have always been as violent as they dare, but the early violence was explained away or excused rather than vindicated, lest it should have an ill effect upon the public mind. The presence in the ranks of such women as Mrs Despard, women temperamentally and by conviction opposed to violence, has tended to discourage and delay publicly given approval, but it has not prevented the application. Now violence is openly advocated – but only the small violences which can be effectively contrasted with the greater ones committed by the Government. This is not advance; it is the search for a new thrill for the public and a new chain for the women who pay the price.

Just as there has been something monotonous in the lines of activity, so there has been present an element of ruthless generalship. The sacrifices that may be justly called for in a rebellion are out of all proportion in a publicity campaign. Where the rebel leader would be extolled for a courageous conquering of natural emotion the advertising agent will seek justification in vain. In this movement the leaders have always appeared to be more tender of heart to the enemy than to the women in the ranks. It is not any sufficient excuse for this error to urge that the leaders concerned sacrifice themselves as well as their followers. The leaders stand to gain much more than the rest, and for themselves under these circumstances the sacrifice may be worth while. It is not a small thing to secure that you shall go down the ages, to the exclusion of all other suffragists, as the winners of votes for women.

It is not easy to win the militant advocates to deal fairly with objections to the present militant policy. Most of them immediately assume that the doubter has recanted and must be dealt with as an opponent. This is not my position. I am opposed to the kind of militancy; not to the fighting, but to the fighting on present lines. Neither is the decision on the question of the value of militant efforts to be made as a choice between the dead level of pre-militant days and the present greater vitality. Any movement having an ounce of energy could have made an advance on the suffrage conditions of 1900. The same reply is sufficient answer to those who argue as though the condemnation of present militancy shut the door on everything but peaceful propaganda. The case is utterly different. It lies here: the great forces of sex revolt were alive in the hearts of women and urgent for expression in the early days of the century. Only an outlet was wanting. The outlet was found; and those who found it were trusted with the direction of its course of expression. The question is not 'Are the forces of rebellion behind this movement?' Of course they are. It is not 'Have the women shown great powers of sacrifice and courage?' I know of those things as much as any. The question is 'Have the leaders justified their trust, have they made the best use of the forces and the women given over into their hands?' And to this question I give an emphatic 'No.' I do not ask if the leaders have made a better use of these forces than was made of other forces by leaders of an earlier day. This again is not the point. You cannot vindicate one sinner by the fall of another. The great forces of revolt were there for the using, and I claim that instead of being used they have been exploited and abused.

It is no use evading the issue by restating the same proposition in the form that momentum was necessary to awaken the dead movement and that this has been supplied. The whole value of momentum depends upon the direction in which it causes things to move. My contention is that the momentum supplied by the kind of militancy developed under the Pankhurst domination has moved along a narrow channel to a purely political goal, and has brought the movement to a lower plane in the process. A choice of bolder and broader methods, an acceptance of imprisonment if it should come, but not a deliberate seeking of it for itself, an energetic seizing of all the avenues of protest, instead of the specialising upon the repetition of one or two artificially contrived ones – this course would have produced a bigger momentum and brought women by a higher and broader road to their ultimate goal.

Militant advocates who use the revolutionary phrases talk of terrorism moving the politician, and of cowards only praying to the devil they fear. But these are cant phrases employed by the directorate for the exact purpose of keeping such young persons as can be deceived by them in a posture of admiration. There has not been either revolution or terrorism in this movement, nor yet any of the red-blooded devilry so much admired by modern decadents; these things have only been aped; these claims are sham. And even politicians cannot be expected to yield so much to the sham terrorism which gives them merely an occasional physical pang, half of which is dread of a ridiculous situation, as they would yield to a dignified massing of protestant forces clamorous for the redress of wrongs really suffered by real victims of present conditions.

I put the position as I see it here; revolt there would have been and must have been. It was inevitable. The tragedy of it is that revolt has been allowed to fall under the unchallenged direction of those who can see nothing but the political outlook and use nothing but artificial and essentially small methods.

I have been twice to Holloway, and have been prominent in a fairly large number of other protests and demonstrations during the last five years. I have been personally responsible for the planning of many militant protests, and have issued many calls to danger duty in the Freedom League. I do not regret my own part in this work, nor that of the women who have answered my call. Until last year my thought on this subject had not matured. But a year of more or less enforced leisure has given me time to go back to the beginning again and revisit the land of promise; it has given me an opportunity of seeing the movement from without and fighting things out with my own soul. And these are my convictions: militancy on the present lines is not effective; it is not justified; it is not justifiable; it is a wasteful and extravagant method of advertisement. It was always small in practice, but now it is small in spirit; and all the world of our enemies sees that it is small.

I shall deal later with the political situation and the return to militancy which finally severed me from the movement; but apart from it entirely I believe that such militancy as we have so far had cannot be further indulged in without damage to the lesser suffrage cause and to the greater cause of the full emancipation of women.

# CHAPTER IX:

# HOSTAGES TO HURRY

The spirit of hurry which dominates both leaders and followers in the militant movement has been justified against attack with much earnest argument. The chief claims advanced are historical, and a reference to the long years of patient effort for which the Woman's Suffrage Societies have been responsible since 1867 is supposed to fully answer any charges of undue haste brought against the modern movement. On the surface of things this record supplies every justification, and, paradoxical as this may sound, if it had been urged in 1885 instead of in 1905 such justification would have been fundamental as well as superficial.

The special work to which the older Suffrage Societies devoted themselves was the work of creating a majority sufficient to pass a suffrage measure. As I have shown elsewhere, it completed this task in the early eighties of last century; at this time it had created its voting machine. When in 1884 a Women Suffrage Amendment was moved to the Reform Bill there would have been no doubt whatever as to its success if this voting machine had been allowed to work. But the suffragists had reckoned without the Government, which, in the person of Mr Gladstone[28] and the chief engineer, stepped in and stopped the machine. This was the moment for the revolt; and upon the heels of revolt should have come changed tactics, based upon the recognition of the responsibility of the Government for the defeat.

There can be no doubt but that at this period very general support of the suffrage demand existed in the country. The records reveal a series of great meetings, extraordinary for that period, branches and committees even in the smallest towns of Scotland, which the modern movement has not yet retouched, and resolutions in favour from municipal authorities and other responsible administrative bodies. The failure of the suffragists of that day to strike when the blow was necessary, and their further failure to develop a new policy to meet the conditions which Mr Gladstone's action revealed, threw them back into impotence. They were in a blind alley. They went on building up a majority that had failed them, that continued to fail them, and that they could not trust. They remained in the blind alley for twenty years; and during that twenty years the movement lost heart and courage, drooped and pined, until it was a dead simulacrum of the thing it once had been. During those twenty years the contemptuous indifference of the politician hardened into a habit.

He came to regard the suffrage question as a perennial. He judged it by its methods and by its effects, and in a great measure he was not to be blamed for accepting it at its own valuation.

These facts change the position materially. When suffragists count up the years of effort and agitation they ought honourably to admit that twenty of those years were wasted by their own incapacity – that the living vital agitation had only existed during the earlier days, and that the dead period before militancy was more due to the suffragists themselves than to the politicians.

When the militant movement began it was therefore face to face not only with the ordinary political atmosphere of inaction and the common masculine sense of objection at first sight to Votes for Women, but it had to leap barriers which the older suffragists had erected. It had to create a new spirit in women themselves and a new Parliamentary atmosphere on the suffrage question. It had to re-convert numbers of old adherents and to reform and re-marshal its army. And while these needs called for vigour and attack and sacrifice, the very fact of their existence called for thoroughness and depth, for a guarding against bias and against over-much impatience. It was necessary to awaken the sense of urgency; but to guard against the demon of hurry. It was necessary to reject the patience that meant inaction, and to guard against the impatience that meant ill-action.

The militant movement made no attempt to grasp the necessity for this discrimination. It was carried over the line of urgency into hurry, over the line of personal sacrifice into the sacrifice of principles and liberty and essentials. It refused to acknowledge facts and conditions or to allow for them, clamouring, 'It ought not to be'; it refused to believe in what was. It will be argued that no limits to hurry could be desirable whatever the attitude of the country because of the stress of industrial oppression from which women were suffering. But this argument cannot be urged in justification of speed-mongering which sacrificed the working woman and the advocacy of her rights as one of the primary hostages given for early success. Further, it is incontrovertible that this movement for the suffrage solution of industrial evils did not come from the women workers but from women of higher economic grade. And in the third place a slower, bigger, and more outspoken movement alone would have had any chance of appeal to the women who are industrially enslaved. From the present movement of hurry they are excluded in great measure by class prejudice, by the expense and slowness of organisation, and because of the fact that their working conditions deny them any leisure for voluntary service, any power of adding to the funds and any opportunity of sharing in militant action.

The spirit of hurry has its rise more in the temperament of the chief leader than in any reasons of historical happenings or industrial stress. The chief characteristic of Mrs Pankhurst is what has been described as her 'divine impatience.' She is alive with it. It has sides that are glorious and inspiring enough to justify the description. It has sides that are anything but glorious. But it is this spirit of unresting haste that has carried the movement into the shoals that are ever ready for the feet of the restless rusher. I believe that each new sacrifice to this spirit in possession has caused Mrs Pankhurst a pang. But the sacrifices have been made. One by one, steadily, as they were demanded, the hostages have been forthcoming. To one convinced of the need for urgency and possessed of the spirit of unrest the sacrifices have appeared as the lesser evils. Autocracy was preferable to delay; a restriction of demand was preferable to delay; convention and narrowness and intolerance were less objectionable than delay: and in turn each of these prices was paid. A daring advertising scheme will always produce quicker results than revolution. Revolution frightens people, and must ever be of slow growth; but a picturesque policy of publicity, especially when it is carefully allied with otherwise impeccable propriety, is capable of raising a mushroom movement in a very short space of time. The pageant fever is almost a universal one. It brings satisfaction to the colour hunger and the histrionic aspirations of humanity. It is always easier to arouse the senses than to arouse the soul; and for this speedier result the militancy of effect has been preferred.

By women under the influence of the hurry spirit, interference is resented not only because it will lessen personal glory, but because by introducing other points of view it will introduce the need for longer considerations of decision and action – it will cause delay. To those not so influenced and less self-opinionated the very fact that there was danger to the rate of advance of the movement in a representative system would have raised the fear that the desired rate of advance might be artificial, and as such ultimately dangerous to the movement itself. It might have suggested also the possibility that there were more ways than one of achieving a given purpose and that it was never wise to reject unheard all other ways but one's own.

This policy of hurry must be judged by its effects not upon laws and law-makers alone but upon the women. In the beginning militancy made promise of leading women out of the land of bondage, but if I am asked now whether women will be the better in themselves for the militant movements I must answer a reluctant 'No.' Here and there are women who will be better, but for the mass the influences are bad. The very virtues of the movement have become dangerous to women; it is sapping their independence, their self-control, their scorn of small and dishonest things. It is blinding their eyes with passion and devotion. It is making them into tools. As a result of the system of autocracy great numbers of the militant women have ceased thinking, have ceased to feel the need for thinking, have become mere receptive vessels. Unstimulated and armed by original thought their advocacy is marked by crudity and ignorance. Half the suffragette speakers one hears reveal an amazing barrenness of matter and an utter lack of individual ratiocination. They repeat parrot-wise the speeches of other speakers. They make use of statements of which they do not know the origin and of which they cannot supply the proof. In the political world they play the game of follow-the-leader; into the woman's position in other wide areas of human endeavour they have never been guilty of investigation. The jumble of economics and assumptions, of social facts and fancies, they repeat because they have learnt them by heart, just as they have picked up the smart platform retorts and illustrations with which the original group of speakers arrested the attention of their audiences.

Take the methods of political trickery which are now so consistently applied. Do they tend to produce a higher type of woman? We know that they do not. The petty vices of women who live in restricted circumstances and to whom the wider worlds of education and public life are closed have formed a theme for numberless illogical tirades against the nature of woman. This movement of over-hurry is bringing those vices into politics. It is developing capacities of equivocation and boasting and disregard for the exact observance of truth. It is falsifying even at the time of utterance the commonly urged claims, not the essential ones or the logical ones, but the claims of sentiment that are popularly employed as to the advisability of enfranchising women.

One of the glib retorts favoured by the suffragette speaker to the 'man in the crowd' who asks why she prefers politics to the seclusion of home life is that women are needed in the political world. She would be a brave woman who would dispute this claim; but it can be used and supported in a very undesirable way. The customary line of argument is that politics needs the purification that women alone can bring and the home is quoted as an exemplar of what ought to be in the political world. This dragging in of the home is often a platform trick employed to awaken sentimentality in the audience, but it is as often a proof of the crude and limited rebellion that has been kindled by suffragette methods. The home of to-day is commonly far from perfect. From its evil traditions of women's subjection and inferiority come some of the worst of our social and economic evils. The suffragette who is content with the home as it is, built upon the subjection of the woman and continued by the infringement of the rights of the child, is not a true rebel but the victim of superficial emotion. Any woman who is really a rebel longs to destroy the conventions which bind her in the home as much as those which bind her in the State. She wants a new home and a new motherhood and a great many more new things as well as a Parliamentary vote. The waters of purification she seeks must flow through the home as well as through the political world. Yet the present conditions are such that the suffragettes who know these truths suppress them for political motives and those who ought to know them are left to blunder in the shallows of superficial things.

The claim that women will purify politics may be advanced from many points of view. It is often based merely upon the old sickly sentiment that has survived from the days when men in search of self-approval promulgated the angel-idiot theory. There are suffragists who claim that women have a higher moral nature than men, and who will accept any statement, however extreme, based upon that assumption. But while these premises are ridiculous and inadequate, there is something to be said for the theory that if a sex has been kept cleaning and scrubbing and scouring and sweeping for a long series of generations, there will be a tendency for the habit to assert itself when that sex secures a wider sphere of existence. From this point of view I have often suggested the theory. The early history of the suffrage movement, and the strange detachedness of the women's party organisations from those of the men, have confirmed the view. The twenty years which elapsed between the last Reform Bill and the first outbreak of militancy and showed the older suffragists as totally incapable of grappling with the political machine, showed also that this failure was due to their unswerving belief in the honesty of their professed friends and their inability to play any of the ordinary political tricks. But the militant movement has changed all this. The modern suffragist is not only acquainted with the dishonest philandering of the politician, she has proved herself capable of meeting him at his own game. She has read him like a book, and then played off all his best tricks. She can talk large or small, according to the need of the moment, as he does; threaten and complain without a change of colour; snatch credit from accident and read special meanings into ordinary events in order to serve her turn. Like the male politician, she can rouse an audience by the use of great phrases, raise the cry of 'Equality' to win enthusiasm, applause, and sacrifice, and then cut down her official demand from principle to present expediency. She herself is disproving her own claim. She is losing her own self-respect in that she knows that she is urging a claim that is false.

198

The misuse of militancy as a medium of advertisement points in the same direction. It shows that women in politics are as easily corrupted as men by the desire to win. The scoring of showy and effective victory is so magnified as to undermine the very object which the victory is required to achieve. The devotees of militantism under the Pankhurst flag have become devotees of the big drum. And militantism is but one arm of the advertising octopus which is feeding upon the spirit of revolt and purification, and gradually eating it out of the movement. Noise and show have come to be the accepted substitutes for argument. Government by suggestion has superseded personal conviction. The impetus of emotion and numbers has taken the place of reason. The woman's boasted standard of morals in public life has come down to the standard that she has so loudly condemned. She has employed all the under-influence, all the stage illusions, all the little vices, all the great blind virtues, to carry her through the maze. The respectable classes have been won – and paid for. The treasury has been filled – by sacrifice of devious kinds. Some people have given out of their abundance for the great show and shouting, and they are adequately repaid. But others have given out of their necessities because of the misused language of revolt, because of the souls to be won from captivity, and these must be counted among the many exploited by a movement that has no scruple about the methods it uses to gain its ends. The woman with money, the woman with courage, the woman with talent, the woman with leisure, the woman with warm life-forces pulsing through her, arresting and attractive, the woman who has made her name, the lady with relatives in high places, the lady with a title – all these have been made use of as pawns in the game. They are all means to an end; tools to be used and forgotten; agencies to serve their purpose and drop out of sight. They regard themselves as patrons, heroines, rebels, and emancipators; they are really the instruments of advertisement used by a great machine of boom. These are some of the strange manifestations of the great purification which women have brought into politics! And all these accomplished facts, all these resulting forces, have been forming the environment of the militant women for years and have been moulding and bending her. She has become the creature and the slave of the speed-mongers. She has been losing herself with every step by which she has approached nearer the legislative goal.

One of the most dangerous influences that have been brought to bear upon her has been that of sex opinionation. The old sinful humility which was inculcated in women is gradually giving way to an assertion of individual and sex value, and to a claim for respect and recompense in the world. This is a tendency to be encouraged. The first thing a girl-child should be taught to say to her brother is this: 'I am as good as you,' but the second is: 'Of course, I don't claim to be any better.' The militant movement has definitely encouraged its supporters to act as though they believed that women were the superiors of men. It has encouraged a system of stupid sex-glorification. The future is referred to with capital letters as The Woman's Age, and language is employed of which the only inference is that in the glorious coming days man will be as much repressed and discriminated against as woman is now.

In a small way this pro-woman spirit may be a good thing, for men – very young men. In special cases, and where the mental machinery is of such quality as to make the effort worth while, this attitude may prove useful in reducing a foolish young man to reason. But the world is not full of foolish sex-opinionated young men, and it will make things no better to fill it with foolish sex-opinionated young women. There is every justification for the woman who runs amok under masculine provocation; there is everything to be said for the steady cultivation in women of a high respect for their own functions and capacities and a belief in themselves; but there is no permanent satisfaction to be obtained by casting man down and asking woman to tread upon him. To reverse an evil condition is not to remove it. The cultivation of distrust in all men because they are men is as evil as the cultivation of contempt for all women because they are women. But there is danger as well as evil in this course of action. Women who are taught to worship women and scorn men are liable to go too far in the opposite direction when under the influence of strong natural emotion. If you have been subjected to a system of mental control under which you have come to regard the average human male as an inferior and evilly-inclined creature, you are in danger of mistaking the first intelligent and honest man you meet for a god. The element of deceit in the canonisation of woman at the expense of man provides a channel for the further degradation of women. This may be regarded as of slight account by the suffragist who needs the infatuated woman in the frenzied rush for legislation, but it will become a large thing when the calm of quieter days gives opportunity for marking its effects.

By such forces are women turned into sexual prigs. By such means are they being prepared for legislative liberty. By such means is the personal emancipation of the individual woman being retarded and sacrificed. The subjection of the individual woman, in her person, in her mind, to any outer force, the infringement of her individual integrity, the degradation of her outlook and aspirations, all these are much more disastrous in effect than mere legislative disabilities. Legal and formal disabilities are chiefly objectionable in that they tend to produce the evil of personal subjection. A woman can be free in spite of law and apart from law; the law can only give her the chance to be free. No passing of legal enactments can set free a woman with a slave mind. No one can be made free by machinery. The machinery can only provide the opportunity.

The price paid to speed-mongering mounts up higher and higher as every fresh aspect of the movement is considered. The whole movement now is honeycombed with exploitation. With one of the strongest cases that could possibly be desired by reformers, with material of the best offered for use, with great human potentialities urgent for outlet, with the qualities of great leaders in themselves, the whole of the better things have been sold or cast away by the dictators for the mere satisfaction of a speedy end of some sort. One used to hear thinking women express the fear that the struggle would end too soon and the great cleansing forces of revolt have too short a time to work. The fear is now that the movement has already lasted too long. It has lasted long enough to lose sight of its great end, long enough to create new evils, and long enough to sow seeds of many weaknesses and limits among the women whom it might have freed. It has lasted long enough to impose another slavery for that which it has not yet removed.

# CHAPTER X:

# CLAIMS EXAMINED

Extravagant claims on behalf of militancy will be brought forward to counterbalance the charges I bring. I want to say at once that I am not prepared to admit anything like all of them, although I have no desire to belittle the effect of what will amount to a national acceptance of the principle of sex-equality. But the claims made cannot be granted without consideration.

Militancy has hastened the day of the first legislative victory.[29] I believe this now; I could have staked my life on it a few months ago. But the return of militancy in November, 1910, has raised up fears as to whether the present undoubted advantage will be permanently retained. If it is, if the sacrifice of the past is not bartered for revenge in the immediate future, women will have votes, some women of those at present qualified, at an earlier day than would otherwise have been the case unless some other extraordinary change had come over the suffrage movement in the interval. This must be frankly admitted as a good claim.

I do not wish to be understood as indulging in unqualified prophecy. The recent breaking of the truce which had given Mr Brailsford and his Conciliation Committee a chance of focusing the results of our work inside the House was ominous. The demonstrations at the Dissolution brought to an immediate end the negotiations with the authorities. They indicated that the desire for retaliation threatens to outrun even the desire for early results. And this way lies the danger of postponed legislation. But the admission of the effects of militancy on hastening suffrage legislation does not necessarily imply that the right use has been made of the militant spirit and machinery, or that the best possible result has been or will be achieved even in the political world. I am of opinion that the legislative victory could have been won only a little later than will now be the case had another guiding spirit been substituted for that which has been employed, and that instead of the way being paved with sacrifice the wider interests could have been royally served at the same time.

But let the claim of hastening legislation be admitted. It is not certain that the results predicted for women will follow. The prophecies of protagonists with regard to the effects of legislation are generally over-rosy. They are made without full recognition of the British capacity for accepting at one and the same time a hotch-potch of contradictory laws and principles and refusing to follow out to its logical conclusion any course of thought.

Nor will the absence of co-relation in British legislation and the untidy conservative methods of the British people be the sole influences which will limit their extravagant expectations. Their own methods, their own rush, will serve to reduce the value of the vote when it is won. The vote cannot secure of itself any single woman's emancipation. It is a tool; and the kind of work that can be done with it depends upon the nature of the tool, and second upon the capacity of the person who uses it. Both these conditions seem to have been forgotten by the militant apologists. They fail to see that large areas in which emancipation is needed lie entirely outside the scope of the vote. They forget that a slave woman with a vote will still be essentially a slave. They do not recognise that the woman with a restricted outlook can only express herself within its limits; and that the crude shallowness, sex-opinionation, and resentment, which forms the basis of their enthusiasm, do not supply the best training for the serious work of emancipation by law-making. The frenzied rush for votes is not carrying women more deeply into the problems that confront them; it is carrying them over the top. Facts and figures, serious investigation, considerations of principle and consistency, these are all foreign to the atmosphere of hurry. The future law-maker would be the better for a period of calm.

But any real legislative advance for women must be based on aspiration after a re-created world. This will necessitate that the enfranchised women, the users of the voting tools shall be possessed of those aspirations and capable of carrying them into practical acceptance. If we look at the body of women who form the suffragist rank and file we find that any hopes based upon the assumption that they are advanced feminists craving to use the vote in the interest of womanhood are doomed to disappointment.

The consistent believers in the complete emancipation of women do not form a large proportion of the suffragists' rank and file. The greater number of suffragists are of the political variety, and many of these have very limited aspirations. Those women who claim equal rights and are eager to accept the full burdens which sex equality must bring are the promise of the whole movement. But they are submitting to a policy of avoidance of fundamentals, a policy of suppression, which must be an ill-preparation for the future. I do not speak lightly in this matter. I have had the evasion and hypocrisy forced upon myself. I have quibbled with questioners. I have spoken on the edge of self-committal and held myself back. I have found myself under the influence of the audience I addressed whittling down what I should have said into what I knew was as much as I dared to say. Such evasion has become a habitual use in the movement. The forces that would make for the best kind of legislation, which would prepare the future elector to destroy and to construct with knowledge and insight, are dammed up at their source; they are sacrificed for a mere temporary advantage.

The women for whose sake the chains of silence are imposed are merely out for the parliamentary vote, preferably upon the present or a narrower basis. They want the vote because they rightly object to the sense of personal degradation which is involved in its denial. The matter is purely a personal one to them; their clamour for change will cease as soon as the personal indignity is removed. There is no revolutionary zeal in this large class; in politics and social and sexual affairs it will stand for things as they are. Between the narrow personal and political suffragists and the true feminists there stands a second much smaller class of women who would accept some such programme of reform as that embodied by Lady McLaren in her Woman's Charter. But while accepted in spirit even this moderate and in some suggestions retrogressive programme is considered too advanced to be advocated in public. It has been neglected and pushed aside by all the suffragist associations, and the militant societies have been the worst offenders. A similar attitude has been maintained on other occasions. It is deserving of note that neither of the militant groups sent any representative to give evidence before the Divorce Commission,[30] and that when, in 1908, Mrs Despard took up the case of Daisy Lord,[31] there was no other prominent suffragist who shared her advocacy, while much disapproval of the intrusion of such a matter into suffrage propaganda was expressed, not by the high-and-dry conservative ladies, but by the 'advanced.' The re-creation of the world by legislative means does not seem likely while these types of women predominate, and the forces at work leave them uneducated and undeveloped.

To the credit of militancy must be counted the general awakening of interest in the question of women's right to self-government. The revolt has brought many people into active touch with the question who would not otherwise have heard of it so soon or in such a startling and stimulating way. It has provided elementary education upon the issue of women's citizenship to the general public. This claim is irrefutable. It can claim further to have brought women into associated service in a rough-and-ready way which has not been wanting in developing social qualities and powers of co-operation. But while in the Freedom League this training has tended to the production of thinking and questioning co-operation, in the Women's Social and Political Union it has produced the subservient self-abnegation of the individual. The movement may claim, too, to have aided in a remarkable degree the development of self-sacrifice and personal courage among women.

Herein lies its greatest value. This particular work has been well done, and done in spite of the rampant evils which have accompanied it. To this it is clear that the militants can always turn to substantiate their claim of having helped onward the development of a free womanhood. The wonderful forces of sacrifice which have been awakened are such as to stamp the women capable of them as greater than their methods, greater than their speech. If to the courage that has risen above fear and laughter and contempt there were but added a statesmanship as big, the movement would have achieved its glorious work in a glorious fashion. The dream would have become a reality. But the contemplation of this very courage, misused and misdirected, is one of the most pitiful of sights. Not only in applying militant tactics is this quality of courage manifested; it has risen to as great heights in the performance of the numerous kinds of dirty and unpleasant work which active suffragettes always find ready for their hands.

Ages of self-suppression and the yielding up of self have developed this capacity in women to such an extent as to make a vice out of a virtue. Woman has not only failed to assert her own right to consideration, her right to be herself, she has given herself away, and given herself away for nothing. The militant movement, while asserting the woman's right to political liberty, has only continued the cultivation of this spirit of self-sacrifice. It has not only exploited the divine thing. It has continued its degradation. The only consoling reflection is that self-forgetfulness has been provided with an avenue of courage in place of the old-time avenue of suppression. This is an advance. It will bear fruit when the evils of emotionalism and hurry have been lived down.

When all the claims are admitted and examined we are driven to one conclusion. Whatever great forces the militant movement awakened at the beginning it is now doing more harm than good. Even the value of the vote as the tool of legislative emancipation has been steadily sacrificed to the getting of the vote. The great inheritance of women is being paid away for the political mess of pottage; and this is robbed of half its practical use and value by the policy and atmosphere in which women are being trained. Only the real feminists can put an end to the worst aspects of this suicidal frenzy for results; but they have allowed themselves to be blinded by emotion and carried off their feet by numbers; they have given themselves to the game of boastful, arrogant hurry and let it go on unchecked. They have refused to see that they are tying their own hands against the future; that as the first cry of urgency has been used, so will the second and third be used to silence and chain them in the same way; that ever they will be selling the great whole for the little immediate part and robbing that part of its great value by dishonest suppression.

These are the dangers. It is for those who are truly rebel women to leave them so or alter them.

# CHAPTER XI:

# THE BROKEN TRUCE

In every movement towards freedom there has come an occasion that called for revolt. It came in the British Woman Suffrage movement; and after a pause of years, in which the movement nearly died for lack of it, the call was responded to. Whatever evils of administration have restricted it, whatever opportunities and greatnesses it has missed, the revolt has prepared the way for legislation giving votes to women.

But with the suffragist advocates of revolt militancy has come to be regarded not as a necessary means to the end but as the only means. Now militancy can never be this. The masterly generalship of the greatest military conquerors has not alone sufficed to win victory. It is obvious that the last stage before amnesty or legislation must be one of negotiation and peace. This is especially the case when the position of the rebels is such that they cannot themselves focus upon the political machine the forces which they employ. The very fact that women are voteless and have no representatives in Parliament leaves a gap between their achievement and the full record of them which does not exist for rebel groups of men.

To the thinking rebel of the early days of this movement this fact was clear. On many occasions we protested amongst ourselves against the waste of our work, and sought for some means of bridging the gap. We felt that although we had shown numbers and energy and determination we had failed to record them within the House of Commons. 'How long this stage will last, we do not know,' we said. 'But before we win we must get an organised vehicle of expression within the citadel. The last stage must be conducted through friends within. We may not like it. Being rebels we cannot like it. But the circumstances render it inevitable. The last stage will be a stage of truce.'

When in January, 1910, both militant societies called a truce, and Mr Brailsford and Lord Lytton gathered together a group of parliamentarians to form a Conciliation Committee, strong hopes sprang into being. For four years we had been in revolt. Now the time for focusing and recording our work had come. Step by step the Government had been brought nearer to leaving the way of legislation open. With a band of representatives working in the House the last stage looked imminent.

Militancy had prepared the way for the conciliatory efforts, but the two could not go on together. One cannot be treating with the enemy and waging war upon him at the same time. If the work of conciliation and inquiry, if the practical preparation for a practicable measure were to go on, the active aggression must cease. To this agreement both militant societies held fast, and the work within the House was pushed forward with enthusiasm, earnestness, and ability.

Our own work, interpreted by the occasional intervention of suffragist Members of Parliament in the interests of legislation and peace, had brought the Prime Minister stage by stage from his original personal objection of the votes for women demand to the stage of officially speaking us fair. It was at this moment that Mr Brailsford's committee took up the task of finding the basis upon which the House would record a majority for a Woman Suffrage Bill and then bringing the Government to remove its veto out of deference to that majority. This work occupied the parliamentary time during the spring and autmn of 1910, and I believe that it would have resulted certainly in the passing of a Votes for Women measure during 1911 if the constitutional issue had not created a crisis. Even still I am convinced, writing before the King's Speech[32] has been read, that a careful husbanding of the advantages already gained could be made to result in early enfranchisement.

Before the Dissolution was announced in November the officials of the Conciliation Committee cherished strong hopes that they would be able to win from the Government a definite pledge of full facilities for this present year. The announcement of the Dissolution had reduced in value the pledge they obtained before it was finally uttered. But there is no shadow of doubt but that it would have been given in either event, and that it was not merely a pre-election pledge intended to remove suffragist opposition during the contest.

Yet before the Government had replied to the request for an undertaking – and although it had fixed a day on which it would reply – as soon as the Dissolution was announced, the truce was broken. I do not deny cause for disappointment. Could any woman in the ranks fail to feel that when the constitutional issue postponed our own settlement? But I do deny that any justification existed for a return to militancy. To demonstrate at this critical juncture was to demonstrate against accident. It was a childish, a wasteful, and an ungrateful proceeding. It was kicking against the general cussedness of things, before which individuals, and much more movements, have to learn philosophy. Neither the Government nor the Conciliation Committee were so far blameworthy as to justify the return to the tactics of protest. The Government had not deliberately chosen to rush the constitutional question, and to dissolve the House, in order to betray the suffragist women of the country. Only the exaggeration habitual to the militant movement could persuade anyone to believe that.

When it came, the Prime Minister's statement was the best that has ever been made by a responsible Minister of the Crown. But before the pledge was given the militant tactics had been resumed. And this course I think was a policy of suicide. It showed that the rebel leaders were not statesmen; it showed that they were determined to demonstrate, that they were determined not to be satisfied. The year of waiting had left them more enamoured of militancy than ever. They had begun to feel the need for the advertisement that it supplied. When the constitutional issue between the two Houses came to sweep the country into a General Election they rose up crying, 'We will not be ignored. The constitutional issue between the two sexes also claims attention.' But the issue was ignored. Such demonstration at such a time did not prevent the swamping. It could not prevent it. The promoters knew that it could not. They wasted powder and shot and women; and they wasted them to get an advertisement for the General Election.

But the demonstration was not so harmless as it was useless. I believe that it prejudicially affected the minds of retiring members and parliamentary candidates just at the moment when their opinions were of most importance to suffragists. I believe that it affected the attitude of the Prime Minister. His pose, when he made the statement, was described as careless, the words studiously brief and off-hand; and it is remarkable that though a Government statement had been promised for this day it was not forthcoming until at a late hour, and then only after it had been specially asked for. I believe that the demonstration of November 18th prejudiced the chances of early suffrage legislation.

I do not suggest that the Prime Minister's statement called for gratitude. But I hold that in the first place it should have been waited for before it was rejected; it should have been heard before it was condemned. And when it was made it certainly called for a continuance of the truce with regard to militancy so that the work of negotiation could be continued and as much got out of the pledge as the most enthusiastic Liberal suffragist could read into it. It is my conviction that this could have been done, that it was within the realm of the possible. But almost before the pledge was uttered another demonstration took place – a thing justifiable enough if it was absolutely certain that nothing more could be won from the Government by negotiation, and a course absolutely absurd and criminal while it was clear that such opportunities still existed.

The demonstrations of November 18th and 22nd were also objectionable in that they showed ungrateful distrust of the Conciliation Committee. I am not concerned to defend the individual members of this body; some of these men are too well-known as staunch suffragists to need any defence from me, and of the rest it must be said that they had loyally supported the efforts of their colleagues. But I do strongly resent the action which was calculated to throw a slur upon this Committee, and especially upon its earnest and unresting Secretary and Chairman. They will be the last to protest on their own behalf, but that does not make the rejection of their efforts any the more excusable. They still hoped to achieve full victory, and their earlier achievements within the House showed that their hope was entitled to be treated as reasonable. Either their honesty of purpose or their capacity or both were called in question by the November demonstrations.

Now a movement of this kind cannot remain stationary. It may remain too long or too short a time in one stage, but when that stage is ended it must step onward or backward. If the stage of conciliation has really failed then it follows that the type of militancy employed to prepare the way for it has failed too, and the next stage ought to be a more vigorous one. The responsibility this implies for the leaders is enormous. It means that they, having rejected the methods of negotiation, are committed in honour to prove that negotiation had done its best and had failed. If they cannot do this – and it is obvious from their over-hasty demonstration of November 18th that they cannot – it follows that they must bear the responsibility of rejecting conciliation before it has been fully tried, of thrusting the movement back into the stage of violence, and of doing this not because it is proved necessary, but because they desired it. This is the only thing that it can mean.

Even as I write the preliminary vague threatenings of more violent action are being circulated through the Press. Before this book is published the first appeal to real violence may have been made. It may not be the real thing, of course. One scarcely expects that it will be more than a spectacular imitation. But whether it be real or sham it will condemn a large number of women to personal sacrifice that in some cases amounts to suicide, and in all cases to the suffering of terrible strain and much possible abuse. The leaders repudiate responsibility for any acts of violence committed by their followers. But this magnifies their offence a thousand-fold, makes it monstrous, cowardly, and untruthful. Women who have been worked up to fanaticism by years of influence are now to be given rein, but the sins of their befoolment are to be upon their own heads, and those who made them fanatics are to escape. This is the pitiable spectacle as it appears to the public. But to those who know the facts the position is worse. Violence under these conditions is not only vindictive and unnecessary, it is victimisation.

I must make this as clear as crystal and as strong as I know how, for in it lies the cause of my final disillusionment. In brief it can be put thus: there was a chance of peace, and these leaders have cast it away. They have thrown away, rejected, a possible early and peaceable solution. This, in all conscience, is bad enough. But it becomes a deed that calls for a vocabulary stronger than mine at its strongest when the significance of the return to militancy is marked. For it does not mean a return to militancy of the old type; it is certain to mean a return to more aggressive forms of protest and attack. In plain English the directors of the Social and Political Union have deliberately chosen to fling away the strength and nerve force, the physical health and perhaps the mental health, of the women who have been trustful enough to leave their destinies in such hands. They have chosen to repeat scenes that they would have us believe they have always viewed with loathing, as the last alternative to a servile submission. They have chosen to destroy their own followers. Do not let any supporters of these leaders talk to me again of the iniquities of the Government. Here is iniquity enough for me.

Let me be understood. I have myself urged that in any living revolt the failure of peaceful negotiation must mean stronger revolt. I know that it must. Everyone who reads history will admit that it must mean either more vigorous revolt or submission. It is not for the application of more vigorous tactics in itself that I am constrained to condemn in unsparing terms the directorate of the Social and Political Union. I am not afraid of violence. I do not condemn it. I have advocated it. But with the last five years of petty partisan militancy behind us I found that I could not honestly or fairly apply it. If the record of the last five years had been different the position of to-day would be different, and a refusal of early legislation might justify violence completely. But the folly of the militancy of advertisement is that it has queered the pitch. An independent society like the Freedom League is not able to conduct its war with the Government upon fair and sane lines while its every effort and intention may be frustrated by the precipitation of the sister society. How can the revolutionist use violent methods of protest against the Government which obviously has been forced into a false position by the criminal impatience of fellow rebels? How can I attack the Government for the delays occasioned by the Social and Political Union?

It is not violence that I condemn; it is the precipitation of a movement that promised to end in peace back into violence. This I condemn, and I will continue to condemn. It is a policy of wrecking, the deliberate choice of delay and warfare. I know that it will be

211

lightly said that the Government would have out-manoeuvred the Conciliation Committee in the end. But I demand proof. It is not right to hang a woman because you believe that she would some day have murdered her husband. It is not right to commit any act of retaliation before the deed against which you retaliate is done. You cannot revenge yourself upon suspicion. To do so is to be guilty of wanton outrage.

I have already said that I hold no brief for the Government. But neither will I appear as devil's advocate against it. The Government has sins of magnitude upon its head. It has been pushed forward from stage to stage of concession like a reluctant bully yielding always under pressure. But on this last occasion it has not been given a fair chance. It could plead 'Not guilty.' But I am much more concerned for the deed itself than either for the Government denied its chance or for the Conciliation Committee flouted and cast aside. It is the deed itself that condemns the militant directorate.

I would have stayed in the movement to the end, struggled against Fate, and suppressed my convictions for the sake of unity and peace, striving ever for an early solution, if this final criminal folly had not made it impossible. Under the revelation it forced upon me the need for speech became imperative. The dangerous strength of the self-made leaders loomed up imminent and destructive, and silence made me accessory to the evil. Whatever the price to be paid for speech I had to speak. The movement had been betrayed. Find what extenuation you can, you who worship and follow, for you cannot deny the fact: the movement *has* been betrayed. Divine impatience has outrun its divine attributes; it has made a stupendous blunder. In the rebellion against this blunder the whole movement stands forth to be judged.

# CHAPTER XII:

# PARNELL THE PROTOTYPE

It would be folly to pretend that the women capable of directing and dominating this movement are common-place women, women endowed with only the average share of gifts. Both Mrs Pankhurst and her daughter are women of striking personality. They are not necessarily women of wide culture nor of great intellectual power, but they are mentally alert and temperamentally tenacious, they have absolute confidence in themselves and in their methods, and they possess in a remarkable degree the capacity for winning the unreasoning worship of others. They are both of them feminine women, and women who rejoice in their femininity. They are women who are feminine in the popular sense of the word, women of slight physique and considerable physical charm, in whom some of the prevailing characteristics of the subject women of past days are still marked. This is especially true of Mrs Pankhurst, who is by far the more human of the two, the more natural, the closer to the hearts of her followers.

The woman of other days was proverbially variable; so are these women in small things – in the things that they think are great they have perfect steadiness of purpose. But their steadiness is not always the steadiness of wisdom; it is sometimes the expression of folly. They will not admit the human facility for making mistakes; they are never wrong; they never give way. They are not calm women, but irritable, yielding to sudden tempests; they believe what they want and reject what they do not want to believe; they like and dislike by instinct and chance circumstance, and change rapidly from one state to the other; they act on the spur of sudden feeling and unthinkingly, but they can always make a justification that sounds sufficient to give the action reasonable basis within a few moments after it has been committed. Perhaps because Mrs Pankhurst is more frank and self-revealing than her daughter these characteristics are more marked in her. But while the younger woman may show her limits less often in speech the elder woman is the more lovable. She is natural, herself, a wonderful woman, self-inspired, possessed with the spirit of hurry and impatience, paying any price her aims demand but paying every price with a pang, unscrupulous in that she will not bate one jot or tittle of the price, human and appealing in that she regrets the payment and sorrows over it.

Miss Christabel Pankhurst is of harder stuff, not greater. The mother is a natural product, the daughter an artificial one. She might have done her work better if she had been herself. She has schooled herself to a pose, formed herself upon a model, and fitted herself to the mould the model supplied.

Angry Irishmen have been incensed that the policy of the Women's Social and Political Union should be described as an application of the tactics of Parnell, while Irish suffragists have been flattered by the description. But no one seems to have grasped how very deeply, considering the difference of circumstances and material, the influence of Parnell can be traced. The idea of an organised militant campaign directed against the Government was not the fruit of any single brain. Some parts of the policy evolved under our eyes as we worked. Some parts were directly attributable to Miss Pankhurst in their final form. Some parts must be left to conjecture as to origin. But even a cursory examination of the history of Charles Stewart Parnell establishes the fact that the militant suffragists have paid him the compliment of more than ordinary imitation.

There were two centres in Manchester in either of which the idea of a militant campaign might have originated, the Pankhurst household and another. I first heard the suggestion in the latter centre and may have been influenced thereby to believe this its place of origin. Because of political views and national sympathies Parnell would be regarded with admiration in both centres, and there is little doubt in my mind, from my acquaintance with the conditions which preceded the militant outbreak, and from a consideration of the work and life of Parnell, that he was the inspirer of Miss Pankhurst, and that in a lesser degree his methods influenced her mother.

This influence of Parnell is traceable in the tactics and direction of the movement – in great things as well as in small, and it is traceable also in the personal attitude of Miss Pankhurst in a degree that cannot be explained except by the hypothesis of study and imitation. The parliamentary anti-government policy is the direct gift of the Irish Party under Parnell, although it had been previously practised by the Irish Nationalists of 1852 and preached by Sir Gavan Duffy. In this we admitted Parnell's influence from the beginning. But in addition to the direct policy of opposition or obstruction of the Government in power, the spirit in which the policy was applied is common to both movements. Parnell believed in angering and shocking the enemy; so does Miss Pankhurst. Parnell rejoiced to think that he was hated by the English; it is one of the aims of the Pankhurst policy to awaken the hatred of the Liberals. The desire for retaliation as well as reform was strong in the one leader and is strong in the others. Parnell is reported by Mr Barry O'Brien as saying in Dublin about 1879:

'I said when I was last here that I would not promise any thing by parliamentary action, nor by any particular line of policy; but I said that we could punish the English, and I predicted that the English would very soon get afraid of punishment.' This is equalled by Miss Pankhurst's declarations that 'We will bring the Government to its knees,' and 'The Government will be harassed in every possible way.'

The parliamentary policy of obstruction is the same, and the employment of the forces of rebellion carries out the analogy. Mr Barry O'Brien tells us that Parnell walked always upon the verge of treason-felony, but never by word or deed committed himself to it, and he thus acquired an ominous weight in constitutional circles and a great measure of influence over the Fenian organisation at the same time. The militant suffragist leaders have had to fit this policy to different conditions. No rebel movement existed for them, it had to be created. They had to conduct a political agitation and at the same time combine with it the pose of revolution. They could not take the exact line of Parnell, a line which left him untouched by personal responsibility for lawlessness, but they chose the next best course. They talked revolution, but did not practise it; they walked on the verge of sedition and never committed themselves to it; they put out one hand to protest and another to propriety. In this way again they followed the policy of Parnell, playing off one section of people against the other, and exploiting to their own purposes the rebel forces that seethed round them.

It is said that Parnell was unscrupulous in his methods, that he looked only at the end, caring little how he got there. This is an outstanding characteristic of the present militant movement. It has developed into ruthlessness and casuistry, it has created the methods of boom, it has bred the evils of government by autocracy and management by suggestion and dominance. The women who work with the militant dictators are used by them, and in this the militant practice resembles that of Parnell, who made all sections of the Irish people help to drive the ship for him. There is a similar resemblance to that attitude of Parnell, which called forth comment when he was presented with the great Tribute of the Irish people, in the regally calm way in which adoration and tribute are accepted by the autocrats of the militant movement. But like all other parallels, this breaks down if pushed too far, for to the policy of dictatorship which Parnell followed he brought the capacity to choose and develop men of ability – the other men grew in stature by working alongside of him – while in the militant movement the women of parts have been either looked at askance or suppressed.

The personal attitude of Miss Pankhurst seems to follow in many important points that of Parnell, and a fairly long acquaintance with her leads me to think that these personal similarities are acquired. There is the same reticence which gave to Parnell so much of his strength, the silence about future work, the same evasion of the statement of a policy, the same aloofness. Parnell does not appear to have won the worship of the Irish at home and the support of the Irish in England and America by argument and explanation, but by the pose of self-assurance and silence. He never explained his policy. He merely asked for an opportunity to apply it. He justified it after the event. He was opposed to the publication of the Plan of Campaign, to anything which might serve as ground for criticism and promote the advocacy of alternative policies. 'He was not in the habit of forecasting the future,' says one of his biographers, 'lest it should interfere with the operations of the present.' Again: 'He saw his way clearly to a given point; he went straight to that point and then surveyed the situation afresh.'

This same faculty for silence and for non-committal utterances Miss Pankhurst exhibited in a marked degree in the early days of the women's militant movement. The women about her talked, but she said little except upon the platform. She seemed to stand by and let things drift and grow, and then to seize upon them and fit them in among those already accepted. She thrust her colleagues into new positions with the haziest of hints on policy, the bare bones of an idea upon which to work, and they came through gasping, sometimes right and sometimes wrong. These experiences led them to wonder if she evolved her ideas from hand to mouth as she went or built them up from the more facile speakers about her and from their experimental action. Either of these suggestions may fit the case, but a close acquaintanceship with the life and work of Parnell would have been sufficient explanation in itself. Such a knowledge of the Irish leader would have shown a woman as capable as Miss Pankhurst the advantages of careful non-committal advance, of retaining the initiative as completely and as long as possible by a wise silence, of leading the women with her step by step a little at a time until they were committed to the whole policy she desired without opportunity for criticism of or initiative in its construction. This certainly was the practice and this the result. With the experiences of the last seven years as my guide I am strongly inclined to accept the theory that Miss Pankhurst carefully modelled her course from the beginning upon that of Charles Stewart Parnell.

In another relation the analogy is suggested only to break down. Parnell is admitted to have hesitated when Davitt suggested the formation of the Land League, and his hesitation was due to a recognition of the difficulty of controlling such organisations and the fear that the strength of this one might be so used as to interfere with his plans. But he took the risk and carried the Land League with him, and while Mrs Pankhurst, troubled with the same doubts, refused to take the risks and imposed the iron bonds of personal control upon the movement that she required and distrusted.

There is a common resemblance in the personal egotism of the Irish leader and the militant dictators. 'Parnell believed that he was able to lead the Irish party, and that no other man could.' Mrs Pankhurst and her daughter believe that they can lead the British suffrage movement and that no other women can. They go further: they say that no other women shall. Parnell could always have been displaced by the vote of his colleagues; Mrs Pankhurst can never be so displaced; she has erected the wall of autocracy in order to make that event impossible.

A wonderful facility for quick decision, for instinctive choice of the right weapon, an adroitness that was almost marvellous, seems to have marked the 'uncrowned king.' There is nothing perhaps so specially marked in the two dictators than this same facility. Parnell could not be cornered: I have never seen Mrs Pankhurst at a loss for an explanation or a retort; and her daughter has carried to a fine art the evasion of any issue that cannot be escaped in any other way.

So close does the duplication in personal attitude and methods go that the very arguments of Parnell are employed by the younger militant leader. Parnell's speeches and the history of his life are full of phrases which are used by Miss Pankhurst and of descriptions that might be given of her. With a very few substitutions whole portions of Parnell's speeches could be accepted by her followers as Miss Pankhurst's utterances. Sometimes the very words re-appear. 'We will stiffen the back of the Government. Then we shall see what the Lords will do,' describes Miss Pankhurst's present attitude exactly.

'He called upon the Government to give assurances for legislation for the next session.' Miss Pankhurst has been doing this ever since I have known her.

'Parnell made up his mind to wage relentless war upon the Government.'

'Parnell never dreams of giving the English credit for good intentions. He is always on the look-out for the cloven hoof. He distrusts the whole lot of them, and is always on the watch.'

The book of inspiration from which the spirit and policy of the militant movement have found direction is the 'Life of Parnell.' In the record of his rapid re-construction of the Irish party there has been found the methods of re-construction of the Women Suffrage Party. The likeness in many ways of the struggle that the Irish wage for self-government to the struggle which women wage for political liberty made the problem of adaptation easy after it had suggested the course of action. The militant leaders are the imitators of the Irish leader, but they have failed to attain his mastery of circumstance, his trust in his colleagues, his capacity for judgment. He did not only know how to conduct a campaign and make use of all the forces within his world to help him to his end; he knew more. He knew when to strike and when not to strike; they strike at all times. He knew how to trust men; they do not know how to trust women. He knew when the war was over and the time for negotiation had come; they have rejected negotiation when it has been offered. He knew how to carry the country for which he worked with him; they have left behind them not only the women who are still unawakened but great classes of women who might have been wakened, and of those who were wishful of giving service they have cast some out of the ranks. He was the leader, the natural chief, the chosen, the master of circumstance; they are the autocrats self-made, the artificially created dictators. He deserved to win. I dare not ask, 'Do they?'

# CHAPTER XIII:

## LOOKING FORWARD

I stated at the outset that my criticism would be merciless, and I do not pretend that it has not been. A defrauded rebel is naturally the bitterest opponent of leaders who exploit rebellion. And though I scorn to urge excuse I do urge justification. Speech was necessary. And one might as well have not spoken at all if one did not speak strongly. If upon later consideration I find that I am guilty of having spoken too strongly in the heat and depth of my resentment against the broken truce, I shall not be afraid of admitting my error. But at present, as I write, I feel that I have spoken as honestly as I can and as sympathetically as I dare.

I look forward to other hopes and other work. I see the need for much hard thinking among women: I see the need for much plain speaking. I shall try to do my share of both. I do not think that the atmosphere of the militant movement, an atmosphere at fierce fever heat, has been good for me or for others. In such heat of struggle one cannot see straight. Outside this atmosphere we may begin again and build the foundations of our future work. I cannot prophesy where the new investigations may lead us, what the fruit of careful thought among the women who have to begin again will be, but I believe that there will come a mature movement, adult, strong, fully-grown, to which these women will contribute. I do not think that any such new movement will forge new chains as the price of winning particular liberties, but rather that it will set itself to prepare the way for full liberty. It is not possible for it to confine its attention to politics, even to the great portentous questions of women's connection with economics, nor to the much suppressed and diffi-cult sex matters: though upon each of these issues it will prepare the way by investigation and will take a strong and honest line. It cannot be an anti-man movement, but rather a movement to make possible supermen and superwomen. I believe . . . [sic] But all these things are hopes, and may be dreams. I have dreamed before – and wakened.

The germ of the political virus is in the air. It is a mad, strange world, and we women are as mad as the rest of its inhabitants. Just when all the signs of the times point to the breakdown of Parliamen-tary systems, when the hollowness of the party sham, and the ineffectiveness of governing machinery is becoming impossible of denial, we find the new clamour set up by workers and women to get their rights in the political arena. If their getting them will mean a clean sweep of present ineptitudes and stupidities then we may hope much from their success – more from that of the Labour Party than from that of the women, for the way of Labour has been prepared while the women have sought to escape the burdens of preparation. But if this new incoming will merely continue and perpetuate the political conditions of the present, then the earnest workers should be about their business elsewhere.

Great opportunities for the exercise of personal liberty can be attained by parliamentary means. But liberty in its widest aspects is always curtailed by legislation. There are two classes of legislation to consider: the one is carried by those who control the legislative machine, and this is imposition; the other is carried by the demand of the people, and this is only majority rule and not full liberty. In this second class the reforms women need would have to come. Yet nothing is ever attained in the class of legislation from a representative Parliament – and the more representative it becomes the nearer this rule approximates to absolute truth – unless it has been preached and promulgated throughout the country until the preachers have become weary and the demand itself trite.

This is a work that is waiting for us. By voice and pen to produce the change of spirit in men and women which will register itself in legislation and which will make for better conditions in areas that legislation cannot reach. Before the bullets can be used by the politicians they must be made; before the women can get a thing they must want it. Let us go out and make them want things; let us show them the reasonableness and the justice of the things they already want but of which they have not dared to speak; and let us go seeking for the right outlet along the many ways that are blind now both to us and to them. We may never reach the big movement for which we seek, but we shall be going towards it; we shall not be buying one liberty at the price of others; we shall not be losing hold of ourselves under the sway of dangerous emotion; we shall not be playing political tricks. Even those who confine themselves to the political world will find their work easier because of us. The vote will be more valuable. Those who use it will be able to grasp more of its powers of usefulness and will use it better. And all along the way we shall be winning individual women to self-emancipation without which all else is as wind.

I do not ask the women who think me a little mad and a little bad to revise their opinion or to come out into the cold with me. I know that I cannot hope to reach these women for a long time, that it may take an abler and a gentler advocate to reach them at all. I do not ask them to cease working for the political tool. It is a good work, if it be well done; it is a task necessary to be done. And it is not by the choice of the mass of the workers that the present conditions have been made. May they get the vote quickly, very quickly, not only that women may have votes, but that they may see an end of the present domination.

To the many women who have written to me expressing their sympathy and agreement since my revolt and resignation have been made known, and asking for a new society of women rebels to be formed at once, I can offer no definite plan. I do not think that it is wise that a new movement should be immediately inaugurated. We must have time for thought before we act again. And I do not think that I am the person to take the initiative. I am prepared to share the toil when the moment for a new concerted action arises; for the time I must work alone.

The choice of avenues of productive feminist work is only too great. An individual woman, any small group of women, will find work waiting to their hands. Are there not helpers needed among the women who have taken up the cause of their sisters the wage-workers? Are there not ways of wakening revolt against the slaveries of wives? Do not the home-women, the last class to win personal and economic freedom, stand in need of service? Is there nothing to be done with regard to the thousands of unhappy babies which unwilling mothers bear, unwanted, into the world? The life and work of the local authorities and the communities under their care become yearly more important. Can we not find work to do here? These and a hundred kindred issues need attention, and are waiting for willing brains and hearts and hands. Some of them are outside politics; some of them are inside the sphere of political influence, and good work done here will react upon the legislative results of enfranchisement, will hasten the pace at which the new voters will be able to go forward.

Those of us who are ourselves afire are prone to think that by our own heat we can make others burn and by our own strength can move mountains. But we cannot. We may work as quickly as we like; the lasting results are slow. Teachers will tell you that there has been no more pernicious system devised in education than that known as 'payment by results.' The child, and the child's mind, have been sacrificed to it. The schools have been turned into a huge machine for coining money out of the Government. It has been condemned and shattered by its own inherent vices. In the women's rebel movement we have suffered under a like evil. We have been playing for results. The woman has been sacrificed to the getting of the vote. If we turn away from this movement and condemn it we must be ready to pay the price. We shall not have publicity. We shall not have the world for an audience. We shall drop to the level of the common-place and do our common-place work. But who will count the plaudits at the end? If we do our work as well as we can, what else matters?

# Part IV:
# *Against the State*

# 'Feminism and Politics'*

Politics does not concern itself with the idea or the ideal, but with the practical application. Aspiration after change, the real revolution, comes before political action and paves the way for it. The apostle of the idea, inspired by a great and glowing dream, must not only prepare the way for action, but must submit to see his dream transformed in the political process into the petty product of the politician; and he must school himself to be well content if the partial legislative registration he wins really squares with his ultimate aim. The idea is the life; it creates. Politics is the machine; it concerns itself with the things that are immediately practicable and possible, the products of compromise, of buying and selling, of weighing and measuring, the safe things, the accepted things, the things that are orthodox.

In our own days we have not only to submit to the limitations of the Parliamentary machine, but to the further limits and dangers that come with the control of the machine by the party system. The separation of Members of Parliament into arbitrary groups, obedient to the party whips and financed by the party funds, reduces the human element in Government – personal independence, individual judgment and conviction – and increases the mechanical. It substitutes the advantage of the party for the good of the State. It causes every proposition or measure to be judged from the point of view of its effect upon the party or the system, instead of according to its inherent value. It tends to stifle honesty and individuality. It substitutes numerical strength for sound reasoning, power for justice, organised machinery for the labour of conversion; the machine takes the place of the mind.

Further limitations result from the superficial control of Parliament by the electorate, the mass. Under present conditions, control by the multitude must mean control by ignorance, mediocrity and commonplace. It must mean for all vital things – things which

* *Contemporary Review*, November 1911.

cannot be carried over the heads of the public – a very slow rate of progress. The rate of advance under democracy is measured by the average intellect and activity; and with us the average is still low. A theory must become a truism before it becomes a law. This is one of the prices we pay for democracy.

From such considerations it follows that a movement which expresses itself in politics only must be a restricted one. It must have narrow and clearly defined boundaries. It must cast many things aside. It must keep clear of all doubtful and unorthodox issues. It must prove itself desirable and innocuous. It must concern itself entirely with the mechanical work of getting certain partial expressions of opinion registered in the form of law.

This is the condition of the feminist movement in Great Britain. It took its first rise in rebellion against the general degradation of women, but in practice it has confined itself almost entirely to politics, and in politics to the winning of the Parliamentary vote. It has shut off, evaded or neglected everything else. So completely in this case has the part obscured the whole that it has come to be taken for the whole, has passed for it in the public eye, and has blocked the way to it among adherents. So that at this present time there is no feminist movement in the country, but only a suffrage movement – and chaos.

It follows naturally that there is no feminist organization and no feminist programme. And though the first is not essential, the second is. It is possible for a movement to exist without machinery, but not without a policy or a purpose – and these latter are lacking. To serve the present need, a definition of feminism may be put forward in general terms, based upon those classics of the movement which, like Mary Wollstonecraft's *Rights of Women* and John Stuart Mill's *Subjection of Women*, were produced before the broad feminist demands came to be sacrificed to politics. With such guidance feminism may be defined as a movement seeking the reorganisation of the world upon a basis of sex-equality in all human relations; a movement which would reject every differentiation between individuals upon the ground of sex, would abolish all sex privileges and sex burdens, and would strive to set up the recognition of the common humanity of woman and man as the foundation of law and custom.

It is clear at once that a movement so defined demands a revolution in every department of human life, and that the channel of politics is all too narrow and shallow for it. A feminist confession of faith commits those who make it to the effort to transform life. They do not set out to revoke laws merely, nor to draw up paper-and-ink documents imposing restraints upon unwilling persons and apportioning penalties for the rebellious among them, nor to register the opinions of the mass; but to make human beings themselves other than they now are, giving them new thoughts, new aspirations, new hopes, new horizons. Feminism would re-make society, would set up new standards, would destroy old customs, would establish a new morality. It frankly sets out to do great deeds of destruction and reconstruction. It asks a new world.

Politics may serve rightly as one of the tools which such a movement brings into action. It may serve as the record of work done, fixing in the form of law the changes of opinion and morality which active feminism will produce. In material matters it may provide a weapon for defence and a tool for the removal of barriers. But it can never be an adequate channel of expression for feminist desires, and its effectiveness must always depend upon the wider feminist propaganda. The real work of feminism lies outside politics, the real harvest of feminism will be garnered outside politics, though both may be recorded in its books.

Against the small things there is rarely any strong opposition, unless in those cases in which ignorance and superstition first exaggerate and then rally in the antagonism of fear. But against the thing of great purpose the opposition is of great extent; the greater the potentialities it possesses, the greater the forces that will gather to hinder them. Such a movement as feminism, momentous and vital, will ever have to meet the onslaught of persistent and unnumbered forces. The army of vested interests will be massed in opposition, and with them the established authorities, the conventions of social life, and the prejudices and misconceptions of the ignorant. A movement seeking to re-model social life, to create another industrial revolution, to purge sex-relations of the elements of barter and property, to set up a new type of home and family-relation, must necessarily shake all established things, creating conscious disturbance and distress where now habit blinds us to the existence of danger and evil. It must be prepared to meet opposition from every quarter, fierce outcry, bitter antagonism, the ridicule and slander of fanaticism, and the dead-weight of inertia.

The early professors of sex-equality met the full forces of opposition. They paid the price exacted from all pioneers. A very slight acquaintance with the early records of the struggle for the emancipation of women is sufficient to assure us that in ridicule, contempt and contumely, in poverty and personal indignity, the price was exacted in full. But the later rebel woman has tried to escape the thorny way, has tried to evade direct conflict with the enemy. She has not sought to rouse the storm that she might then go forth to do battle with it, but to leave the great forces of opposition sleeping while she passed quietly by on the other side. She has sought the line of least resistance for her advance, and has reduced her creed to a minimum to take advantage of it.

Of all aspects of sex-equality the political is the least vital; cut off from all other demands and considered apart, as an end in itself, the claim for voting rights is calculated to awaken less opposition than any other detached element of the full sex-equality programme. For this reason it was given precedence and prominence over all other aspects; for this reason feminism was cut down to suffragism, sex-equality to votes for women on any terms. This was the line of least resistance: to win some measure of power in politics for women, and then, armed with this, to seek the further goal of sex-equality. Many convinced feminists deliberately accepted this policy, threw in their lot with the mere suffragists, restricted themselves to advocacy of the Parliamentary vote, and concealed cautiously those further aims which they sought to approach by these means. This policy may be described as one of cowardice, caution, or statesmanship; on this point there is a difference of opinion. But it is generally admitted that in its results the policy has reduced the feminist movement to a vague chaos of confused opinion, and has confined the efforts of the rebel women of the last half-century almost entirely to the political world.

With most women who recognise that the general movement has been narrowed down to politics, the recognition is accompanied by approval. These women claim that the limitation was statesmanlike and desirable, and that it was calculated to reduce opposition to a minimum and to effect a useful concentration of the attention and efforts of women. They point out that much time and work is wasted through diffusion and multiplication of interests, that it is best to follow the elementary rule of doing one thing at a time, and that this political demand falls naturally to be asserted first. It is argued further that in every successful campaign numbers are necessary, and that in this case numbers could only be obtained by the limitation of the demand. The great body of women neither understood nor desired feminism, but could be won and united in support of the Parliamentary vote. The final justification of the limitation is embodied in the statement that the other vital issues are merely postponed until women as voters are armed with power to secure settlements more quickly and effectively than they can hope to do now. It is even suggested that the winning of the greater rights may not be postponed at all, but rather hastened by their temporary banishment from the programme of women's claims.

It is necessary to examine these arguments in order. In the first place, it may be admitted at once that the limitation of the public demand has reduced the opposition. This must follow naturally where there is less to oppose. It is obvious that a programme which includes such demands as radical marriage reform, the economic emancipation of women, and the complete control by woman of her own destiny, must be more provocative of opposition than a simple demand for enfranchisement. Similarly, the reduction of opposition would become the more marked the more the political demand was detached from great realities, the more the vote was presented as an end in itself, and not a means to an end. But a reduction in opposition is not the only thing to be sought. Opposition may cease altogether – to the great disadvantage of a movement. A loss of inspiration may accompany the limitation, and it may reduce the forces in favour as much as the opposition is reduced. This is the particular fate which overtook the feminists who limited themselves to suffrage. Previous to the militant period, which supplied an artificial and emotional stimulus, the most marked characteristic of the suffrage movement was its deadly, apathetic dullness. The supporters of sex-equality had reduced their public demands so far as to cut themselves off completely from vital things, from the lives women lived, from the injuries they suffered. As a result, women's suffrage aroused no more enthusiasm among women than the merest philosophical abstraction. It did not touch the mass; the few whom it did touch it left cold.

There is much to be said for the substitution of an orderly co-operative effort in the place of the spasmodic and unorganised exertions of scattered enthusiasts; and the limitation of the sex-equality demand to the right of voting might have been of service in this direction if the single demand had been attractive enough. But it lacked attraction; it had not the qualities of bigness or nearness. To most women it seemed a long way off and very small. Until the militant revival brought excitement and exaltation, there was no more unattractive movement in the world than the British Women's Suffrage movement. It was dead with dignity and stiff with limits and doubts. It accepted sex-disabilities by its very decorum. It had no imagination. Active women desiring to serve their country or their sex drew apart from it, and sought a more useful sphere of work in industrial organization, in the existing political parties, or in social service. The majority of the believers in women's suffrage never troubled to join the ranks; those who were members were merely acquiescent. The movement asked so little that everybody could support it, so little that nobody thought it worth while to work for it or pay for it. The country was full of academic support. And the suffragists gradually learned that numbers are of no avail to a cause unless they are earnest enough to get into motion, that what is wanted is an active, not a static, force.

The most weighty argument brought forward in favour of the limitation is that which claims that there has been no real postponement of feminism, since women armed with the power of the vote will make such rapid progress as will more than wipe out any apparent delay. But this position is based upon two very doubtful assumptions. In the first place, it is assumed that the women who will wield the new power will be desirous of using it to achieve the further emancipation of their sex. There is no special support forthcoming for this assumption; it is not justified by the common facts. The great mass of women suffragists are suffragists, and nothing more; and they are nothing more because those who saw further than they do have concealed their beliefs and kept silence when they should have preached a full doctrine. These women to whom the vote is an end, who see nothing beyond it but darkness or a millennial dream, have not been taught to use the new weapon, and will come to its use raw and unskilled. The vote will be of little value to them, or to the world through them. It is but a vehicle. The wish behind the vote is the power. If this wish has not been created, if problems have not been studied and solved, we can expect no quick harvest from the mere possession of the voting tool. A long period of propaganda – the very propaganda that has been so cautiously avoided – must intervene between the passing of a Women's Suffrage measure and an effective demand for feminist reconstruction. We shall be lucky if in the interval the Statute Book escapes being cumbered with measures which are opposed to the root-principles of sex-equality, and that upon the demand of newly enfranchised women. Seeking temporary or superficial advantage, they will succeed only in creating fresh bonds to trammel their sex in the future.

To avoid such a dangerous aftermath, the vote must be regarded and presented as a means to an end; and that end must be considered, discussed, and defined. This clearly necessitates the drafting of a programme, which in turn calls for a removal of the suffragist censorship of thought and word. Only those who accept the vote as an end in itself can be satisfied without a programme, and the fact that suffragists have been so long unconscious of this need shows that upon these women we can rest no hopes of speedy change.

The second false assumption involved in the argument is that full sex-equality can be achieved by the aid of political power. This is not true. The assumption shows both exaggeration and misconception of the function of the political weapon; it assumes power where there is only an opportunity for the exercise of power. Sex-inequality persists to-day because people have become used to it and believe in it, or think that they do. It depends much more upon custom than upon law. A change of the customary habits and usages of the nation is what is required, and this must be preceded by a change of opinion, a change of outlook. Such changes cannot be wrought automatically by the waving of the political wizard's wand. It is much more difficult to change custom than law. A law may be passed in defiance of, or in advance of, public opinion; a habit cannot be changed except by a radical revolution in the mind. But the revolution in outlook and habit once made is permanent in value. It secures the end; it is in itself the accomplishment. On the other hand, the passing of laws may give us only dead measures which the unconverted individual will evade, which will serve to irritate without accomplishing, which may end in aggravating the evils they were intended to remove. Those alterations in sex and social matters which feminism demands depend much more upon persistent and rational teaching than upon any change of law or Governmental machinery. Even in industrial affairs this is true. Where changes can be wrought by law, the law must be preceded by propaganda.

Additional evils which have escaped the consideration to which they are entitled are involved in the policy of the limitation of feminist efforts to politics. It has been forgotten that struggle between antagonistic principles cannot be evaded – except at a price; an artificial truce can be obtained only by the suppression or sacrifice of one of them. When one of these principles is established in common use, an avoidance of struggle can only be purchased by the sacrifice of the unestablished or unorthodox principle. This is what has been done by feminists who have confined their advocacy and effort to the Parliamentary vote. Their goal and their doctrine has had to be buried in silence. They have had to acquiesce in the things that were, giving ostensible support to evils against which they dare not disclaim. In seeking to purchase an early political victory they have sold themselves into a false position. It must be a bitter reflection to those who have paid this price to reflect that after nearly half a century this early victory is still to be won.

In any circumstances the policy adopted would have been a doubtful policy, and it was made more doubtful and dangerous for feminists by the very nature of the sphere in which they sought to work. Compromise is as the very breath of politics. The gold and silver of the mind it coins at best into copper, at worst into dross. There is a tragic difference between the child of the reformer's imagination and the product of the political machine. In this atmosphere suffragist caution tended to become cunning, compromise to become bartering, and selection hypocrisy. There was no original intention of betrayal, but only of postponement; yet the pressure of

231

the political machine, the effect of the political atmosphere, has been to produce a position of complete falsity. The choice of silence upon all other issues was made deliberately. But it was not found sufficient to be silent. The tricks of evasion have had to be employed, and these have been followed by untruth. When the advantage of the suffrage campaign exacted that price, it was paid. An innocent selection of a primary issue to which other issues were to be temporarily sacrificed by feminists – though the selection may have been dictated by motives that were narrow and mistaken – was not in itself dishonest. But as played out in the political arena, the game has become dishonest; the conditions have produced falseness. From one unfair and unwise start feminists have become involved in a very quagmire.

One practical consideration remains. It is argued that in achieving sex-equality political emancipation fails to be accomplished first. This may be true; a weighty case can be stated in favour of the claim. But it does not follow from such an admission that all other aspects of sex-equality must be suppressed in favour of the vote; that there should be no programme of after work; that the vote and nothing but the vote, should be advocated until it is won. Every political party in the State, each of them with a programme containing many items, places one measure at once in the forefront, and gives it temporary predominance. But this is all; it does not sacrifice every other project; it does not evade and deny its further aims. It makes a standard of them; it turns them into recruiting agents. Women could have put the vote first in the list of feminist demands upon the legislature without putting every other sex-reform out of existence; they could have put it in the front of the stage without clearing the stage of everything else. It is possible that the enunciation of a full programme might have hastened the first gain. To ask much in order to get a little is an accepted rule in Parliamentary affairs, and one which is commonly and successfully applied. With feminists, as with others, a full statement of desires and intentions means both gains and losses, for every item in the programme will gain supporters as well as lose them. If the cause be good and the case sound, the argument and discussion consequent upon publication would be every day increasing the number of supporters and reducing the number of the enemy, so that an increasing balance of advantage would accrue.

It is clear that the full weight of the support of statesmanship cannot be claimed in favour of the limitation policy. It may be that the balance of advantage and argument is on the side of free speech and frank acknowledgment. At all events, it cannot be denied that much more would have been accomplished along the way if feminism had been clearly proclaimed. Instead of a series of barren years, we should have had a series of victories to mark the passing of the years. Feminists would not have stood aside from women's movements which clamoured for their help, and were in principle entitled to it. They would have been capable of taking advantage of every emergency either social, political, or industrial, as it came along, and after enfranchisement had been won they would have been prepared for the speediest progress. An accumulated series of advantages which cannot be calculated – advantages of strength and numbers, and understanding and time – may have been thrown aside by the concentration upon the single political issue and the suppression of all else.

Directly resulting from the policy here examined has come the magnification of the functions of politics. While all definite instruction and examination of other sex-inequalities has been denied or discouraged, the zeal of youth and the enthusiasm of sympathy have been led to cast a glamour over the vote, making it a wand of wizardry. It has come to be accepted among young suffragists, and taught by older ones, that the vote is the key to every locked door, the ladder into every heaven, the foundation of the new world, its security and its symbol. The exaggeration may not have been wholly conscious or deliberate, but it has followed naturally from the narrowing policy of concentration. It has had this strategic advantage, that while it set forward no programme and left nothing definite for the enemy to strike against, it supplied the inspiration of a great dream for those who were unsatisfied with mere suffrage. The suffragist demanding a vote really desired a vote and nothing else; the enthusiastic champion of womanhood demanding a vote desired and expected a passage into paradise.

Such magnification of political functions may serve a temporary purpose, but it is harmful in many ways; it is harmful in what it excludes as well as in what it involves. It shuts out study, thought, independence, the quickening force of personal conviction; it opens the door to obsession and to ignorant intolerance. In place of mental activity we have blank minds; instead of knowledge, shibboleths; instead of thought, dogma; instead of argument, a catechism learned by rote. The women kept in this state are less in themselves than they might be, and they are less capable of serving their cause; and thus womanhood is robbed twice – in their persons and in their efforts. This is the first bad result.

But we must add to it a further undesirable tendency. The magnification of the functions of politics leads to a belief in what may be called emancipation by machinery. The vote, and the voter, are endowed with the divinity of kings, and they become the highest authorities, the final arbiters of every issue. The right of interference is set up as a prerogative of the voter, and the day of the possession of the vote by women is looked forward to as the day on which they will be able to use this power. Women who are spending their days condemning the subjection of women to men, appear to be seeking a subjection of both women and men to their ideas. They rely no longer upon the word of the preacher, but seem to be heading straight for a period of sex-reform by compulsion – the last ditch of the modern reformer. This is not by any means a weakness confined to women suffragists, though they are contributing in very large measure to this dangerous and tyrannical tendency in our present political life.

So far has the political aspect of reform obsessed the modern woman's imagination that it is necessary to emphasise the work that waits for the workers in other spheres. Habit has blinded her to the evils which lie entirely outside politics or in the solution of which politics can play only a secondary part. But many of such evils are vital. Take first those in economics. The problems of the wages of women workers, of equal pay for equal work, of the right to economic independence of married women, of the right of the woman to apprenticeship and training – all these are of primary importance, and they are all in great measure dependent upon forces outside politics for their solution. Legislative intervention in these matters can only come after much trade union organisation, much preaching of the new doctrine, much reform in our domestic industries, and a fundamental change in the outlook of working-men upon the issues affecting the work of women. Take, second, the questions of criminal law amendment, of sex-immorality, of illegitimacy, of divorce – it is patent to any careful observer that law alone, unfounded upon public opinion or sentiment, is totally incapable of producing permanent change. You cannot make a man moral or a woman strong by Act of Parliament. You must work a change in man and woman; you must set a new standard; you must remove the cause of evil, if you can lay it bare. Living law can only follow slowly after the change of public sentiment; with dead law it is foolish and vain to cumber the Statute Book. This argument should carry its appeal to those who have concentrated upon politics, and paid the price of winning political power – unless other weapons than the political are employed, the political weapon itself is robbed of its effectiveness. This is true not only in the cases briefly considered, but in the greater number of problems which call for the attention of women reformers.

These numerous considerations incline one to plead strongly for a reconsideration of the feminist position. Now that we are close on the eve of seeing the first suffrage extension to women, it is impossible to remodel the suffrage movement or societies. But the feminists within these societies should work out this problem for themselves; should make for themselves and for their fellows an opportunity for some serious preparation for the future; should put an end to their own personal responsibility for any type of dishonesty. There is not only political work to be done; there are years of accumulations of social and industrial work waiting. There are areas of civic and national activity in which the feminist principles have never been quoted, where the feminist solution has never been put forward. The most important departments of public life have need of feminist illumination. There are numberless individuals to whom feminism is not even a name, but who are suffering from the lack of the salvation it would bring them. In the interests of these neglected areas, of the women and men who are in need of them, of the bodies of earnest women who are penalised unfairly and unwisely in the struggle for the vote, the feminists should come out into the open. They should make their programme and proclaim it. They should face strife and controversy. They should seek their strength and peace not in silence and evasion, with all their train of evils, but in the security of conviction and the soundness of principle upheld before the world.

# 'Women and Government'*

That women who desire emancipation from the old sex-servitude should desire to see that emancipation expressed in concrete manner in the machinery of life is reasonable and commendable. But the common attitude to-day seems to be to rely upon the machinery and to leave the emancipation alone. The small class of thinking women recognise that the present suffrage agitation is only of indirect value, that it is of service so far as it tends to create the new spirit by the struggle for the new machinery and to stimulate a new practice by the exposure of the old, and only so far. But even among these women an undue importance seems to be attached to institutions and systems and mechanical devices. The reality is lost sight of; the machinery blocks the way.

This obsession shows itself in many ways. It shows itself in the exclusive concentration upon the winning of the Parliamentary vote. This is the obvious example, though in truth it is only an aspect of something bigger and more significant – the assumption by women that they can obtain and enjoy emancipation under existing institutions, and simply need to set up a paper-and-ink equality within them to be secure. This assumption is practically-universal; with nine out of every ten thinking women it passes as an axiom. They limit their speculations to life moulded by the present institutions, to society based upon the present conventions: they assume that this is the material through which and with which they must work.

It is my purpose to ask whether this attitude is justified, and I take democratic political machinery for my first inquiry. Before I begin it I desire to assure the reader that I am writing, not as a dogmatist, but as an inquirer, and that I am not prepared to substitute for the machinery I criticise destructively any personally devised alternative

* *The Freewoman*, December 21, 1911.

machine. I do not intend to make any concessions to those to whom the nakedness of a machineless land is an offence. Those who want machines may make their own machines; I am concerned with the realities behind them.

Out present governmental machine claims to be democratic and representative. Now, apart entirely from the fair argument that it cannot be either democratic or representative in the full sense of the words until it includes women in its franchises, I claim that the words used are inaccurate and untrue even for those who are supposed to control the government. The voters of the country are not represented in the Houses of Parliament. They do not get from the Legislature the laws that they want. They do get from the Legislature the laws that they do not want. They do not control the police or the Post Office, or the army or the navy. They do not control the private member of the Commons; and, much more definitely, they do not control the Cabinet. To listen to the speeches of some Suffragists, one would think that voters did all these things, getting from a perfectly oiled machine the perfectly formed legislative product. But this is not true. It is not too much to say that our democratic governing machine is an utter failure. It does not perform the work which it was constructed to perform. It is a penny-in-the-slot machine that won't work.

Our democratic machine suffers from two classes of faults: the first are inherent in all democratic governing machines, and the second are peculiar to the one which we have produced. The latter may be briefly dismissed. They are: Government by the secret Cabinet caucus, control of the private member by the party, the collusion of the two parties in the alternate governing game, and the numerous conventional devices by which liberty of speech and independence of action are denied and restricted within the House of Commons. If our democratic system were a perfect and ideal machine, the addition of these devices would render that machine inoperative. This is recognised by a younger school of politicians who are devoting their talents to the work of purifying the machine. Many women sympathise with this attitude, and declare, absurdly enough, that all the present corruption and dishonesty will be swept away with the coming of women into the political world. Let me admit for the moment that it may be that women will purify politics. How long will it take? And what reform of value are they likely to obtain in the interval? A survey of history will show that there have almost always been some aspiring politicians seeking the purification of the machine, and equally that governing machinery has always continued in spite of every mechanical change to be corrupt and dishonest. It is pertinent therefore to ask why women seeking emancipation should try to get it through this particular existing governing machine.

But even if women should accomplish the Sisyphus task and purify politics, even if they should come into possession of the democratic machine perfected and completed with adult suffrage, redistribution, and all the other missing devices, it is still pertinent to ask if it would serve their need. To answer this question it is necessary to consider the essential and inherent imperfection of all democratic machines that have ever been devised.

The democrat believes that by natural right every unit in the State is entitled to share in the national government. To achieve this ideal it has been supposed that it was merely necessary to give to every citizen a tool of some sort to play with. But this is another example of hiding the reality with the machine. What each unit in a democratic country needs is not a tool to play with or a name entered and numbered in a book, but a share of power sufficient to ensure self-protection. Under a real democracy no normal citizen could be subjected to coercion except for criminal incursion upon the rights of others. The bureaucrats have always met the democratic clamour by saying that such a system was an impossibility; and so far every democratic governing machine has proved that they are right. In practice every democratic system reduces itself to government by the majority and coercion of the minority, or government by the privileged and coercion for the unprivileged. Every democracy in action has become a bureaucracy; there is only a quantitative and not a qualitative difference between these two systems. The widest device of popular government still leaves a section of the people under compulsion, and it becomes interesting to ask what units are likely to form this slave section. At this stage I will content myself with the suggestion that there can be no certainty of full human liberty for women under a system from which the element of coercion cannot be removed.

The democratic machine is unwieldy, and with every extension of its powers and franchises it becomes more unwieldy. This means that it is always overweighted, that, as a result, legislation is always behind the demand, is unco-ordinated and unconsidered, and that there are always some victims suffering from these imperfections. The law under which we live at any given time is the registered opinion of the past. It may be the narrow prejudice of the middle ages, the outlived morality of the last century, the half-truth-become-a-whole-lie of the last generation; but it is always the dead hand of the past. The more unwieldy the machine the more complete becomes the chasm between the living thought of the living race and the dead thought that is embodied in law. The mind and the soul grow and grow, to new heights, to new understanding. But the law crawls ever behind. Pulling there from behind it does not only hold the world back, but its administrators punish and crucify whoever rises beyond its conceptions and transgresses its outworn creeds. And this tendency is increased by the unwieldiness of all democratic machinery.

A vote is a thing of value when one has room to use it, when its possession confers some real power upon the holder. It is a thing of no value when the arena is so crowded that no effective use can be made of the weapon, and when by multiplying the voters the fraction of power which attaches to the use of one vote is negligible. With universal suffrage the vote value is reduced to zero, and the real power is transferred definitely to the bureaucracy that controls the working of the machine – the officials, the political cliques, the vote-catchers. It will be argued that under the worst conditions these fractional powers of the voters can be added together to control the bureaucracy. But this is a fallacy. In practice it has been possible at all times to divide the electorate in such manner as to make the claim of control a farce. The one real power that the combined fraction wielders do possess is the power of dealing death, of destroying. It can unmake what it cannot control. And it is to be noted that this power of dealing death has always belonged to the populace, and has been used under and against every tyranny. We have travelled rather a long way from the autocratic government of John, from the oppression of Charles, to secure to ourselves only this same old right. For it is obvious to the most superficial that the right of destruction of a government inheres in the people themselves, and not in the democratic machinery. We already possess that which such democratic systems can give.

The value of political power may be assessed anew after these considerations; the disproportion between the cost and the gain may be seen in a new light. The machine-mongers have had a long day. Because women have been chained and beaten by government they have appealed to women to win a share in government. But is this the only way to liberty? Is it the best way? Is it a way at all? If government exists, women are of course entitled to share in it. Their right is not the question at issue here. It is granted. The question at issue is whether it is worthwhile, whether some other movement outside politics, independent of the governing machine, would not provide a surer and a speedier way to full human liberty.

239

# 'The Feminist Revolt: An Alternate Policy'*

To remove servile conditions or conditions of imposed disability rebellion of some kind and degree always has been necessary. Change is born of aspiration and discontent; these are its creative forces. But they do not become fruitful in silence and inaction; only when by protest and organisation they have found voice and form, only when they are expressed in rebellion can the desired revolution follow. It is true that the statement of a grievance has sufficed in some rare instances to procure redress – but this is peculiarly uncommon. The attitude of governing bodies generally tends to make necessary a further degree of rebellion than that which the malcontents have contemplated or desired.

But the necessity for organized movements of protest does not wholly proceed from the conservatism of governments; it is in great part due to the inertia of the mass of humanity, to the multifarious and conflicting interests and detachments of the governing and the governed, to the indifference and ignorance of the victims, and in these modern days to the many avenues of interest and amusement, opened by wider knowledge and applied science, in which pleasure, forgetfulness, and solace absorb mind and years and energy.

\* \* \*

Those who undertake any campaign of reform must be prepared to serve a novitiate to propaganda. For a reform which depends upon individual conviction and acceptance progress may be early measurable and steady; there may be laurels for wearing every day. But a very much greater length of service and strength of appeal is demanded before success can be obtained when the reform sought requires a legislative enactment, and the demands are multiplied

* Typescript, Box 404, File 3, TBG Collection, Fawcett Library, n.d.

when the enactment is claimed by a body of non-electors. This is especially so at present when the parliamentary machine is permanently overburdened and an accumulating overplus of ungranted demands marks the end of every session. It is easier nowadays for politically powerless persons to establish a new creed than to carry a new law.

In order to obtain effective support for any demand it is necessary to enlist in its behalf emotion and numbers. This can only be done by awakening public interest and sympathy. Protest, propaganda, persistent appeals and demands, energetic organisation and advertisement, must all play their part. The evils to be redressed and the advantages to be gained must be set forth in every possible way so that sympathisers may be moved to adherence and adherents to activity. But paramount among the forces which must be employed to produce momentum for a reform movement is that of feeling. The average British person is not moved by appeals to abstract justice nor by aspirations after better things as he or she is moved by suffering. As a nation we have no desire for change unless there is a hurt to be remedied. We must believe ourselves hurt or liable to be hurt or see someone else hurt or endangered before we will organise to bring about new conditions. The hurt must be forced upon our notice or we will hide away from it lest it should disturb our comfort. But produce a victim, a victim from whom we are not allowed to escape, and we will act. A victim will stir us to the deeps and give momentum to the deadest of old Causes. We are a nation of sentimentalists. When an evil is so thrust upon our notice that we cannot escape from it we will legislate it away.

This fact has to be recognised and reckoned with in every reform movement. It had to be recognised and reckoned with by the first militant suffragists; no doubt assailed us upon this point. We knew that the mere act of voting would never appeal to the imaginations of women as in itself so desirable a thing as to call for strenuous effort and bitter sacrifice. It was also clear to us that the vote as a symbol would appeal only to those who were already self-emancipated and not therefore in need of awakening. Our task was to stir the imaginations and enlist the feelings of great numbers of indifferent and unthinking people, the great mass of the community. To do this we recognised clearly that we must appeal to the emotions; that we must produce evidence of injustice in practice; that we must show victims to the eyes of the nation.

This policy has been put into practice; victims have been provided to move the hearts of the people. But from the beginning the task has been carried out on false lines and founded on a wrong basis. Those who from the early days have kept in their own hands the control of the militant suffrage organisation decided upon a policy of making victims – of creating them specially to meet the need. They did not seek for true cases of victimisation caused by the conditions of which we complained but set out to create an arbitrary supply of artificial victims. They made it a policy of the society to train women to seek martyrdom in order that they might pose later to waken enthusiasm among other women and to stir the sympathy and admiration of the multitude. They abandoned the natural way of producing the forces of revolution and devoted themselves to an artificial one.

It has been argued that this method was the only one which left the control of individuals and events in the hands of the militant directors and that it provided that the women best fitted to act as propagandists should wear the martyr crown and interpret the new gospel to the multitude: and these claims must be granted for what they are worth. Vaguely as they are commonly stated by apologists of the system of victim-making they can be reduced to this crude form – the method chosen has provided greater prominence and greater power for the leaders than the one rejected. This scarcely needs emphasis. A true victim has to be taken as she is found. She is not a follower to be directed and controlled and she may never become a follower. Her wrongs have made her a means of appeal to the public not the leaders who exploit her; she cannot be given her period of publicity and then pushed into silence. She must share the pedestal with the champion of her wrongs; and this although she may be socially, physically and conventionally, an undesirable person. On the other hand the follower can be chosen and cast off, can be made and unmade, and is always under direction. She can be driven to action at any moment for advertising or retaliatory purposes. She can be chosen because she has a title or family connections which will be of service. Under all circumstances she is the creature of the leaders and her sufferings redound to their credit and add to their glory while she herself passes through the fiery furnace – and into oblivion. For such reasons as these the false system has been preferred to the true.

There are other dangers which can be urged against the employment of the natural forces of revolution, and consideration of them has played a part in determining the course of events. . . . Every victim would bring into prominence some particular phase of the women problem which would have to be threshed out and its connection with the acceptance of sex-inequality in national politics established. A steady production of victims, such as alone would be effective in arousing the public conscience, would bring up every aspect of this problem for review. It would inevitably carry the movement wide of the strict political path, enlarge it to embrace

many issues now neglected, define and carry into prominence many
matters now evaded and feared, turn it into the dark and devious
ways of industrial and social wrong and amongst the very cripples
and criminals of our one-sexed system, and thus bring it into close
and vital connection with the realities of women's lives. To the
feminist propagandist and rebel nothing would seem to be more
desirable; to the politician nothing more objectionable. It is always a
heavier and a longer task to dig deep enough to uproot a tree than to
lop off one of its branches; but the politician prefers the latter
effort. . . . Every new problem will bring new converts, but also
new opponents; new opportunities for argument may strengthen the
case and yet bring new dangers of delay; the fewer exposures [mean]
. . . fewer prejudices will be aroused; the smaller the demand the
fewer interests will stand in its way of advance. Thus the politician.
And after five years experience of the militant suffrage movement it
is clear that, though its leaders have tried to tread a middle path,
giving one hand to the work of revolt and the other to the work of
the politician, the latter spirit has dominated the whole of their
operations. They have been cautious to the verge of cowardice.
They have avoided all possible connection or contact with those sex
and economic problems through which the meaning and the purpose of the suffrage movement can alone be interpreted.

The production of artificial victims as a method of appeal to the
emotions of the multitude, taken apart entirely from the considerations examined above, could never be regarded as sound. It is not
even politically advisable. It fails at the first test. It proves nothing in
favour of the Cause in which it is adopted. The fact that there are
women willing to sacrifice themselves in order to advertise the
demand for votes for women may establish their earnestness and
sincerity but it cannot be held as proving that their Cause is good.
The world is used to mistaken martyrs; its records of the past are full
of them – fanatics who have been willing to suffer any measure of
pain and despoilment for a superstition, a tyrant, a pretender, or a
mad dream of an overwrought brain. The world has learned to
admire the martyr while seeing the mistake . . . it is not mentally
blind enough to accept self-sacrifice as a proof of logical reasoning
and noble intentions. The sight of women deliberately seeking
martyrdom has moved to disgust and ridicule as well as to admiration. Where the full symbolism of the struggle has been appreciated
it has been felt that such sacrifice demanded recompense but to
others the whole policy has been a joke or an irritation. The
weakness of the artificial method has tripped up its supporters at
every turn. Nothing but the enthusiasm of the few has been proved
by self-sacrifice; and that has come to be looked upon as an emo-

tional craze. The heart of the multitude cannot be deeply stirred by victims who victimise themselves. It is more frequently moved to anger than to admiration of those who set out to create victims.

There seems nothing clearer than this: the proof of the existence of real victims of a system will condemn that system and make for reform. Every demand for reform originates in some case of suffering. All reform movements are born of such cases and embody the spirit that is created by them; the victims are at once the justification and the cause of organised rebellion. Hence those who cut off a movement of revolt from the victims in whose sufferings it has originated cut it off from reality and from its beginnings, set it apart from life conditions and make of it an unreal thing, a shadow, an imposture. The suffrage movement stood apart from life and reality during the latter years of the constitutional efforts; it was high and dry and academic and life moved on without it. The first outbreak of militancy seemed to promise a change; there was hope that the movement would come down to earth and the common life of common women and become vital there. But the hope has failed. The militant movement has kept to a straight narrow way and lest it should touch life it has cloaked itself with artifice and hypocrisy. The deliberate manufacture of victims to fill the void created by this policy of cowardice has been a futile effort. It is clear that it does not condemn the system of sex-inequality nor yet provide any sound argument for action to the minds of those who have to be moved. Indeed from one point of view this deliberate manufacture of martyrs may be taken as presumptive evidence against the demand. It is a pretence, a worked-up and unreal explosion, a dramatic display – and as such a thing to be suspected along with the movement which produces it. This argument is not uncommonly employed and it has stifled much possible sympathy at its source. The artificial method of awakening the spirit of rebellion has not succeeded. It has not strengthened the case for the granting of Woman Suffrage; it has not deceived the public. A certain political advance has been won by the united efforts of all suffragists during the last five years, but this dwindles into a disproportionately small result when compared with the effort put forth and by contrast with what might have been achieved had other lines of revolt been adopted.

The arbitrary discrimination against women if emphasized by exposure and protest on every possible occasion could not fail to produce a very serious effect upon the public mind. The material for bringing about a complete revolution in the position of women is only too generously furnished by the events of every day. The daily newspaper reports supply more victims than any movement could make use of; the daily Police Court records of proceedings are full of their cases; women who have suffered personal injury, industrial wrong and legal oppression can be numbered by the hundred every week. The magistrates are constantly dealing out legal punishment or legal protection to these women; and the failure of the law is seen in that they constantly return. In the higher Courts of Law instances of one-sexed law and one-sexed administration are not wanting – cases of infanticide, of serious sexual crime, of divorce. Every one of these would give a sound rebel movement its opportunity; every one of them would supply a victim by means of whose suffering the evil of present conditions could be taught. There are constantly occurring also instances of sex-differentiation in industrial and social affairs. Men are dismissed and women set to perform their work at half the wages – in which case both men and women are victimised. Married women are compulsorily excluded [from] . . . some branch of labour, or are submitted to illegal taxation; women are denied training and apprenticeship by the men working in the same trade and then treated as 'blacklegs' because, being untrained, they are forced to accept lower wages; prominent Labour politicians advocate the solution of the unemployment problem by the substitution of male for female labour on every possible occasion; important scientific bodies refuse qualified women admission to their ranks; the married woman while denied the honours of parentage is submitted to punishment when she fails in the fulfilment of its duties – in all of these cases again there is ground for complaint and a clear connection can be established between the injustice and the political inequality of the sexes; a strong protest would at once arouse sympathy and secure some advance towards redress. According to the nature of the case and the circumstances which accompanied it the lines of protest could be determined. On one matter the protest could be made within the Police Court, on another outside, in public meetings and the public press. A bad case could be used to arouse a whole town or district or trade. Strikes and boycotts could be employed on new feminist lines. Where the authorities interfered with the free statement of a case the campaign could be carried to the stage of defiance. Contempt of Court might be faced, even libel actions, to bring a case under the notice of the whole nation. Under such circumstances there would be no need for any deliberate seeking of imprisonment; it would come naturally when the case at issue was so serious as to awaken great interest and indignation. Men and women alike would be carried into active agitation for change. From every side the little forces would gather into one overwhelming torrent of purification.

This method of awakening true revolution would have one great advantage over an artificial method. It would pave the way to the final goal with other reforms. The present attitude of the organised suffragists of Great Britain, that of cautious concentration upon the voting disability alone apart entirely from every other legal and social injustice, commits women to years of barren effort in which neither the vote nor any other feminist advance can be won. This is not wisdom; it is a spurious imitation of wisdom. It has been thought that the right of women to use the parliamentary vote would be the sooner won if the feminist demand for sex-equality were whittled down to a fictitious simplicity. But such action has cut off the suffrage movement and the suffragist workers from their armoury and their inspiration. The campaign of manufactured victims has waked in the movement a semblance of vitality: it has been only a semblance. Revolt upon artificial lines has left things as they were. The movement is still separated from the real life of the women of the nation; it is still a thing apart, detached; it is still by a policy of short-sighted cowardice closing up the avenues of its own re-birth, giving its best forces no outlet, maiming itself, restricting the area of its own influence and effort.

To those who look beneath the surface it is clear that the demand for equal voting rights for women and men cannot be separated from the rest of the feminist demands for sex-equality. They are bound together, all parts of one great whole. The woman who desires her human rights in politics must desire them in social life; the woman who claims that there shall be a standard of equal return for citizen services without regard to sex in the State cannot deny the claim for equal pay for equal work in the industrial world; the woman who claims the right to control her own life through the law is committed to claim the control of her own person in marriage. The severance of the political demand for voting equality from the same demand in other departments of life was undertaken as a method of hastening political liberty; but it would appear to have failed of its purpose – women have given nearly half a century of service to the suffrage agitation – and it certainly has tended to postpone all other liberties for an indefinite time. It has led to silence where there should have been speech, to evasion and neglect where there should have been constant and careful attention. The price of putting all other sides of the movement away has been paid to the full; the victory has not been won. Its worst result is that the majority of suffragists have been left by this policy crudely ignorant and fearful of the very problems they must finally solve.

This is a condition which cannot longer be defended; it is a condition which spells suicide for the present movement if it be continued unchanged. The artificial line of revolt may be abandoned even at the eleventh hour. There is nothing but usage now to recommend it; it can do no more than it already has done. The limitations and weaknesses of it have become manifest to its own most strenuous supporters and the world stands unmoved by its later developments. At first there was indignation when the victims were merely arrested and sent to prison; then the forcible feeding had to be endured to keep interest alive; now the brutality to which some women have been subjected in the demonstrations has to be canvassed abroad; but all these efforts are ineffective because the original falsity of the position is understood. The clever advertising and booming of the larger militant society is mainly responsible for the remnant of live interest with which recent protests have been met. The movement is interesting now to the people who come out for the show and to the intimate workers in the ranks who are overmastered by emotional methods of control. For the rest of the world it has no more interest than a puppet-play. The movements which lack reality always suffer the same end and only a recourse to some alternative method of revolt which will link the suffrage demand to the real lives of women, to real evils from which they suffer, to real crying needs for the lack of which they die, only this will save it from decay and death.

# Part V
*The Consumer in Revolt:*

*Selections*

# The Consumer in Revolt*

## CHAPTER I:

## AN ECONOMIC DIVORCE

There are some unions made by necessity from which there is no escape, and one of these is the union of the consumer and the producer. The parties to such unions cannot ignore the bond between them without hurt. . . . Since all their problems are two-fold they cannot find solutions for them by working from one side only. Their ultimate interests can only be fully served by co-operative action.

These are truisms; but our modern world would seem to have forgotten them. They are not observed in practice. They have fallen, like the conventions of our morality and the phrases of our religion, into the position of pious lies which serve a soporific purpose on certain occasions when hypocrisy is called for by custom, and are at all other times relegated to the great realm of neglected things.

This blind neglect of a patent partnership between consumer and producer may not have been caused wholly by our artificial industrial system, but it has certainly been continued because of it. In the simplest case presented by economics the producer and the consumer are one, and obviously there can be no opposition of interests between them. In the case where several producers exchange wares, each being both a producer and a consumer, the opposition of interests is merely superficial, and is reduced to disappearing point by the dual relation in which each individual stands to the others. An honest product at an honest price must be the rule in such a community. At the next stage the problem is complicated by the

* Stephen Swift & Company Limited, London, *c.* 1912.

251

presence of the non-productive worker, the one who transports, prepares, cleans and cooks, but does not directly produce anything. The value of the labour of this class has been very grudgingly recognised by the actual producers, as is shown by the fact that the great body of clerks, cleaners, and final preparers – such as house-wives – are still of a lower economic grade than the body of productive workers themselves. Also it is to be noted that these non-productive workers are at the mercy of the productive workers as to the quality of the products with which they are supplied; they are concerned with products as consumers more than as workers. The divergence of interests indicated here cannot be adequately dealt with from the point of view of the workers, it must be considered from the point of view of the consumers as well. The final stage of complication is reached with the presence of non-workers. Children and infirm and old persons have existed always, of course, and these natural dependents upon the workers have been regarded generally as blood-burdens of some well-marked group of workers or of some individual worker. But to this class of natural dependents there was added a further class of artificial ones which grew to large proportions under the influence of pretentious caste systems and by the aid of monopolies until it reached its culminating point and came to control all industry for its own advantage without sharing in labour. This class of non-workers who control industry through their accumulated wealth has diverted the whole economic system from its primary purpose and thrust the consumer and the producer into a false antagonism.

The economic system now exists, not to satisfy the needs of the consumers as a whole in the best possible way, but to reward the idleness of one body of consumers with a larger share of the fruits of labour than labour itself enjoys; it exists to support a privileged class of non-working consumers on the shoulders both of consumers and producers; it exists to make profit out of the labour of the one and the necessities of the other. The capitalist may pose as a philanthropist when Labour is rebellious, and show how much the community benefits by his promotion of industrial ventures, suggesting that he produces goods for the consumer and provides work for the worker out of his generosity; but the moment a venture ceases to produce something over and above these two things – produce and work – that moment it is abandoned. Capitalist ventures exist for profit; when profit ceases such ventures cease too. It is not to promote industry nor to provide products for consumption that the profiteer steps between the two natural and necessary elements in the econo-mic world – it is to promote profit-making, the getting of something for nothing. And seeking this end the profiteer has not only diverted the whole force of industry into false channels and confused the whole problem by his presence and exactions, but he has succeeded in dividing the two natural partners in economics the one against the other.

We are all more or less profiteers, and we are all more or less victims of profiteering. . . . The basing of industry upon the false principle of getting something for nothing, of getting more in return than is given out, has insidiously permeated every part of our economic machine and thence woven itself into our general conduct and our habits of thought. But broadly all may be classed as workers who give time and brain and muscle to economic or social service in any form, whether as mill-hands or managers, teachers, farmers, transit-workers, or traders. Those of us who are more highly paid than our services deserve are profiteers of a kind, however conscientiously we may fulfil our tasks. But the great class which forms the main body of the profiteering incubus upon society are those who perform no useful work at all or whose payment for the functions they do fulfil is extravagantly excessive.

The profit-making atmosphere is around us all, both producers and consumers. Each class is formed of profit-makers in potentiality if not in actual practice. Each class seeks to get more than it gives. So we find that while admitting their mutual dependence upon each other both producer and consumer have tried to stand alone; each of the economic partners has attempted to secure advantage by the exploitation of the other. We have had in turn an economic competitive system of production and service by which the consumer was bred to ignore the worker, and an organised revolt in which the worker has retaliated by ignoring the consumer. All the devices of modern industrialism have been turned to the satisfaction of the consumer's cry of 'More! More!' and 'Cheaper! Cheaper!' without any thought of the producer. All the strength of the revolt of Labour, with its organised army of voters and its scouting party of intellectuals, has been turned to the satisfaction of the producer's demand for higher wages at whatever cost to the consuming public. Each complementary element of the economic partnership has tried to ignore the other element. Each has taken counsel alone, acted alone, sought to benefit alone – and failed alone.

For the most obvious fact of the moment is that both the economic system and the revolt against it have failed, that neither of them has produced for that partner whose cause was espoused the benefit desired. The competitive system was supposed to exist for the consumer, yet the harm done to the consumer by this system is as great as the harm done to the worker. It had been accepted as an infallible doctrine by the apostles of free competition that the struggle between the promoters of production to secure the custom of the consuming public would result in the production of the best and cheapest product and in the elimination of the inferior and over-priced article by a process similar to that of natural selection. But this prophecy has failed. The system which claimed to find its justification in satisfying the needs of the consumer while ignoring the rights of the producer has resulted in a flooding of the world's markets with adulterated goods, imitations and shams that are tricked out for show and made attractive by a false cheapness . . . it has resulted in waste and dishonesty so universal as to be inescapable; it has so reduced the level of production that it is almost impossible to secure a pure product for the ordinary consumer in spite of safeguards, inspection and guarantees. Briefly, it has failed to fulfil its primary object. We must add to this that the great mass of consumers are wage-workers or dependents of wage-workers, and that the demand for false cheapness tends to reduce the rate of wages upon which the power of consumption of the greater part of the community entirely depends.

It was assumed by the apostles of competitive commerce that in practice this system would achieve cheapness by the stimulation of invention and ingenuity and by the application of new methods of saving work and waste, and that the advance so won would be of benefit to the whole community. The great improvement in the methods of production during the last half-century may be quoted in support of the former contention; and rightly so. Science has been fee'd as the ally of commerce, the bounds of knowledge have been widened, thousands of inventions have been brought into use, and waste products have been turned into sources of profit. But experience goes to prove that all the advantage of improvement has been confiscated by the profiteer and all its disadvantages have been borne by the working and consuming general public. In the first place, just as much ingenuity has been devoted to the reduction of wages and workers as to the development of better means of production; in the second, it is only when further reductions of wages are impossible or when such reductions have failed to accomplish their purpose that the alternative course of expending capital upon improvements has been employed . . . Thus it has ever been that prices reduced by competition have carried reduced wages along with them. The wages bill of any industrial concern – with a few exceptions rare enough to be startling to the observer – is always the first item cut down to meet a fall in prices. It is clear, therefore, that as the great majority of consumers depend upon wages for their power of consumption, wage-won cheapness can be of no advantage to them. The craze for cheapness defeats itself; labour is cheapened by the cheapening of the products of labour; the power to purchase falls with the reduction in price, and the deluded consumer is left exactly in the same place.

The revolt of the worker against the oppressive conditions of labour and the smallness of its reward is the last evidence of the failure of the system which involves these evils. No institution can endure which depends for its success upon the unwilling service of large numbers of intelligent human beings; and it is to this pass that our economic machine has come. The workers give their service unwillingly, resent its conditions, and scorn its wage-reward. Knowing that the system depends upon them they claim that their support should be the first charge upon production, and protest against the device by means of which they receive but a tithe of the wealth resulting from their labour. To a natural necessity, however immoral and irrational it may seem, the majority of intelligences will yield, but to an artificial system that is unjust there can be no permanent willing obedience. It is not from the wage-workers alone that this condemnation has come; to some of the clearest minds of this generation the present system has revealed itself as unsound and unsocial; and there is distrust and doubt and questioning even among those who are most advantaged by it. A simple recital of its code and basis and purpose is a full condemnation. And these facts are known universally. They are admitted freely during times of stress, as, for example, during the recent coal strike. They are the basis of all intelligent constructive effort, of all honest discussion. Every one is learning that no economic system can be stable that is so glaringly immoral, that exploits the consumer by whom it lives, that condemns its workers to poverty and distributes its greatest rewards to those who do not work at all. The profit-making machine is breaking down. The divorce of the consumer from the producer and the unnatural alliance between the former and the profiteer has failed. From no point of view can the consumer regard the bargain as having been worth the price exacted.

The revolt of the workers against the exploitation of this false system is of long standing; in its present form it is three-quarters of a century old. But from the beginning – except for the presence here and there of a prophet who was disregarded or whose message was misapplied – it has been a narrow one-sided revolt which has refused to recognise the duality of the economic relation. . . . As the competitive system professed to give over the world to the consumer, production going on at just such a rate and in just such a manner as was determined by the consumer's demands, so the revolt of the workers has based itself upon a demand for a similar control. 'The world for the workers,' has been its cry. It has been as narrowly sectional as the system it attacked, divorcing itself just as completely from its economic partner, ignoring just as absolutely all rights but its own. The immediate result of this policy has been a narrowing of the boundaries of appeal and a provincialising of the movement by the shutting out of large bodies of workers whose chief interest in reform were from the consuming side. The ultimate result has been that the workers' revolt has failed. It has failed as completely as the competitive system itself to effect its purpose, and failed because like that system it divorced two interests that are naturally inseparable and sought its own advantage without considering the rights of its economic partner.

The movement of the workers has fixed its eyes upon the criterion of money-wages and refused to look before or behind. The great body of consumers, because it included in its ranks the small body of exploiters, has been as resolutely ignored by the Labour movement as the wage-workers themselves have been ignored by the competitive system. The fact that the worker, as agent of the profiteer, was responsible with him for the universal defrauding of the consumer was conveniently forgotten. The fact that the whole body of workers are consumers and are concerned for the purification of consumption whether they have grievances as workers or not was given no weight. Indeed, there has never been any hesitation in sacrificing the consumer to Labour's demands, but rather there has existed a tendency to count upon the general public clamour caused by suffering as an element in the winning of the fight.

The narrowness of outlook which has marked the movement may be indicated by the setting up of that ridiculous claim that the actual producer is entitled to the full product of his labour. . . . I have constantly heard it interpreted literally, entirely ignoring the non-productive workers of the community or assuming that they shall be dependents of the producers – as is the case now with wives – ignoring also the wear and tear of machinery, the wages of management, the payment of labour and replacement of machinery employed in transit and distribution, and the communal charges for the upkeep of public services and the support of children and the infirm. There are the makings of a new aristocracy here, under which all those who were not actual producers of economic commodities would be branded as of an inferior class.

This policy of narrowness has not been defended; it has merely been assumed to be right. The wrongs of Labour – low wages and bad conditions – against which the rebellion was organised have been held as sufficient to warrant the sacrifice of all else in the common-weal to their redressing. The sacrifice of those consumers who were workers has been defended because it is assumed that they stand to gain finally by the labour revolt, that the suffering inflicted is unavoidable and perhaps for their own good. As for the non-working consumers it is argued that as they have long enjoyed an undue advantage, any action which constrains them to yield up more wealth to the workers is to be commended. The assumption underlying both justifications is that the worker in rebellion is sure to win, that the present methods are sound and will produce their effect, and that such sacrifice as is entailed in the struggle will be compensated by success. To this assumption, totally unsupported by experience, is added another: that it is perfectly safe and proper to leave all wider considerations of the consumer and the community aside until the present system has been remedied or destroyed. The underlying thought appears to be that it is essential under present conditions that the worker should concentrate upon his own interests . . . and that when Labour comes into its own the consumer's problem will be solved automatically.

In spite of steadily increasing evidence to the contrary this policy has been followed by every branch of the movement of revolt among the workers. The Trade Unions and their federations, the united associations of industrial reformers banded together for action in the industrial or the political arena, the Socialist societies, the Parliamentary Labour Party – they have all confined themselves almost entirely to the producers' side of the economic problem. The Trade Unions, which have from the first restricted themselves to the raising of wages by combination and collective bargaining, have now added to their methods that of political organisation; but to their objects they have added nothing. They are still concerned primarily with the problem of raising money-wages and secondarily with improving labour conditions. They are bodies organised against the reduction of the wage of the worker; the degradation of the same worker by his employment as a maker of false products awakens no resentment; the part he plays in robbing the consumer by adulteration and shady practices awakens no shame.

The Socialist parties have preached a wider doctrine than that of the Trade Union movement. They have exposed the root cause of the poverty-evil by indicating how the whole industrial system is exploited for profit-making. They have laid stress on the relation between production and consumption, between work and wealth, pointing out that upon every consumer there lies the duty of work, the duty of giving to the community an equivalent for the value received from it. They have advocated the substitution of a system of production for use for the present system of production for profit, a natural and morally acceptable system based on reason and justice for one that is reprehensible and unjust and degrading. So far they have played the part of capable doctors diagnosing the disease, and it is only when they commit themselves to the advocacy of a great State monopoly as the only alternative to small private ones that disagreement arises. To a growing number of reformers this seems to be a foolish and futile barring off of many good ways in order to crowd all effort into one very doubtful one. But this aside, and in spite of the great part they played in committing the Labour movement to years of futile waiting upon parliamentary action, the Socialists have done excellent work among the discontented workers in introducing a wider view of industrial action and a deeper study of the problems involved. But in their practice and in the direction of their teaching the Socialists have been almost as completely obsessed by the workers' side of the economic problem as the Trade Unionists. 'We are all consumers; we ought all to be workers,' they say in substance. 'Our sufferings as workers and as consumers proceed from the same source and are results of the same cause – the monopolist system of production for profit. It is necessary to remove that cause, and we will organise as workers to do so. All consumers who are workers or dependents of workers are concerned equally with us in this side of the problem and they can secure emancipation by co-operating with us. As for the other consumers they are parasites; if they suffer through this revolt it is of no matter to us. The workers suffer through their very existence, and are oppressed and enslaved on their account. These non-workers suffer not because of any wish or will of ours, but because of the false position which they occupy; they will disappear when we abolish profit-making, and all other problems will disappear with them.'

There have been Socialists who have avoided this error of forgetting the dual economic nature of man. The eyes of Robert Owen were clear enough to perceive, before the day of class-conscious socialism, the two-fold nature of the economic problem, and his co-operative and colonising efforts were the results. The socialism of William Morris and of the school of artist-socialists generally saw the problem as one of two dimensions; they asked of the new dispensation joy in work and a fair recompense for the worker and beautiful fruits of work for the consumer. The degradation of the worker in the making of false goods and of the consumer in the consumption of them were seen by these men in their true light. But in the main this side of the movement has lain asleep, there have been no developments, and little effort calculated to bring any. The problem of wages has blocked out everything else.

This indicated a common fault in our reform movements: that they are prone . . . to be of one dimension, to have no breadth, no capacity for seeing more than one aspect of a problem. A truth is discovered that is true from one point of view and for one set of circumstances; and everything is strained and bent and cut down to fit with the partial truth. . . . In this case it is much easier to deify the worker into a wronged saint oppressed by the devil of profiteering than to balance the claims and wrongdoings of the two victims and construct a policy that shall be just to both while checking the anti-social tendencies in both. The Socialist parties have taken the easier course, taken it unconsciously because it was the easier, because it fitted with their doctrinaire outlook, and because super-ficially it was the most productive road to take since there was in existence a workers' movement in which they could reap an early harvest.

The influence of this large organised body of workers has thrust the workers' side of the question to the front . . . [but] there has been no similar body of organised consumers in revolt to make balancing claims from the other side. As a result the Socialist bodies have reacted to their environment by concentrating upon questions of wages and working conditions and their immediate effects. Nor has the influence ended here. The Parliamentary Labour Party has been dominated and narrowed by the purely Trade Union character of its financial directors . . . Under this stimulus much has been done in one way which would have been better done in another, much that ought to have been done politically and industrially has been left undone, and some things have been done that had been better not done at all. Under this stimulus also it has become the fashion among Socialists to claim for the workers' revolt a larger social value than it deserves, and to assume that this social improvement is an accepted and intended part of Trade Union policy. It has naturally followed that the anti-social tendencies contained within the Trade Union movement have been deliberately ignored, or at the best commented on mildly. And this is bad both for the workers themselves and for the reformers and their work as well as for the neglected and exploited consuming public.

If there had been in existence a consumers' movement equal in assertiveness and size with the Trade Union movement, this undue inclination to one side would have been redressed by the introduc-tion of a balancing influence throwing into relief the aspect of every side of the problem as it affected the consumer. . . . Even the most intelligent of our self-appointed world-saviours would appear to be greatly dependent upon experience and external environment for the discovery of evils. Those things that are thrust upon the public notice they see and find remedies for; those things that are suffered in silence either escape their notice or receive inadequate attention. It is by a cynicism of natural law that from the deeps in which they have been left by neglect these unmarked realities issue forth to make the reformers' remedies useless. So has it been in this industrial struggle. The whole Labour army, with its workers and reformers and revolutionaries, from the Fabian Society to the Syndicalists, has been committed to a one-sided activity. For it the question of industry is one of settlement between the worker and the monopolist, the producer and the profiteer. There is no duality; these two alone are concerned in a single fight; the consumer does not exist, except perhaps as a looker on. This is the basis upon which the plans for the fight have been made, and because of its falseness and insufficiency the fight has been a fight of failure. For the consumer has been remembered by the enemy and used to destroy or divert every Labour attack.

There can be no doubt about the failure. The lot of the workers has not been materially changed by all the industrial sacrifices they have made for eighty years, by all their organisation and political adventuring. There has been no permanent betterment in the cardinal matter of wages. The servile masses still remain; they are still upon the verge of destitution; wages are still at bare subsistence level. There have been transformations in certain areas, ups and downs of prices and wages have played a double dance, the burden has been taken off Everyman the worker and placed upon Everyman the consumer – with a little extra weight added to pay for the labour expended in making the change! But there has been no real relief. Profits still range away high above wages, increasing while wages remain stationary or drop. An increased supply of gold by decreasing its value has increased the value of everything else and increased prices in all directions. But while every other kind of raw material has been advanced in price upon this excuse the raw material of labour has been excluded; the wages of labour have not increased. With his unaltered supply of depreciated gold the worker must seek means of obtaining his normal supply of appreciated products. Neither industrial action nor political action has given the quietus to this thieving chicane. Neither of them has proved to be the method of industrial salvation; and both together have proved futile.

Industrial action alone filled up the first fifty years of Trade Unionism. It cost the workers themselves millions of money and the nation an ocean of waste and suffering. But it failed. It was not enough. Reluctantly the collective bargainers came to recognise that something more was wanting, and turned themselves to the political machine. Labour Representation in Parliament was to be added to, or to supersede, industrial action; the ballot was to be the worker's weapon instead of the strike. It was to make the strike unnecessary, or if strikes still continued necessary they were to be made successful by political action. This was the theory which resulted in the formation of a Labour Representation Committee, and later in the election of a group of Labour Members to the House of Commons. But political intervention has not modified the position by one iota. . . . The profiteer takes from the consumer all that the worker is able to extract by strikes or political action. From our experience of the last six years it would appear that reliance upon Labour politicians for wage-raising is doomed to failure. All the legislation to which these representatives have given their special blessing has been of the pauperising, benevolent kind which leaves wages where they are and prices where they are, and gives out doles to the impoverished. The Labour unrest of 1911–12 teaches us the further lesson that when industrial action is taken the political representatives of Labour are not to be relied upon to assist it to victory. To the workers they have proved a broken reed; and they have proved as willing as the capitalist to play jugglers' tricks with prices and wages, and to place all the burdens of disturbance and change upon the shoulders of the consumer.

The net result of all the Labour effort, of all the toil and sacrifice, has been to take from the worker in his capacity of consumer all that he has been able to win in his capacity of rebellious worker. He has worked a treadmill of which the revolutions have left him in the same place. . . . The industrial movement simplified down to a movement of workers against profiteers has failed ignominiously. And I believe it has failed just because of this false simplicity, just because it has been divorced from the consumption side of the problem, just because it has failed to recognise the dual nature of economics.

History shows that it has been the conscious or unconscious policy of the profiteer to keep these two apart – the worker and the consumer. . . . Exploiting each of them he so juggles with facts as to make each of them help him in the robbery of the other. He lives upon both, and when one resists him he merely transfers the burden which is rejected by the one on to the shoulders of the other. By means of his agency and pretensions, and with a certain degree of plausibility, he is able to persuade each that the other is an enemy. The worker regards the average consumer as a weak-kneed creature, the ally of the profiteer, who is ever assisting him to reduce the wages of labour by clamouring for cheaper and cheaper goods. The consumer regards the worker as a lazy and greedy self-seeker, who sacrifices the consumer ruthlessly to his demands for higher wages and is ever assisting the dishonest capitalist to place fresh burdens of price and adulteration upon his shoulders. Thus these two units, which are alone essential in the economic world and are alone

261

capable of settling its problems, are divided one from the other, one against the other, and the solution of the riddle they have to solve is indefinitely postponed.

\*　　\*　　\*

. . . The deduction which seems to lie plain upon the surface is this: that while the masses stand in a dual relation to each other and to their common enemy, the profiteer, they must organise their activity and resistance also along dual lines; that they need for the full expression of human needs a consumers' as well as a workers' movement which, acting in concert along parallel lines, one on either side of the profiteer, may thus reduce him to impotence.

# CHAPTER II:

# THE VICTIMISATION OF THE CONSUMER

It would appear that when an evil is universal it tends to go unchallenged, however evil it may be. When all women were subject to men there was no voice of rebellion heard in the wilderness. When all workers were serfs there was no sense of shame in sustaining serfdom . . . The thing that exists on all sides comes to be accepted as a part of the unchangeable order of the external world . . . Thus the very universality and persistence of the victimisation of the consumer has caused it to be as persistently neglected. It has existed always in modern times whatever system of production has been in vogue – competitive, monopolistic, protected or unprotected. The great consuming public has been for every system at once the support upon which it relied and the victim which it defrauded. And it has not been the great masters of industry alone, the promoters of monster enterprises coining millions of profit, who have been guilty of false manufacturing and false trading. The middleman, distributing goods for a livelihood, has done his share, and in the doing of it developed a whole code of trickery which is recognised and practised as part of the normal distributive machinery. The worker has given his assistance to the work: as the agent of the profit-making employer he has conducted the business of fraud, as an unconscientious worker he has given the consumer bad workmanship, and he has contributed to the wastefulness of the system by the limitation of output and the waste of material, thinking thus to 'make work' or to 'get even' with his employer. . . . All sections of the great productive and distributive army are tainted with this corruption, so that the consumer must either take constant risks or pay an exorbitant price for guarantees of honesty. . . .

The demands of the consumer are the *raison d'être* of any and every economic system, and for a system to fail to satisfy the consumer is for it to have failed utterly. . . . A clock that does not keep time but has been made use of as a paper-weight is a clock that has failed; and as a paper-weight it is unduly expensive. Our economic system stands to be judged by its capacity to fulfil its purpose, and by that alone, and the judgment being against it the machine is doomed.

In simple form the consumers' demands may be summarised as comprising these: a pure product, clean and honest, being what it professes to be; a product at a fair price; a sufficient variety of products to allow of reasonable choice; and a sufficiency of all kinds of products. From these demands we deduce that a system which produces impure, false, and ugly products is to be condemned, that an artificial inflation of prices is similarly reprehensible, as is also an insufficiency of products resulting in want or a contrary condition resulting in waste. And our present system, judged by any one of these tests, must cut the sorry figure of a failure.

The consumer who attempts to put into practice the demand for a pure product must be prepared to struggle through an appalling morass. Great quantities of every kind of foodstuff are sent daily into the markets of the world adulterated with inferior matter or with matter positively dangerous to the consumer. Through the Local Government Board, the Board of Agriculture, and the local authorities of the country, a system of inspection of food and drugs is carried out in defence of the national health, and facts and figures are available which give some indication of the extent and shamelessness of adulterating practices. Each Annual Report of the Local Government Board presents an account of the attempt made by an insufficient staff administering unsatisfactory regulations to deal with an evil of which the fringe only can be said to be touched after all official effort is exhausted. . . .

[TBG presents several examples of adulteration of foodstuffs and medicines.]

\* \* \*

Inspection and legal definitions of adulteration appear to exist only in the matter of food and drugs. Other adulterating and dishonest practices carried out to the hurt of the consumer are unchecked except by civil actions for damages, by agreement in the trade concerned, or by the occasional exposure of a trade rival or an enterprising journal . . . . [For] the ordinary consumer who detects adulteration or trade trickery there seems to be no remedy except that of the individual withdrawal of custom from the offender; and this is a method that is always slow in producing any effect, and it is not always applicable. For those above the average working-class level the established policy is to deal with what is known as 'a reputable firm,' which means a firm that trades upon its honesty and for an enhanced price gives the consumer a guarantee that its wares are pure. But this method of protection is strictly limited, and for the great number of consumers, under present conditions, there is no certain escape from adulteration and petty cheating and dirt and shams . . . .

[TBG presents examples of adulteration and mislabelling of such goods as clothing, furniture and other household furnishings.]

\*     \*     \*

The tricks employed by every branch of the distributive trade are legion. They cannot be enumerated. But they include the sham 'Sales,' for which bales of special shoddy goods are purchased and goods in stock are specially soiled and then sold at a normal price as 'Special Bargains,' the short-weight and short-measure tricks, the scandalous over-pricing of fripperies and fancy goods, the substitution of one article for another and of one quality for another, the mixing of inferior goods or material with superior, as in the window presentment of fruit – all the best at the front for show and all the inferior quality at the back for sale, and the false packing of fruit and vegetables. All these and a host of other devices are employed to deceive the unwary consumer.

\*     \*     \*

Unrestricted competition and the desire for profit at all costs and by any means, however dirty, has produced these results. They are so unsavoury and so fundamentally wrong that it is not to be wondered at that any system of re-organisation which offers to limit or remove them becomes desirable by comparison. In this spirit even so hopelessly unjustifiable a development as the growth of monopoly has been welcomed by some sections of the public. But such welcome is premature. Competition is but a weapon of the profiteering system; it is the system itself that is the evil. And the system acting through trusts and combines, either in this or other countries, has rather been one of added than of reduced exploitation. Trusts in this country and in America have neither abolished adulteration nor improved conditions of labour, indeed they have seriously devoted themselves to reducing labour and its reward, and the deliberate intention of their formation has been to raise prices to the consumer. Trusts are wholly a selfish protective development of the profit-making machine, adopted to check competitive suicide so far as it injures the profit-makers, but with no intention of reducing those evils which competition has brought to the consumer and the worker.

In the process of the formation of trusts indeed a greater burden is laid upon the consumer. Dividends have to be paid upon all the old capital as well as on the 'water' added during the process of buying up; and all this extra profit the consumer has to find. The more effective and complete the trustification the more certain that this additional tribute of price will be exacted, and if the formation of the trust has not wiped out or bought out all rivals the additional tribute will merely be obtained indirectly by adulteration. . . . The methods employed by the trusts to keep their markets against all comers form a veritable inquisition and react at all points to the disadvantage of the consumer. All kinds of conditions are imposed upon the distributor, and if he refuses to submit to them he is ruthlessly taxed or squeezed out. Thus a virtual compulsion to buy is imposed upon the consumer, who is left totally helpless to reject goods either because of prices or quality.

The consumer must always be sacrificed by competition or by monopoly so long as production is diverted from its natural object, and this sacrifice is imposed upon the consumer by all who take part in economic service whether as profiteers, manufacturers, distributors, or workers. The workers have served the economic system, have sold themselves to it for a wage, have prostituted their strength and talent and ideas to its ignoble and demoralising service. From the worker who manages to the worker who makes they have all served the economic Satan. . . .

. . . The working-man is accessory to all the corruption, humbug, and dishonesty of our detestable economic world. To the agency exacted from him as an employed worker he has added a few dishonest tricks of his own. Time killing is one of them, and the doing of shoddy work from sheer laziness is another. The *ca' canny* policy with which he seeks to restrict production, and the deliberate prolongation or creation of work by special devices at which he excels and in which he shows an amazing indifference to the destruction of the work of his own hands, are not personal weaknesses, but deliberate, organised, anti-social exactions for all of which the consumer has to pay in the end. So that the pretensions of the worker come to this: that he is oppressed by the profiteer, but that he in turn, as the agent of the profiteer and as a free human agent, oppresses and robs the consumer, proving himself his own enemy and that of the community. It is in normal times that he preys upon the consumer along with his employer and reduces the general output of wealth in addition to aiding in the robbing of the individual; and the same result, the placing of an increased burden upon the consumer, follows from his agency in bringing about abnormal times by strikes and all kinds of industrial disturbances.

The immediate object of a strike may be entirely justified, the final object of the organisation of the workers may be entirely commendable. It is with the effects of these agencies and not with their objects that we are here chiefly concerned, and with that effect from the consumer's point of view. And from this point of view it is evident that all strikes heretofore have been evil. The price of every strike, whether it is successful or not, is paid by the consumers. The dislocation of service and supply is paid for by the consumer in money and inconvenience. The rise of prices comes out of the consumer's pocket. The loss of wealth occasioned by the stoppage of machinery and idleness of workers creates scarcity of products from which the consumer suffers again. Our system seems to breed harpies ready to prey upon the consumer at every turn, and strikes and lock-outs are often of real financial benefit to this type. Many middlemen and some of the employers chiefly concerned reap rich harvests out of the consumer while the worker is starving. . . . Only a most utter forgetfulness of the fact that he is also a consumer could make any worker satisfied with a successful strike; as for an unsuccessful one it is of grave disadvantage to every one except the class that it is intended to hurt, and to these it brings a harvest of gold.

The strike on past sectional lines failed long ago. The strike *plus* the vote has been barren so far and is losing its hold upon those who preached it ten years ago. The alternative general strike which has been substituted on the last occasions – the railway strike, the transport workers' strike, and the coal strike – has failed under our eyes. It brings up the striker against forces with which he is making no attempt to cope and he gains no real benefit from his rebellions. He is as far off now as ever from the realisation of his demands. If he is able to force up wages prices follow to eat up the advance. If prices fall wages are beaten down. The worker is either worse off or no better off as a result of all his industrial effort. Only all the time during which he seeks to fight the oppressor single-handed his yoke-fellow the consumer is being made the scapegoat of all his blunders and experiments, of all his successes and of all his failures.

# CHAPTER III:

# WOMAN, THE CONSUMER

. . . Not the world for the worker, but the world for the consumer, is the natural law – and it contains the higher ethic and the greater joyousness. We shall always have consumers whose service to humanity cannot be measured in work and whose claims are irresistible. The claims of the young and the old may be measured in terms of work, they are served because they have worked in the past or will work in the future. The infirm, to whom we pay bitter-tasting pittances to-day, must be dealt with according to their necessities and not to any standard of work, unless they can be made whole or abolished. But those . . . who struggle ahead of their world and generation, the thinkers and dreamers and artists who carve out the way – for these no standard of work will suffice. A world based upon work would ask them to sell their gifts for bread as they have to do to-day, and it would test them by the limits of the market and reject them.

It is the human being that is sacred, not the worker. Such sanctity as the worker acquires comes from his service to the world of consumers. He is raised above the level of the non-working units of the community because the fruits of his toil satisfy human needs. So far as he does this he is worthy, but it is the fruits of his toil and not the toil that make him so. Work in itself has no inherent sanctity. It may be imbecile waste. Much of our modern work cries out clamorously for abolition; it is ugly, exhausting, and sordid; the sanctity of it is imperceptible, for it serves no good purpose and its degradation brutalises the worker and slimes the very face of the land. A rational society would turn its best brains to the task of carrying all this kind of toil into oblivion by the substitution of machinery for human labour and of self-service for the service of serfs. Much necessary work can only fit into a decent scheme of things when it is possible for it to be done by the pushing of a button at a very great distance.

This worship of work as work is utter folly. A deed well done, a new truth or beauty revealed by handicraft or thought, a new power given into our hands by the wonder of machinery, a thing that is good to look upon and serves its purpose well – for these things and the doers and makers of them worship is fitting. It is in such creation that we reach the highest our little life allows. But for the rest work is to be abolished, not to be gloried in; it is to be accepted as the price of existence, not as its crown, and reduced at the earliest moment to the absolute minimum. In these democratic days work and the worker are become an unholy obsession under which humanity and the individual have been weighed down to inhuman depths. The industrial world, with its products and its problems, its profiteers and its proletariat, looms too large in life. We are bewitched and bedevilled with the economic struggle. We have no time for joy. . . . The business of life is living. Work is a mere means to that end.

The long and flagrant neglect of the consumer . . . leads to a niggard view of life itself, to the submission of the individual to the petty tyranny of false things, to the wasting of joy and beauty and a thousand golden opportunities, to the infection of multitudes with a taste for tawdry trash, to a willing acceptance of the worst poisons and pretences that the prostituted system can produce. The consumer of to-day will consume anything. There is no standard among the masses. . . . In books and amusements and dress and furniture and food, in manners and morality, it manifests itself. We are a shoddy people; and all the things we do and are partake of our shoddiness.

It is a common phrase on the lips of certain reformers that the cause of women and the cause of the workers are linked together and that each stands to gain by the advance of the other. But the full significance of this statement does not appear to have been even glimpsed by most of those who have made use of it. So far as the women's movement is a sex revolt it stands apart from all other movements; so far as it is an active demand for opportunity and fair working conditions for women workers it is a part of the great workers' movement; but its peculiar value in economics lies in the fact that the great body of women are consumers, that they are not wage-workers, and that they look upon life from the consumer's point of view. Thus the workers' movement and the women's, between them, represent both economic elements; each supplies what the other lacks; each desires what the other can give. The worker is dominated by the point of view of the producer and the woman by circumstances and by nature is committed to champion the case of the consumer. And the active combination of separate organisations representing these two outlooks seems to offer the only highway to economic salvation.

There has been an economic divergence between the sexes almost from the dawn of history. Man and woman have played different economic parts, and playing them each has seen the problem of supply from a different view-point. The broad economic demarcation between them began when man specialised as a hunter and fighter and woman as a producer and a domestic worker. The man

269

provided protection and was the bringer of meat; the woman did all the rest – the whole of production, agriculture, housing, clothing, cooking and domestic handicraft. The first act of production was protective; it was a woman's instinctive attempt to satisfy the needs of her child. And from this beginning the whole process of production was directed and developed for the consumer, its natural object being life-preservation and its natural agent woman.

As a producer woman became a more desirable object to man, just as man the producer has an enhanced economic value for the woman of to-day. The cunning of man's hands has made him master during this later period, but the cunning of woman's hands would appear to have helped to her enslavement . . . the first exploiter of labour was man, and the first labourer exploited was woman. We find that she is both a sex-slave and work-slave among a great number of those races in which the appreciation of her economic value has led to polygamy. We find her a beast of burden as well as the bearer of children among many primitive peoples. At this stage she remained long enough to learn the habit of servile work.

The next change of function in industry gave over to man by gradual changes almost the whole of the productive work of the world, and left woman a non-productive worker engaged in a hundred final processes of preparation and burdened with the cleaning and body service of the human home and family. This change was not wrought quickly. Much productive work such as brewing, baking, weaving, spinning, and other domestic handicrafts, remained in the hands of women until the coming of the industrial revolution. The modern demons of machinery stole these remaining trades away from her. Even so, however, the same process which carried all productive work out of the home carried many women out with it to be producers in factory and workshop. But the majority of these women were and are *femmes soles*, women standing on their own feet, independent individuals, and because of this fact and in spite of their increasing numbers they have escaped recognition. Their existence cannot be denied, but it is consciously or unconsciously ignored. The status of women is the status of wives among women, nay, not even that, but the status of the majority of wives. The men of an age form their attitude towards women from those with whom they are brought into closest relations. They generalise all women into wives – wives to be, wives in practice, wives out of work. And whatever is the normal position of a wife that is accepted as the position of all women. By aid of this fallacious habit men have been able . . . to turn blind eyes upon the women who were self-supporting economic producers. As a result 'man' and 'producer' have become synonymous terms.

It is impossible to say at what stage the producer began to make pretensions. It may have been the early productive woman who claimed superiority because of the fruits of her hands; man may have had to choose labour to escape the yoke she sought to impose. But the probabilities are against the theory, and as we know it, the pride of production is wholly a masculine vice. The male producers recognise themselves as the essential workers and all others as of secondary value; and at the brutal bottom of things they are right. What they do not recognise is that they are not to be credited with honour or privilege, because accident of sex or circumstance made them productive workers rather than distributive or preservative ones, and that neither are all productive workers males nor all males productive workers. Indeed, it is one of our most urgent problems that the disproportion between the number of productive workers and the number of consumers should be decreased among men as well as among women.

It is directly from the producer's sense of superiority that the undervaluing of the work done by women proceeds . . . the present contempt for women's work within the home is not due to or justified by inferior workmanship. It is directly traceable to the pride of production which has come to coalesce with masculine pretensions of sex-superiority.

This economic divergence in function between men and women has produced a psychological divergence in outlook. Man ceased to strut in his war-paint as the fighter and took to strutting in the home and out of it, in politics and social life, as well as in industry, as the producer. In much of the 'dignity of labour' twaddle that we hear speaks the voice of the male trumpeting forth his value, that woman may be suitably impressed. This is of course balanced by the sentimental clamour that woman makes about her babies. But her utterances have commonly been pitched in the minor and have been more irritating than impressive.

. . . public affairs naturally are now entirely dominated by the producer's point of view. Our latest word in political democracy is representation for the workers, the men who do the actual work of production. The master-producer, agricultural or manufacturing, has dominated the legislature of this country since the days of Simon de Montfort. Capitalistic industry, that with its tongue in its cheek talks of the needs of the consumer, is mainly concerned with making production useful to the small class that controls it. The revolts and rebellions and re-constructions which are planned and made are producers' movements and producers' changes. The producer . . . turns every two-sided problem producing-side up and declares that it has no other side because he cannot see one. . . . Human affairs

271

that ought to be considered from above and below and all round suffer from a partial understanding and presentment, and partial remedies are prepared to cure their partial defects.

This unreasonable bias of things is in great measure due to the exclusion of women from public life. Women are essentially consumers rather than producers. . . . The name of the national purchaser is woman. Women are the final buyers of nine-tenths of the fruits of industry. They are the spenders of the greater part of the national income. To them it is not so much wages as prices that matter, not so much hours of labour as the quality of the product labour produces, not so much labour itself as its fruits. Under present conditions, with the narrow cutting off of women's interests and the stress of economic poverty, the questions of quality have been pushed aside by the paramount question of prices, of quantity . . . . Narrowness, ignorance, and lack of experience beyond certain strict limits, play their part in preventing greater outcry about adulteration and shoddy. The segregation of women, each shut apart in her own home, tends in the same way to delay protest and organisation. But the forces are here ready to be used; and the economic revolt is delayed and defeated for lack of the use of them.

*      *      *

. . . Not only does the exclusion of women from public life postpone the co-operative action between workers and consumers, and its consequent harvest of reform, but it is matter worthy of inquiry as to whether the subjection of women has not been in great part responsible for the diversion of productive industry from its natural object. The doctrine of profits is closely allied to the doctrine of the superiority of the producer. The individual producer claiming an unfair dominance over non-productive workers was setting up privilege. The producer's predominance in affairs made possible the attitude of mind which allowed the individual producer to exchange his goods for other workers' services at an advantage to himself. This individual producer was the first profiteer. There is but one step between him and the capitalist producer who exchanges the products of many workers in the same way. It seems obvious that the domination of the world by the producer was the historical preliminary of the birth of the profiteering system, and the logical deduction from this fact is that had the consumer shared the world control the diversion of industry might not have occurred. It would thus seem that a very heavy price has been exacted from humanity for the sex-subjection of women and the economic divorce which it has occasioned. Woman the consumer has been revenged for the degradation of woman the creature of sex. And it follows that the economic re-organisation of the world can only come when woman is active and free.

# CHAPTER IV:

# THE FAILURE OF THE
# LABOUR REVOLT

Those who commit themselves most deeply to any scheme are the leaders. By the very strength of their advocacy they achieve leadership. But those who have committed themselves most deeply to any scheme are most reluctant to admit its failure. . . . There is a sense of disloyalty to their past selves involved in conversion to another faith, and there is an admission of fallibility such as all democratic leaders – knowing their King Mob by bitter experience – are very loath to make. Hence it follows that any change of policy in a democratic movement, any development into new regions or along new lines, is opposed by the leaders . . . . They seek to keep things stationary, or to restrict advance to such courses as secured, and will assure, their leadership . . . . Change of policy may be but the prelude to change of leaders. Dependent upon the votes of the masses for position, they seek alliance with the majority, slow and moderate, and safe, in ordinary times, and if capable of swift judgment and cruel rejection when the time of change has come, generally habit-bound and sentimental. This dependence throws them against change for safety. They must resist the extremists to hold their places, to prolong the day of their tenure. Then among the malcontents are the younger men knocking at the door of office, with better equipment and newer ideas. But the body of the older men resent the aggressive haste of the young . . . . They desire for their leaders 'safe men' who will deal with the Union business on the old lines, and comfort or inspire them with the old phrases of sentiment and promise. It is to be noted, too, that the administrative leaders of any movement commonly become incapable of wide vision because of their very immersion in administrative affairs. They are so busy making the machine move that they have no eyes for the changing directions and motions of the other machines against which it is required to move. Long absorption in this work of detail commonly leaves a man unfitted to take any wider view at all of the general problem before his organisation. He becomes a mechanic, and cannot supply the vitality and insight of the recreator. He can continue; but he cannot reconstruct.

The labour leaders are not less susceptible to these circumstances than other leaders, and we find them at this critical juncture in industrial affairs rejecting scornfully the charge of failure, resenting criticism, and refusing to consider any alternative or supplementary suggestion which is offered to them. Like the majority of leaders they see personal disloyalty in the unrest among their followers, and they refuse to give attention to the discontent which long-continued and repeated failure has brought into existence.

At the different stages of the Labour movement there have been different formulae for action. At one time all hope was based upon industrial action alone. . . . Organisation, Collective Bargaining, the Strike: this was the cycle of effort. It must be admitted at once that collective bargaining has served to confine within certain limits the competition of workers in their search for work, and has therefore kept wages from decrease by competitive pressure. But all that can be done by combination and pressure from the workers' side has been achieved already. The whole product of Trades Unionism is the difference in wages between those which would be paid to unorganised competing workers each beating down the other in his eagerness for work, and those which must be paid to the same men organised and refusing to undersell each other. Beyond this combination of workers alone will not go – beyond this it cannot go while each demand of the worker can be resisted by the profiteer with the half-conscious assisting clamour of the public, and while all the wage-successes of the workers are transferred to the shoulders of the consumers, and thus rendered empty and valueless.

This fact was glimpsed by some Trade Unionists forty years ago. It was driven home by bitter experience of failure during twenty more years before there was any real response to the demand for change. Then came the Socialist into the field to point the moral of this failure as lack of political action, and after another period of industrial effort and futility the political weapon was added to the old industrial one and the fight resumed.

This had been the theoretical formula since the formation of the Labour Representation Committee in 1900: the industrial weapon must be supplemented by the political one if Labour is to win the fight. But while this was the accepted theory, the practice during the first nine years of the period has been almost wholly political. Money, work, thought, enthusiasm, within the Labour movement, have been devoted almost entirely to the elaboration of the machinery of parliamentary action, to the fighting of elections, and the returning of Labour Members to Parliament. Socialists have much to answer for in this regard. They were the active movers in the creation of a parliamentary Labour group, and their work was not entirely without self-interest. . . . 'Commit the Trade Unionists of the country to parliamentary action in anything,' it was argued, 'and they are committed to the principle of State intervention, from which it is but a step to State control.' In this spirit the Trade Unions were permeated and the new development given velocity. The Taff Vale[1] decision might have been especially devised to add fuel to the fire so created. This was all that was needed to concentrate attention upon political action, and to give to the exaggerated prophesyings of the State Socialist enthusiasts the colour of severest truth. And it is only since 1909 that doubts of the expediency of this exclusive policy have obtained any serious attention.

Now there is a back-swing of the pendulum. The moderates – in which camp some of the most prominent professing Socialists are found – all emphatically declare that it is in the combination of industrial and political action that the worker must put his trust, and not in either of them alone. But in the three years since the party of doubters began to find expression this policy of conjoint or co-operative industrial and political attack upon privilege has been tried. And it has been a very nadir of failure. It has almost made it appear that Labour with two arms is weaker than with one. For the political arm of Labour has been used to hamper the free action of the industrial arm.

Half a hundred reasons have been tentatively suggested for the strange incapacity that has manifested itself in parliamentary Labour ranks. The Labour members are accused of traitorism, of snobbery, of stupidity – and each of the accusations can be supported by weighty instance and argument. There is no doubt that Labour in Parliament has failed to do what it might have done; that it has cut a figure of painful futility, of scandalous inertness. But the weakness of the Labour position is not a weakness of men. Men might have won for the organised workers illusory victories which these Members have thrown away, but they could not have altered the essential nature of the problem they are out to face. With all their political and industrial activities they are still solely representative of the one side of the economic problem; they are still persistently refusing to assert themselves as consumers as well as workers, and so protect themselves from both sides.

The latest manifestation of dissatisfaction with the results of the long Labour struggle is the uprising of the Syndicalist. The Syndicalist has had enough of what he calls 'political hugger-muggery,' and has devised a special form of voluntary organisation of industry which combines the principle of revolutionary direct action with that of sectional craft organisation. The coming of the syndicalist movement is momentous. It is the first direct modern evidence of a British decision against the age-long procrastination and partiality and inadequacy of Parliament. It suffers from the faults of all first moves: it is crude and limited and unconsciously deceptive. But it is by its very existence the most promising indication in the industrial world of to-day. It is the revival of the challenge to parliamentarianism for which there has been need for many years. It will serve to put all the pretensions of government, of State Socialists and benevolent bureaucrats, under examination. It will lead all serious thinkers to seek a definition of the value and sphere of government, matters too long left to the doctrinaire Socialist and accepted on his authority.

But the weakness of the Trade Union position lies entirely apart from the question of parliamentary action. . . . Every time the army of profiteers is forced to retreat by Labour it retreats upon the workers in their aspect of consumers. . . . [The workers] force up prices for themselves; they force along adulteration for themselves; they beat the profiteer in order to pay him his own price!

\* \* \*

[Comparing changes in rates of wages since 1900 with variations in prices] . . . It is . . . quite safe to conclude . . . that to-day a pound is required to buy what seventeen shillings would have bought ten years ago. Taking a 30s per week wage, this is equal to a decrease in spending power of 4s.6d, or almost a sixth. To balance this increase in prices this amount should have been added to wages during the same decade. But instead of this the official figures indicate that there has been a very slight increase in certain trades, that there has been actual decrease in others, while the mean result shows wages as practically stationary, but with a downward tendency.

. . . that it [the decrease in purchasing power] is not a necessary condition is indicated by the disproportionate rise in profits which has accompanied it. This rise in profits . . . goes to show that wages could be raised or prices lowered if the right action were taken. The pauperising of the public is not a necessary process; it is not required even for the continued persistence of the profiteering system. There is profit enough to raise the masses above the economic standard of 1900 and still leave the profiteers in possession of an over-generous plenty.

Two considerations of importance emerge from the examination of these figures. The one is that the Labour movement appears to possess only the power to resist actual decreases in money-wages, that in addition to its blank impotence in regard to prices it is not able actually to raise money-wages to any appreciable extent. The second consideration is even more arresting. It may be that the steady rise in prices since the Labour movement began to concentrate upon politics is not wholly accidental. Labour, being detached from the economic aspect of the struggle, did not attempt to follow rising

277

prices with demands for corresponding advances in wages. It trusted to the vote. And so it would appear that we are now faced with a profiteering system which relies more completely for exploitation upon increased prices than upon decreased wages.

It is as consumers that the people are to be chiefly victimised in the future . . . A slow and steady increase of prices to which wages will never catch up, but between which and wages the distance will increase, is indicated as the most probable development of the immediate future. Prices may be raised by the action of external forces, as by the increased supply of gold, and advantage will be taken of these to justify trade impositions. But the naturally implied rise in the price of labour will not follow. Similarly any external changes which decrease values will be used for the personal advantage of the profiteers, but wages will not rise nor prices fall in just correspondence with them.

To meet this newly emerged danger the worker must awake from his dream. The false simplicity of the movement on which he relies must be demonstrated to him. . . . He must put himself into touch with the outlook of the consumer. He must realise . . . that he plays two parts in the world, and that in the playing of each he is harried by the enemy, and therefore upon each he must learn to fight.

But it will be argued that this is possible without the formation of a new movement, that if the Labour movement turns its attention to the problem of prices its existing forces will suffice to stop the working of the price-dodge for the eating up of wage advances. The worker and the consumer being one, it is merely necessary to enforce upon the worker the need for a development of industrial activity along new lines. This conclusion is greatly to be desired. But much more is required to bring about reconstruction. The Labour movement is essentially a producers' movement. It represents the superior crafts, the aristocracy of labour. It leaves out entirely the great body of unorganised manual labourers at the bottom; it leaves out almost all women workers; it entirely ignores the existence of the great consuming classes of home-women; and it has made no appeal whatever to the brain-workers and professional workers of the nation. As labour is organised to-day these classes are debarred from admission to the ranks by economic circumstances, conditions of membership, methods of propaganda, and similar causes. But all these are, in one way or another, deeply interested in the problems of consumption, prices, the quality of foodstuffs and other products. Representative sections of these classes ought to be organised as consumers, and when federated as the workers are federated they would form a second sympathetic army with which Labour could work out a joint policy for mutual advantage. . . .

The workers may doubt whether the consumers coming from these complementary classes of the community are likely to prove reliable allies. They may point to the criminal indifference which has been manifested by the general consuming public to the industrial suffering involved in processes of which it has willingly consumed the fruits. The dangerous trades revelations have aroused no large section of the consumers; they have heard and turned away in great number, but they have never heard at all in still greater numbers. I hold no brief for them. The sacrifice of the lives of workers, of health and strength and happiness, to this insensate system ought to have wrought the consuming public to a frenzied seeking after means of protest and reform long ago. They purchase life with their pence. They condone murder and mutilation with indifference. They appear as callous as the profiteer. But they are the only allies to whom the worker can turn, and they are victims too. . . . Their enlightenment involves at first a big problem of education, but after that the working towards union is sure because of the natural partnership between the two economic elements.

\*    \*    \*

# CHAPTER V:

# PAST EFFORTS TO SECURE UNION

It was clearly seen long ago that active union between producers and consumers was essential to economic justice, and that no system of production could be permanently grounded upon any other foundation. The history of the uprising of the common people is marked by repeated re-discovery of this truth. . . .

It has run its course through religious communities, communistic and socialistic settlements, 'Union Shops,' co-operative societies, industrial colonies, and their variants, down to the present day. But it has never been successfully applied in its entirety, and most of its promoters have devoted themselves to some particular sectional development, and ignored those broader possibilities which it contains and which are of the most vital importance. Generally the attempts made to bridge the gulf created by our profit-making system between the consumer and the producer have been restricted to industrial experiments concerning themselves with administration. Many of them have failed. But if the full measure of success of which they are capable had been attained they would still have left the economic divorce the predominant condition of the greater part of the world. . . .

In our own country it is to Robert Owen that the expression of the ideal and the first efforts to attain it are due. His experiments at New Lanark, his factory reform agitation, his Socialist millennial dreams, his co-operative and colonising ventures, were all dictated by this spirit of new industrialism. The Grand National Consolidated Trades Union was no mere sectional wage-getting combination out to make the best terms for its members without any regard for the rest of the community; it was inspired by a wider vision of human solidarity than we find in the Labour movement of to-day.

The early productive co-operative societies, or Union Shops, inspired and directed by Owen and numbering 400 in 1833, were organisations seeking a settlement of industrial discontent by direct co-operation between workers and consumers. Owen's rejection of the State was of a piece with his wide vision. He saw that it was held by the exploiters and that it was slow to move. From these two facts he deduced that it would take a long period to win the people fair recognition in politics, and that their incoming would only drive privilege back upon other lines of defence, while it would make the political machine itself more cumbrous and dilatory in its workings . . . .

Owen was in advance of his time. The organisations he founded demanded bigger men and more men than he could obtain. They probably demanded, too, some of that experience of effort and failure which the century just closed has supplied. All the Owenite organisations dwindled away under stress of government pressure, financial difficulty and practical disillusionment. . . . But they left behind them a leaven of thought which vitalised the modern co-operative movement instituted by the Rochdale Pioneers, and prepared the harvest for the later Socialist rebirth.

The co-operative movement is a workers' movement and a consumers' movement. It is an organised effort made by workers to distribute and produce for themselves, thus eliminating for themselves the private profiteer. In theory, therefore, the movement is sound. . . . The weaknesses lie in the application of the idea. In the first place the workers engaged in the productive and distributive co-operative societies' shops and factories are not necessarily the co-operators. These workers are engaged, paid and exploited, in the manner adopted towards the workers in similar capitalist enterprises. The conditions of service may be better or worse than those of private traders, according to the class of trader with whom comparison is made and the particular co-operative society. . . .

The great body of co-operators are not co-operators in the spirit of the founders of the movement. They are dividend co-operators, seeking a safe and easy way of saving, and a share of the profit which would otherwise go to the private dealer. . . . They employ and make profit out of labour for their own benefit. . . . They are workers seeking for themselves a consuming advantage. This prevailing condition is no doubt due in great measure to circumstances beyond the control of the promoters of co-operative societies. The pressure of economic conditions upon the body of workers makes them at once hard task-masters to other workers and eager seekers after some personal security. The problem of selling at market rates while paying above the market wage has not been solved; there has been a sacrifice of the wage-worker. The union of interests between worker and consumer has been seriously weakened by this policy . . . .

The Co-operative Union and the Women's Guild are the educative and ethical parts of the movement. They have come into being because of the sense of partial failure and neglected opportunities and responsibilities. That they have come into existence from within the movement is a sign of promise which makes it possible to believe that the capacity for a gradual evolution towards a higher form lies within co-operation itself.

But if co-operative societies were fulfilling the ideal of their

inspirers and founders there would still be need for further development and additional organisation. The awakening of the consumers
is not only needed to ensure the undertaking of particular trading,
distributing, or producing. It is needed to take active educational and
aggressive action in the fighting line of the movement of discontent.
This fact has never been seriously faced by co-operators. . . . So far
as they are propagandists, and in spite of the fine record and high
ideals of their best men and women, they are limited in outlook and
action. They are not willing to take active part in militant industrial
action. . . . Their strength lies in their commercial undertakings,
and these limit the possible avenues of their activity to purely
administrative economic processes.

. . . What is wanted is the organisation of workers on the one
hand, and consumers on the other, to provide the means of making a
new economic world. Associations [as] limited in objects and membership [as] those in existence cannot be expected to meet the new
needs. New movements are required to work out the change by
aggressive protest and boycott and strike, by combined peaceful
pressure, by exposure, by education, by action through existing
agencies and institutions, by the inventions of new systems and
methods, by a great federal partnership of two great movements. In
such a great union both Co-operation and Trade Unionism will find
a place. But to neither of them can the whole task be delegated, and
in neither of them reside the whole powers which will be required to
carry it out.

Colonies and communities suffer from their withdrawal from the
general life of the race. They have been free in most instances from
the exploitation of other workers. In them the problem of supply is
more or less communistically settled by a universal acceptance of
work and a universal equality among consumers. The Communist
or Socialist colony has been a very serious and very real effort to
bring the consumer and the worker into a natural material harmony.
The underlying idea upon which segregation from the mass of the
people has been based has been sound also. It has been an effort to
eliminate the profiteer and the conditions created by him . . . So far
it has been sound, but only so far. . . . Turning one's back upon the
profiteer is not eliminating him. It is leaving him in possession of a
fair land from which some of his most dangerous opponents have
voluntarily withdrawn. . . .

These co-operative and colonising experiments have been founded upon sound economic principle and inspired in their beginnings
by a wide vision of human needs. From the same root have sprung
the Socialist and Communist movements. As the one type of
economic reformer devoted itself to limited practical experiments,

the others devoted themselves to propaganda, permeation, organisation, and political action. But the official Socialist movements, while sound in theory, were biased in practice. They came to life in the producers' world dominated by privileged producers and clamant with the rebellion of producers who were oppressed. They have been influenced in work and outlook by this external condition . . . When this one-sided course has failed them the Socialists have fallen back upon a policy of benefits and doles, of State interference and benevolent legislation. Socialist education and permeation have brought into existence on this side certain laws which are based on bonuses – upon the principle of State aid, and this is the one development of the modern Socialist movement which can be claimed as having special regard for the consumer. It takes as its basis the one who needs, and not the one who works. . . .

The policy of doles from the State has been an admission, generally unconscious, of the insufficiency of the general propaganda of the Socialist movement. Vaguely the weakness on the consumers' side has been felt, but long habit and over-much use of trite phrases has deadened the perceptive capacity of the members, and they have not been led to any re-examination of their practice. The dole policy itself has proved inadequate and illusory. . . . Action *for* the consumers instead of *by* them cannot be so well informed and soundly based at the best. Intervention from without is not what is wanted, but uprising from within. The Socialist will indignantly reply that his party is at once the champion of the worker and the consumer, and that therefore it acts from the inside. This is true as to Socialist theory, of course; the Socialist has a foot in each camp; he seeks to socialise industry, and that can only be done by harmonising the relations between the producer and the consumer. He has chosen to substitute the State for the consumer in most of his theorising as well as in his practice, but we are concerned here mainly with the latter. And by this test of practice the Socialist is shown to be a workers' advocate rather than a social reformer or revolutionist. . . . Their action is at once inadequate and ineffective. State bonuses have to be paid for by taxes: so far as these fall upon the profiteers they are transferred to prices or deducted from wages; so far as they fall upon the masses they act as direct reducers of the power of consumption. All that is achieved is that the burden is removed from one shoulder to be returned in another form to the other.

Every re-consideration of the problem brings us to the same conclusion. Economic reconstruction is no matter for the workers alone, whether they act through Trade Unions or Parliament. If they could succeed alone in obtaining security for themselves the probabilities are that we should be committed to a mere substitution of economic masters, the organised producers taking the place of the profiteering capitalists. But they cannot succeed alone. . . . The economic changes that are necessary in the interests of sanity, justice and humanity require that additional forces shall be added to those at present in existence, and it is clear that these new forces must come from the consumers . . .

Two small attempts to deal with the organisation of the consumer have been made in this country, but neither of them has been broad-based upon the rights of the consumer nor capable of strong appeal to large bodies of people. They have been little sectional movements, the promoters of which missed the whole view of the problem and grasped at some particular limited policy for which consumers could be organised. The short-lived Consumers' League sought by 'White Lists' and 'Labels' to satisfy tender-hearted buyers as to the conditions of labour in stores and factories, but it never extended its scope beyond the merest tentative limits, and it made no general appeal to the public. The Women's Industrial Council and the Christian Social Union have made efforts in the same direction. The latest proposal for the organisation of the consumers come from a prominent anti-suffragist gentleman, who desires women to give up their demand for equality in order to fulfil their responsibilities as buyers.* The idea behind this little revival, which appears to have been attempted wholly among anti-suffragist women, has been to provide useful social service that would keep women out of politics, while at the same time disproving the charge that anti-suffragists are generally women of anti-social tendencies. It is not to be wondered at that this limited proposition, promoted in a spirit of partisanship, should have been still-born.

In America the Consumers' League owes its origin to an inquiry undertaken by the Working Women's Society in 1890, and it has achieved much more than the British movements ever attempted. The White Lists and the Labels have here been much more generally used and much more effective. Conferences and exhibitions have sufficed to bring large numbers of women into the movement, and universities and clubs have been permeated. A standard 'good store' has been defined by which the conditions of employment, hours, wages, sanitary arrangements, are fixed. Compliance with this standard entitles a store-keeper to figure upon the White List, and representatives of the League make supervisory visits to see that the standard is kept up. In 1905 there were sixty-three consumers' leagues in twenty States of the Union, and one large national league

---

* He is now actively engaged in organising black-legs to save the Empire.

in which all the local leagues were federated. Various differences in policy were manifested in the different States, some leagues specialising on the protection of children, some on improving the conditions in shops, some the conditions in factories and among home-workers, and some combining different efforts.

The French *Ligue Sociale d'Acheteurs* was formed in Paris on the American model in 1902, but it is marked off from the Transatlantic movement by its association with the Trade Unions. . . . This league has specialised upon the conducting of accurate inquiries, and its work and its members have been made use of by the Labour Board of the Ministry of Commerce in the forming of new regulations and the working of special inquiries. The French consumers have given much attention to child labour, to the conditions of domestic servants, and to the checking of the spread of consumption through industrial neglect.

Switzerland, Holland and Italy have their consumers' movements. The Swiss League, formed in 1904 in Geneva, spread rapidly, for in 1906 there were local leagues in Berne, Bienne, Neuchatel, Zurich, Saint-Gall, Aarau, Winterthur, Lausanne, Fribourg and Bâle. . . .

These consumers' leagues are younger and smaller manifestations of discontent with the economic system than the great workers' movements which have been under brief review. They are marked out as being societies organised by consumers as consumers, as the first sign of awakening consciousness among consumers. They are the little beginnings, the first steps. They must not be measured by their accomplishments, for they have scarcely yet found expression, but by the spirit that is making a channel for itself through them. . . . Up to the present these leagues have achieved but half-expression, seeking to fulfil the consumers' responsibilities without claiming the consumers' rights. They have been directed wholly to the protection of producers by the intervention of consumers. . . . Their recognition of their connection with economics has been purely one of responsibility. This indicates that though the consumers have become strong enough to initiate independent action, they have not yet emancipated themselves from the predomination of the producers' outlook upon economics. They have not yet learned that it is their task and will become their joy to reject the burdens now placed upon the consumer, and that this must be done in their own interests, and in those of the worker, and as a step towards reconstruction. At present this consumers' movement is a mere handmaiden to the producers' movement. It must cast off this limitation before it can perform its work.

\*     \*     \*

# CHAPTER VI:

# THE WORK TO BE DONE

The needs revealed in our inquiry may be summarised under three heads: We need a new consumers' movement through which the rebellion of the consumer[s] against the present system may be expressed on their own account and in the interests of labour; we need a new recognition of the rights of the consumers from the workers, so that the labour movement may become a social, as well as a self-protective organisation; and, finally, we need an active national and local combination between these two divisions of the economic army in revolt, in order that each may moralise the other, and each may contribute to the joint victory which neither can win alone. The question now reduces itself to one of practice: How are these needs to be satisfied that the end in view may be attained?

The new consumers' movement claims first attention. It is necessary to consider upon what basis such a movement can be formed, and from what sections of the nation active support should be forthcoming. Though they are small in numbers and young in experience the consumers' leagues are the only consumers' movement upon which we can fix. They are examples, rough beginnings. They indicate dangers to be avoided as well as good policies to be imitated. It is of the first importance that the new organisation of consumers shall be a fully conscious dual movement directing its energies to the defence of the consumer. This must be its clear and complete purpose. It must be to the workers' movement as a balancing movement, and not as a subsidiary one. It must put the consumer first. It must set out to emancipate the consumer by the purification of production, by the recognition of the rights of labour, and by the final elimination of the profiteer. But it must not come to Labour as a handmaiden offering service . . . It must enter into an alliance between equals, and the terms of the alliance must be fair: the assistance of the consumers must be pledged to the workers in every fair phase of their fight; the assistance of the workers must be given to the consumers in like manner. This will mean that there must be a mutual acceptance of responsibility leading to mutual confession of past wrongdoing and mutual self-denying ordinances. . . .

The consumers' leagues are to be preferred as the nuclei of the new organisation to any other existing groups or sections because they are the only existing consumers' movements. . . . They have not lived long enough to limit or define themselves permanently; they are still young and plastic; they have not become doctrinaire; they have barred no doors of effort, but merely specialised in those directions in which circumstances indicated the possibility of successful action. Their general appeal to all consumers is what is necessary. It would be foolish and futile to attempt to organise the consumers according to arbitrary classifications such as those which sectionalise the workers. There is no need to divide off coal consumers from jam consumers or pure-food enthusiasts from rebels against high prices. The general movement must be broad-based, and its appeal must be calculated to reach the responsive and awaken the ignorant in every part of the nation. The many tasks which such a movement will have to face can be attempted in no set order throughout the country, but will naturally fall to be dealt with according to local circumstances and decisions. Sectionalisation will come internally by the gradual growth of special committees. There will very probably be need for a committee to deal with prices, another to deal with adulteration, another with workers and conditions and wages. Experience may call for these to be again subdivided, and bring into existence supervisory committees for special trades and occupations. There will need to be a section devoted to the training of inquirers and the carrying out of inquiry. Protest, publication and propaganda work will call for special attention. And all these various interests and activities will be centralised in a general council.

Such an organisation is required in every city and town of the kingdom just as much as a trades council and its federated unions of workers . . . the coming into existence of a consumers' movement would establish a hundred points of contact with the existing organisations of workers. There would be differences to adjust and assistance to seek. There would be deputations and conferences and temporary alliances. There would be consultations and joint making of plans. There would be working out of ways and means when a practical reform desired by one party seemed opposed to the interests of the other. The consumers' council would stir up the trades council about the quality of bread. The trades council would send recommendations to the consumers' council respecting the conditions of the workers in the jam factories or the fashionable dressmaking establishments. From this mutual helpfulness there would come a recognition of wider uses and powers and relations, and in all probability a permanent joint advisory committee, which would be the clearing-house for difficult matters and the place of settlement of the broad terms of alliance, would be instituted.

These local movements, with their committees and general councils for given districts, will need to be linked up into a Great National

League through which unity of standard may be attained and simultaneous action directed upon particular issues. The circulation of the White Lists relating to factories would fall into the hands of the national body, and the general orders for the application of the boycott; by Black Lists it would secure permanent record, and call for special action to back up or prevent strikes. Such a central body might also collect and collate information, and make use of it through the reform movements generally, and as the spur to hasten official action by the authorities or voluntary action by other bodies of interested individuals.

The strength or the weakness of the attitude of the consumers will depend very much upon the quality of the work which goes to their awakening. . . . There must be no narrow bias among the protagonists. To be of real avail this movement must be made truly representative of the nation. Every body of consumers must be appealed to, and special efforts made to bring in those bodies which are not touched by the present Labour movement. . . .

Organised Labour professes to represent all workers. But this claim is extravagant. The great body of wage-earners who are organised as workers belong to the best types of manual workers; they are such men as would have belonged to the old crafts and guilds. They form the middle stratum of the workers. Above them are the workers who are paid salaries; below them are the workers who are largely unskilled and universally unorganised and sweated. The Trade Union movement has neglected the latter type, and the former has neglected Trade Unionism. To both of these sections of workers a consumers' movement can offer what the workers' movement has not within its gift. The 'black coat' brigade, which has never recognised itself as a brigade of workers, being fairly satisfied with regard to conditions of employment, is conscious of great grievances on the consuming side. It is intelligent enough to object to adulteration, and needy enough to resent the imposition of rising prices. The general level[s] of education and domestic expenditure have been rising in this class for a generation, and both these forces have tended to permeate it with discontent. Charges of pretension and snobbery are levelled against these workers, and the charges are superficially true. But the assumption of superiority because of professional work, brain work, or the status of management, does not go deep. It is sufficient to close the door to Trade Unionism, but it would very probably melt away during a few years of experience in a consumers' movement. . . . [Active work] would show the consumers of this class that the charges which they issued against Labour could be returned, that while the workers were not sinless, neither were the consumers. . . .

To the lower-grade workers the appeal of the consumers' movement would be even stronger. To the advantages it would offer them
as consumers who suffer most both from inflated prices and adulteration, there would be a new strength given to their position as
workers. Trade Unionism has been impossible to this great class
because of low wages. Its members have not been able to pay for
organisation, and they have not had the spirit by which the impossible is attained. That spirit is not bred on low wages. Thus it has come
about that the great Labour movement has been of no use to these
workers. . . . they have shared in no advances of wages, but have
been hit hard by every increase of prices, whether caused by advances of wages to their luckier brethren, or by strikes, or by
taxation, or by those capitalistically convenient fluctuations of the
market. But the coming of the consumers' movement should bring
about a new situation for the unorganised masses. It should not only
mean that prices will be kept down and a supply of honest products
become available, but it should provide an opportunity for organisation. A very large percentage of the sweated workers are employed
in the preparation or distribution of those very goods upon which
consumers will naturally fix their first attention. Foodstuffs and
clothing would fall into this class. In making their demands for clean
and honest products, the consumers, whatever be their previous
opinions, will be brought into close relations with this body of
sweated workers. They will begin to see the relation between
adulteration and under-paid labour, and finally recognise them as
evils of the same class. They will be compelled to add to their
demand for a pure product at a fair price, the demand that the makers
of the product shall be given fair wages and healthy working
conditions. . . . It is, of course, impossible for the consumers to
emancipate these workers, just as it is impossible for the workers to
emancipate the consumers. Each class and sex, each individual, must
work out the way of liberty for itself. But an outside body might
enter into a partnership which would provide the opportunity and
remove some of the handicaps. This the organised consumers can do
for the sweated worker.

Woman, . . . in whom the interests of consumption predominate
through the ages of training. . . , must be brought into this new
adventure . . . . It is the one movement which will awaken the
average woman to her relation to the rest of the community, and to
the vital matters affecting her which call for her presence in public
affairs. Among the sweated workers women predominate, but the
greatest body upon which the new movement must draw is that of
the home-women. It has been a familiar grumble among working
men that their women-folk do not sympathise with the reform or

revolutionary movements in which they engage. The attitude of discouragement has been characterised as selfish and anti-social, and the whole sex decried because of it. But personal experience of such cases generally reveals the fact that no effort has been made to widen the artificially limited outlook of many of these women, and that there has been no recognition whatever of the difference of economic function and its corresponding difference of view-point. There have been no attempts to seek out those grievances against the economic system which were practically confined to this section of the community, and to use these as the basis of organisation. There have been attempts to organise these women upon men's lines to carry out the producers' ideas and policy. The Women's Labour League was such an attempt, based upon the examples of the orthodox political parties, but as a woman's movement it has not succeeded. It consists chiefly of appreciative wives and daughters of Labour men who make use of it to voice their husbands' opinions or to please their fathers. . . .

It cannot be denied that these women have been hard to rouse. But that they can be both roused and organised has been demonstrated. The Women's Co-operative Guild is a consumers' organisation, and it is 27,000 strong. The Beef Trust in New York brought out the home-women to riot against extortionate prices. In Germany during 1910–11 many disturbances were caused by women's protests against the criminally inflated prices of foods. That this movement of discontent among the home-women is growing is indicated by the recent attempts that suffragists and others have made to seize upon it as a means of education and particular propaganda. Special house-wives' meetings have been held, and there has been an issue of special literature dealing with the housewife and politics. This new move-ment needed among the consumers is nowhere needed so much as among the home-women, and it needs no other body so much. The influence which the national purchaser can wield over the profiteer cannot easily be exaggerated, for without her he cannot exist, and he must choose between ruin and obedience to her behests. It is, therefore, a most vital thing to the proposition here advanced that the woman in the home should be brought to take an active and increasing part in the organised rebellion of the consumers.

It must be evident that a movement making an appeal to all these unorganised sections of the community and tackling industrial problems from a side now neglected cannot but have a high value. Containing these new elements, . . . it will bring new brain and blood to the service of the common good. It will close the bottom-less pit into which the fruits of all the Labour efforts of the last century seem to have been cast. The improvement which Labour has sought so long, only to see it recede before every advance, has had to be sought very often apparently against the general advantage, and more than any active force of misrepresentation or opposition this has told against Labour in the minds of that great part of the people which is entirely without economic consciousness. It is not one of the least of the great results of the suggestion here made, that by bringing about co-operation between workers and purchasers such apparently anti-social action would either be rendered unnecessary or presented in an entirely new light.

By the work of propaganda and inquiry which must necessarily precede the making of this new movement, much education will be conveyed to those who are within the Labour ranks. From these seeds, from more general discussion, and from the demands which the organised consumers will make upon them, there must come a great change of outlook and tactics amongst the workers. The necessary criticisms of their past indifference to adulteration and the production of deceptive rubbish will arouse the wider social spirit now lacking, and set willing individuals afoot to bring their unions and federations into line. . . . It is recorded that the builders of Barcelona went on strike against the building of shoddy houses, refusing to share in the degradation involved in this act of robbery and waste . . . . In Glasgow in 1840 the painters' union presented a memorial to the Master Painters protesting against the scamping of work in which they were expected to assist. . . . As the memorial brought no redress it was followed by the issue of a mammoth warning to the public, in which the tradesmen explained the whole system of plunder by means of examples. The Seafarers' Union in protesting recently against the inadequate supply of boats on passenger steamers showed a social as well as a defensive spirit. Similar Labour protests against corrupt practices have been recorded in individual cases in sufficient number to indicate that there is a possibility of active co-operation between workers and consumers to secure the purification of production.

All such actions undertaken hitherto have been isolated, and if organised at all, organised only from one side. In the future they must be encouraged, linked up into a system of exposure, and organised from both sides. The victimised consumer and the degraded worker must join hands, making their plans together and acting in unison. . . .

The possibilities and position of the strike will be changed by the new co-operation. Strikes from one side are failures. They are wasteful and barbarous protests justified not at all in their ultimate results, but only because they keep the spirit of protest alive. But a double-edged strike, a strike from two sides, in which, while the workers strike, the consumers employ a positive or potential boycott, will be an engine of a different kind. A boycott *plus* a strike is more than the strongest employer or the strongest combine would willingly face. . . .

It may be well to indicate other lines of action open to the economic allies by a few examples. The local authorities might be influenced in several directions: they might be brought to take over directly those services with which both consumers and producers are dissatisfied, or which cannot be adequately conducted on a profiteering basis under existing conditions. They might be brought to incorporate a fair-wages clause in their buying contracts as well as in their constructive ones. They might be won to assist in the forcing of good conditions upon employers with whom White Lists and Black Lists are of no avail, and to whom an active public boycott must be applied. The element of mutualism itself may be made of great strategic advantage. When a strike or a dispute likely to cause dislocation is in prospect, and before it is bruited abroad, preparation for the struggle could be fully made by the allies. Such preparation might take, among other forms, that of having ready for issue suitable explanatory literature for the purpose of counteracting the misrepresentations which are now so universal, or it might take the form of accumulating supplies in order to prevent artificial inflation of prices and scarcity. Action of this nature might be organised directly through the membership of the alliance, through the municipalities, the co-operative movement and kindred agencies. . . . there would need to be some organising of funds for emergencies, as when the taking over of a business upon co-operative principles by consumers and workers jointly had become imperative, or the running of an opposition business against a refractory employer called for an initial outlay of capital.

There may be discussion among Socialists as to how far the new consumers' movement will be really an agency for expropriation, and how far it will merely assist to ameliorate the evils of the present system. It does not appear to me to be a matter capable of doubt. Provided that this movement is a live one, and that it is brought, as it must inevitably be, into close contact with the workers, the real circumstances of our present economic exploitation cannot be hidden. . . .

. . . there need be no grave fears of the misdirection of the new movement. There is only one factor in our economic system which is entirely harmful in its effects. This factor, the profiteer, has been able to deceive and oppress both worker and consumer, his two victims, only by keeping the two victims apart. If both are organised in self-defence and joined in alliance, both will resist the burdening against which each has protested singly in vain. If their organisations act in concert there will be no possible conclusion to their activity other than a diminution of profit. Advances of wages cannot be passed on to prices if the consumer refuses to pay them. Falls in prices, or losses due to abolition of adulteration, cannot be refunded to the profiteer out of wages if the wage-workers resist under these new conditions. The dual economic contract, between partners backing each other in both cases, makes the old failure impossible. Joint action must mean reduction of profit. . . .

But it will be said that the profiteers will meet this policy by the wholesale setting up of combines, from which the consumer must consent to purchase or starve. But this policy, too, can be met. The consumers and workers together can start their own manufactories, and such ventures would be economically sound and safe. The basis of any industrial undertaking is the market, and the factory with a secure market need fear no bankruptcy. . . . Whether at the end the profiteer be squeezed out willingly or unwillingly can make no difference to the fact that he will be squeezed out. Nor is it impossible that some profiteers will abdicate willingly. Pressure from both sides being brought to bear upon the intruder, with a steady diminution of profit as a result, there will be a growth of willingness to dispose of businesses peaceably. The influence of the allies will have reduced the value of profiteering. . . . But the value of the enterprise will be enhanced to the worker and the consumer by every change which brings the profits down. It is possible, therefore, that sections of workers and consumers may agree to buy out the old owners, paying a life rent to the existing family or a management salary to an active director, as the price of complete ownership. But the methods of transfer would vary with circumstances and conditions, and upon these it is dangerous to prophesy. They may range from buying out, or gradual decapitalising, to sudden expropriation. The system of ownership to be advocated for the transferred properties is one of co-partnery between the workers and consumers. . . .

The question of State action towards this end, or of the opposition of narrowly State Socialists to the policy outlined, I have not considered here. . . . This book is intended to open up the question in a manner provocative of discussion, and it makes no pretence of being a complete or exhaustive survey. . . .

There may be those who would advise the attempt to attract the consumers into the existing Socialist and workers' organisations . . . [but] the great need is for a movement separately and individually a consumers' movement, not for a proxy or conglomerate movement dominated by workers. . . . Like women, [consumers] . . . have been overshadowed and remained dumb; like women, they will have to find out their own truths and convey them to their fellows.

The value of the two movements retaining separate identities while working in constant co-operation must have emerged already in the arguments set forth. But certain aspects of these advantages may be stressed. . . . More ground will be covered by education, and it will be covered adequately from both points of view. . . . In bringing pressure to bear upon the profiteer each section will be stronger by the backing of the other, but freer for action if self-contained. . . . But the major reason for the separation is that each movement has its own work to do, in addition to work which it must carry out in co-operation with its partner. The new consumers' element stands for a force that is needed in the life of the nation. . . . There is need for a very clear exposition of the doctrine of life by work, and not life for work. There is need for the more individual philosophy of enjoyment as opposed to the half-conscious servility of the doctrine of labour. We do not live by bread alone, nor do we live alone for the making of bread. There must be free scope for the development of the spirit behind the consumers' revolt, and for its demand, not for the right to work, but for the right to enjoy, with the necessary corollary of the reduction of work to its ultimate minimum. Material things have lain on the soul of man like a nightmare. He has soiled himself with work that he might soil himself with wealth, and he has enslaved his fellows and polluted the things he made because of this obsession of getting. There is another interpretation of things which will be born of a logical extension of the consumers' movement, and will set humanity with its feet on material things and its head and heart free for higher endeavour. And from such a humanity we may hope for that mental and moral growth which now we glimpse in visions and are irrationally afraid to set down in words.

# Notes

## Introduction

1 All the Billington-Greig works are available in the Fawcett Library, London; a few copies of *The Militant Suffrage Movement*, *The Consumer in Revolt*, and *Towards Woman's Liberty* can be found in a few university libraries in the United States. Some essays which the editors have seen only in manuscript may have been published in journals; *The Militant Suffrage Movement* originally appeared serially in *The New Age*; *Consumer in Revolt* may also have first appeared in one journal or another. Wherever possible, the editors have provided publication dates; in other cases, the editors have used the date Teresa Billington-Greig wrote on the manuscript; in still other instances, internal evidence has been used to suggest dates.

The Billington-Greig papers were delivered to the Fawcett Library by Fiona Billington-Greig after her mother's death in 1964. Teresa Billington-Greig had put her papers in boxes, some of them in labelled folders. For a description of the Collection and the problems the researcher or editor encounters, see Margaret Sweet's 'Introduction' to *The Catalogue of Additional Papers of Teresa Billington-Greig*.

A major part of the Billington-Greig papers – especially the autobiographical fragments – were uncatalogued when the editors copied them in 1983, and some rearrangement of the sequence of the papers was inevitable in the cataloging process; as a result, the editors cannot always make citations to a particular box or file, but instead identify material either by the title which Teresa Billington-Greig gave it or by the first few words of the original selection.

2 Teresa Billington's birth certificate gives the year 1876, but since she always believed that she was born in 1877, the editors use the latter date throughout to avoid confusion.

3 For the descriptions of her mother's physical characteristics, information on her mother's and father's relationship, family life, friends, and her parents' last years the editors have drawn extensively on a number of interviews Miss Fiona Billington-Greig granted them in April and June 1985; these are not cited in individual footnotes unless Miss Billington-Greig is being quoted.

4 The ILP was not a political party, but an organization seeking labor reform and socialist legislation. In 1900 the ILP joined with other labor and socialist groups to form the Labour Representation Committee, the parent of the political Labour Party in Great Britain. To distinguish the two organizations, the political party is sometimes referred to as the Parliamentary Labour Party.

5 Teresa Billington-Greig, 'A life that has covered . . . ,' unpublished memoir, n.d., Billington-Greig Papers, Fawcett Library, City of London Polytechnic. Hereafter, material in the Fawcett Library's collection of the Billington-Greig papers will be cited as follows: TBG Fawcett.

6 Teresa Billington-Greig, 'Rebel Childhood. I,' unpublished outline, n.d., TBG Fawcett.

7 Dora Montefiore, a wealthy widow, an early supporter of the Women's Social and Political Union (WSPU) in London, began a personal protest for women's suffrage by refusing to pay taxes, and when the bailiffs came to take her furniture and other valuables, she barricaded herself in her home. On 24 May, 1906, TBG and Annie Kenney led a group of women to the house to offer support and supplies. Two days later, they returned with a still larger group and one of the Suffragettes was reported to have addressed the crowd from a stepladder. A member of the Social Democratic Federation, a Marxian group, Dora Montefiore later left the WSPU to join the adult suffrage movement.

8 Mary Gawthorpe, *Up Hill to Holloway* (Penobscot, Maine: Traversity Press, 1962), p. 253.

9 Frederick Pethick-Lawrence, 'Character Sketch: Miss Teresa Billington,' *The Labour Record and Review*, July 1906, pp. 97–98.

10 J.J. Mallon, 'The Portrait Gallery: Mrs Billington-Greig,' *The Woman Worker*, 3 July, 1908, p. 127.

11 TBG, 'The Live-World-Changers,' in 'Settlement: Humanitarian Movements – Amelioration or Reconstruction period,' unpublished notes, n.d., TBG Fawcett.

12 Notes and comments on her reading, made in TBG's handwriting, can be found in several fragments: 'Read in Youth – about 1900,' 'Materials Required in Blackburn,' 'Possible Early Influences,' 'Notes on subjects of interest at different ages,' 'Manchester,' 'About 1901,' and 'Social and Political Awakening,' unpublished notes and memoirs, n.d., TBG Fawcett.

13 TBG, *The Militant Suffrage Movement: Emancipation in a Hurry* (London: Frank Palmer [1911]). Future citations of material from this work and other TBG works reproduced in this volume will be given in parentheses following the quotation.

14 TBG, 'The Things That Matter,' typescript of synopses and proposals for a series of articles, n.d., Box 404, File 6, TBG Fawcett.

15 Box 404, File 3, TBG Fawcett.

16 Box 404, File 6, TBG Fawcett.

17 TBG, *Towards Woman's Liberty*, (Letchworth, Herts: Garden City Press [1907]), pp. 41–50.

18 'Points of Personal Attack,' typescript with corrections in TBG's hand,

n.d., Suffragette Fellowship Collection, Z6070, Group D, vol. 3, p. 61, Museum of the City of London.

19 E. Sylvia Pankhurst, *The Suffragette Movement: An Intimate Account of Persons and Ideals* (London: Longmans, Green & Co., 1931), p. 263.

20 TBG, 'Mrs Billington-Greig Answers Her Critics,' letter to the editor, *The Vote*, 11 February, 1911, Box 404, File 1, TBG Fawcett.

21 *Ibid.*

22 Pankhurst, *op. cit*, p. 195.

23 TBG, *The Consumer in Revolt* (London: Stephen Swift & Company [1912]).

24 Box 404, File 3, TBG Fawcett.

25 Tape 1, editors' interview with Fiona Billington-Greig, 15 April, 1985.

26 TBG, 'Girolamo Savonarola,' unpublished manuscript notes, n.d., TBG Fawcett.

## The Genesis of a Feminist

1 The exact chronological order of TBG's adolescent experiences remains unclear, for she recounted them in different orders in various texts and outlines. The editors made use of whatever internal clues TBG provided.

2 Helen and William Billington's shop-keeping ventures in their early married life failed. At some time in TBG's childhood a shop in Preston closed, and after a time William Billington obtained a job with a boiler-making firm in Blackburn, where Teresa spent her late childhood and adolescence.

3 By 'Repeal,' TBG means the repeal of the late seventeenth-century Test Acts which penalized Roman Catholics who refused to make declarations denying transubstantiation and the authority of the Pope.

4 'Lord' Polly, the eldest daughter of TBG's uncle George Wilson, was nicknamed by William Billington, who had been amused by father-daughter exchanges which always seemed to begin 'Oh, George!' or 'Lord, Polly!'

5 In this selection and in 'Mrs Pankhurst and the WSPU,' the editors have occasionally reversed the order of sections of TBG texts for the sake of continuity and clarity and, in some cases, because of TBG's marginal instructions. Her chronological order has not been affected.

6 The Manchester University Settlement at Ancoats was a charitable organization serving as a link between the university and the people of the city's slums.

7 For ILP, see note 4 to 'Introduction'.

8 James Keir Hardie, socialist Scots miner, was first elected to Parliament in 1892. He was one of the founders of the ILP and an outspoken supporter of the woman suffrage movement.

9 The Ethical Movement began in 1886 to promote social and political reform. Substituting belief in moral/ethical behavior for more traditional religious doctrines, they held that changing the social environment

would create a moral society. For a time, the Ethical Society provided schools, lecturers, and non-religious services for naming children, marrying, and burying. A number of prominent socialists were attracted to the movement.

10 F.J. Gould was an Ethical Society educator who had a school in Mile End.

11 Anti-sweating legislation was promoted to protect overworked, underpaid laborers, many of them women, who were employed either in piece-work at home or in unsanitary, overcrowded workrooms.

12 The Single Tax, an idea advanced by the American Henry George in 1879, was a proposition that the only tax should be one on rents collected by landlords and that all other taxes should be abolished. Based upon the premise that the land belongs to all people, the concept of the Single Tax was popular in England in the 1880s and 1890s.

13 Margaret and Rachel Macmillan, active in labor and socialist organizations, were pioneers in the field of nursery education. Margaret joined the ILP in 1893, was a member of the Women's Labour League, and served on the Bradford School Board where she campaigned to improve children's health and welfare. In 1904, Rachel published *Education through Imagination* where she argued that nursery schools would help to overcome the cultural disadvantages of working-class children.

14 Robert Green Ingersoll was a popular nineteenth-century American lecturer on such topics as freethinking, civil rights, heretics, Thomas Paine, and Walt Whitman.

15 G.W. Foote was a secularist who followed Charles Bradlaugh (see below, note 26) as President of the National Secularist Society in the late nineteenth century. The Society was a movement of working-class people who did not believe in Christianity but felt they needed some substitute. In the political realm, they advocated land reform, disestablishment, and 'public economy.' By the 1890s, the Ethical Movement had begun to replace its influence.

16 Some of the texts included in this selection may originally have been composed for the Women's Freedom League jubilee or for TBG's uncompleted biography of Charlotte Despard. See also note 5 above on the order of the material.

17 By the Education Act of 1870, the state agreed to fund two kinds of elementary education: 'voluntary schools,' those established by religious or charitable organizations; and 'board schools,' those established in the absence of voluntary schools and partially supported by local taxpayers. Both kinds of schools were required by the Act to provide a half-hour of prayer and Bible study. The Non-conformists – in general, those adhering to religious bodies other than the Church of England and the Roman Catholic Church – made certain that the Church of England catechism should not be taught in board schools. The Non-conformists also were unhappy that board schools could not be established in districts where other schools were already operating and thus that their children might be indoctrinated into an unacceptable interpretation of the Bible. The Church of England objected to a proliferation of board schools,

whose funding was superior to theirs.

In the Education Act of 1902, with the Conservatives (traditional supporters of the Church of England) in power, the school boards were abolished and the County Councils, as represented by Education Committees, were given jurisdiction over all elementary and secondary education – both voluntary and board schools – with power to determine the secular curriculum and the appointment and dismissal of teachers. The Act further made a clear provision for the protection of children's freedom of conscience.

An organization of Non-conformist churches, the National Council of the Free Churches, unified the opposition to this Act because they did not want their taxes used to support Church of England and Roman Catholic schools. Among the non-violent actions the National Council advocated were refusal to pay taxes and persuading some County Councils to refuse to carry out the provisions of the Act. A few of the churches formed caucuses to increase Liberal Party representation in Parliament.

18  In another version, TBG says simply that an ILP friend who knew Mrs Pankhurst recommended that she go directly to her.

19  Boggart Hole Clough was a large open area in the city of Manchester where the ILP had been holding meetings for several years. In early 1896 the Manchester City Council had purchased the land, and in May its Parks Committee forbade the use of the area to the ILP, arresting one John Harker for ignoring the Committee's ban. Dr Pankhurst defended Harker, the ILP continued to hold meetings in the area, audiences grew, fines were imposed on speakers and others, including Mrs Pankhurst.

20  Eva Gore-Booth was a young Irish poet who came to Manchester after having met Esther Roper, a young Manchester feminist and activist, in 1896. Together with Roper, she worked with the Manchester University Settlement, the North of England Society for Women's Suffrage, and trade union women. Gore-Booth was a strong influence on Christabel Pankhurst's decision to work for woman suffrage.

21  The Social Democratic Federation (SDF), founded by H.M. Hyndman, a Marxian, had a program calling for nationalization of all means of production and legislation by referendum. Many of its members were middle class.

22  Begun by a group of Owenite working-men in Rochdale, Lancashire, in 1844 cooperative societies flourished especially in the North. They promised consumers good products and a share in profits in food stores, insurance, and other such enterprises. They also provided a variety of educational and political activities for members. The Women's Co-operative Guild attracted highly educated women who wanted to use the organization as a way of educating working-class women to be better home managers and mothers.

23  Clarion Scouts, Clarion Fellowship, Clarion Clubs (cycling, camera, glee, field) were begun by Robert Blatchford, socialist author and editor, in 1894 to make use of the energy of young socialists especially to bring socialism to agricultural areas. The ILP were sometimes

uncomfortable with their activities, for the young people were wont to stick up posters about socialism on everything they saw. As the suffragists did later, the Clarion groups distributed leaflets by bicycle.

24 As the name suggests, those who honestly supported an adult suffrage bill desired the extension of the franchise to all adults instead of first extending the existing franchise, with its property qualifications, to women. Primarily members of labor organizations, socialists, and the more radical members of the Liberal Party, the adult suffragists argued that the Bill sought by the women's suffrage societies would enfranchise women of property who would vote for the Conservatives. In no small measure this argument served to prevent the most powerful trade unions from giving wholehearted support to woman suffrage bills before World War One. On more than one occasion, the suffragists claimed that the adult suffrage argument was being used as a red herring by politicians who were absolutely opposed to enfranchising women but could not risk open hostility to the idea.

25 Two WFL members, Alice Chapin and Alison Neilans, attempted to destroy votes in a ballot box at the Bermondsey by-election in the autumn of 1909 by throwing ink and photographers' chemicals into it. Some of the material splashed in the eye of an elections officer trying to stop them. At his cry of pain and surprise, another person used ammonia to wash out the chemicals. Although the eye was not permanently damaged, Miss Neilans and Mrs Chapin were sentenced to several months in prison.

26 John Wilkes, accused of seditious libel by Parliament in the eighteenth century, was elected to Parliament, expelled, and re-elected. Charles Bradlaugh, convicted with Annie Besant of publishing and circulating 'indecent' material on birth control, engaged in a struggle with Parliament over the Parliamentary Oaths Act, during which he was elected to Parliament, denied his seat by Parliament and re-elected. In 1882, he forced his way into the House of Commons and administered the oath to himself.

27 In British political parlance, 'the Government' means the Cabinet, headed by the Prime Minister who is almost always the leader of the political party with a majority in the House of Commons. By TBG's time, the Cabinet had assumed almost complete control of the legislative process, deciding which measures would be given time for debate and making votes on certain bills a matter of party loyalty.

Because from 1906 onward a Liberal Party Government had been in power, refusing to give the suffragists any solid promises of support for a woman suffrage bill that the Commons would pass, the WSPU policy was to oppose all Liberal candidates for Parliament regardless of their attitudes as individuals on the issue.

28 Charlotte Despard was a wealthy, philanthropic widow, a member of the ILP and a Poor Law Guardian, who had founded working-men's clubs and child welfare centers in one of London's poorest districts. In the summer of 1906, she became joint Honorary Secretary of the WSPU. She was a popular speaker and participant in a number of demonstra-

tions. Distressed by Mrs Pankhurst's autocratic leadership, she joined TBG and Edith How-Martyn in leaving the WSPU and forming the Women's Freedom League in the autumn of 1907. She was elected its first president. In 1918, at the age of 74, she ran unsuccessfully for Parliament.

29 Although this selection is not technically one of TBG's autobiographical fragments, and is, rather, a draft of a speech composed for the WFL's fifty-year anniversary in 1957, the editors have included it because of its account of TBG's part in founding the WFL. Several rewrites of paragraphs and entire sections are attached to the draft in the Fawcett. The editors' choice of material may not coincide with TBG's final version.

30 (For Montefiore, see above, note 7 to 'Introduction'.) The WFL began to organize and coordinate a tax-resistance effort shortly after its split from the WSPU in 1907. In their section of *Women's Franchise* (19 December, 1907), the WFL called for volunteers for 'passive resistance,' suggesting that women who paid any direct taxes – property, house duty, income – protest by refusing to pay as long as they were without representation in Parliament. A separate Tax Resistance League, sponsored by the WFL, was formed in 1909.

31 In the fall of 1907, the WFL began a series of protests in the Police Courts, the first one featuring TBG and Irene Miller. When a woman was brought before the Magistrate, a protester would stand and make a set statement. One presented at Greenwich in November 1907 was as follows: 'Your Worship, before this case proceeds further I must rise to protest against the administration by men only of laws made by men only, and enforced by men upon women and children. As long as women are denied the elementary rights of citizenship, we protest that this is trial by force, and constitutes a very grave injustice.' (*Women's Franchise*, 28 November, 1907, p. 253)

32 TBG founded an Equal Pay League in Manchester in April 1904 for the purpose of obtaining equal pay for women teachers, primarily by lobbying the National Union of Teachers. The group later united with the National Union of Women Teachers, which won equal pay over fifty years later.

## The Militant Suffrage Movement

1 The extension of the franchise in 1867 gave British male householders the vote, which raised hopes for more representation of the working class in Parliament. In 1869 the Labour Representation League was formed to support working-class candidates, but over the next thirty years only a few working men were elected in spite of a further extension of the franchise in 1885. In 1900, under the leadership of Keir Hardie, representatives of the ILP, the Trades Union Congress (TUC), cooperative societies, socialists, and other working-class organizations gathered to discuss ways to elect labor members to Parliament. The Conference set

up an executive committee, the Labour Representation Committee, to establish 'a distinct Labour Group in Parliament.' In 1903 the Committee began a national campaign fund not only to support candidates during elections, but to provide a stipend for those from the working class who were elected. After the election of 1906, the successful LRC candidates in the House of Commons organized with party whips, chose Hardie as chairman, and took the name Labour Party.

2 The National Union of Women's Suffrage Societies (NUWSS) was a federation of groups – some of them formed as early as 1865 – united under Millicent Garrett Fawcett in 1897. Over a period of forty years, they had depended on lobbying, deputations, and other persuasive tactics to influence individual MPs in favor of extending the suffrage to women. These non-militants TBG frequently calls 'constitutional suffragists.'

3 For adult suffrage, see above, note 24 to 'Genesis'.

4 i.e. the Prime Minister and the Cabinet. See above, note 27 to 'Genesis'.

5 Sir Henry Campbell-Bannerman was the Liberal Party Prime Minister from December 1905 to April 1908.

6 5 December, 1908. Cicely Hamilton (*Life Errant*, 1936) confirms TBG's claim that the audience turned upon the hecklers.

7 For forty years all the woman suffrage bills brought before the House of Commons had been those sponsored by 'private members,' MPs who were not members of the Cabinet. For some time, private members who wished to sponsor a bill not part of the Government program for a particular session of Parliament had had to participate in a drawing to determine the order in which it might be considered if Government business allowed any additional time. Most woman suffrage bills died because the Government denied sufficient time ('facilities') for debate or encouraged various parliamentary maneuvers (e.g. a form of filibuster called 'talking out' a bill) which prevented a vote on the measure.

8 If a seat in the House of Commons fell vacant between General Elections, a by-election was held, usually within a few weeks. A 'Government candidate' was one supported by the same party as that of the Prime Minister and the Cabinet.

9 Charles Stewart Parnell, an Irish Protestant, was first elected to Parliament as a Home Rule candidate in 1875 and was a major force in Irish politics for many years. TBG summarizes his policies below, in 'Parnell the Prototype'.

10 This phrase refers to allegations that the WSPU was receiving funds from the Conservatives (Tories) in order to help defeat Liberal candidates as a part of their anti-Government policy.

11 See below, note 21 on the Conciliation Committee.

12 The 'trinitarian group' consisted of Emmeline and Christabel Pankhurst and Emmeline Pethick-Lawrence. TBG also used the phrases 'triune directorate' and 'trinitarian dictatorship' to refer to these three women.

13 Herbert Henry Asquith, a Liberal, was Chancellor of the Exchequer from December 1905 to April 1908, when he became Prime Minister, a post he retained until May 1916.

14 For Mrs Montefiore: see above, note 7 to 'Introduction'.
15 Annie Cobden-Sanderson was the daughter of Richard Cobden, a nineteenth-century reformer. She was a member of the ILP and left the WSPU for the WFL at the time of the split.
16 Holloway Gaol was the women's prison in London. Prisoners committed to the First Division were usually political prisoners and permitted certain amenities (e.g. books, visitors) denied those serving in the Second and Third Divisions. One of the militants' major grievances against the Government was that, in spite of the fact that they considered themselves political offenders, they were committed to the Second Division (common criminals) most of the time and occasionally to the Third (prisoners of 'undesirable character').
17 The Honorary Secretary in attendance at this meeting was Charlotte Despard. See also note 28 to 'Genesis' above.
18 For Tax Resistance Campaign see above, note 30 to 'Genesis'.
19 Emmeline and Frederick Pethick-Lawrence had a flat in Clements' Inn which was the original London office of the WSPU.
20 The 'grille' screened women seated in the Ladies' Gallery in the House of Commons. In October 1908, Muriel Matters, having chained herself to the grille, began to address the House and while attendants tried to break her chains, another woman began to speak; ultimately, in order to remove Miss Matters the entire grille had to be taken down.
21 When the Liberal Party lost its overall majority in the House of Commons in the General Election of January 1910, one of the male champions of woman suffrage, the journalist H.N. Brailsford, saw an opportunity to advance the cause by the formation of a committee to write and work for a suffrage bill which all could support.

By April a committee had been formed with Lord Lytton as President and Brailsford as Secretary. It included fifty-four MPs – 25 Liberals, 17 Conservatives, 6 Irish Nationalists, and 6 Labour – and they agreed to introduce the measure as a private member's bill. The Committee's Bill would have given the vote to every woman householder and every woman who occupied premises valued at £10 per year. However, women whose husbands had qualified as voters and whose qualification would have been based upon owning or occupying the same property as their husbands were not eligible. Thus, most analysts agree, only about one million women would have been enfranchised under the Conciliation Committee's 1910 Bill.

In spite of this limitation, Brailsford and Lord Lytton persuaded the woman suffrage societies to support the Bill, and the WSPU and the WFL declared a suspension of all illegal militant activity while the Committee steered the Bill through Parliament. This is 'the truce' to which TBG refers.

In early July, the Bill passed its Second Reading, but the Commons also voted to refer the Bill to a Committee of the Whole House. Then, on 23 July, Prime Minister Asquith wrote to Lord Lytton saying the Bill would not be given time for further debate during the session. The militant societies, hoping that the Bill might be taken up again at the next sitting of Parliament, continued to observe the truce throughout the summer and fall.

However, on 18 November, when Parliament began its autumn session, Asquith announced that attempts to resolve a serious constitutional issue (see below note 22) had failed, that the current Parliament would be dissolved on 28 November, and that Government business would take up all the time available in the interim.

Having been prepared for this news, the WSPU had organized a mass deputation to Parliament and, in spite of the efforts of TBG and the other members of the WFL's Executive Committee to persuade their members to keep the truce, a number of WFL members joined an attempt to rush the House of Commons as soon as the news of Asquith's announcement reached them. The women were met by a large contingent of police who used a great deal of force, including blatant sexual indignities, in six hours of rioting. This incident became known as 'Black Friday.'

On 22 November, Asquith promised facilities for the Conciliation Committee's Bill in the next Parliament. Dissatisfied with the language of this pledge, the WSPU led approximately 200 women to his residence at Downing Street where more violence occurred. After another clash with the police, the militants agreed to observe the truce once more in the hope that the Conciliation Committee might have a better opportunity for success in the new Parliament which would convene in February 1911.

22 Resentment in the House of Commons against the veto power of the House of Lords had been growing for many years and came to a head in late 1909 when the House of Lords broke with tradition and vetoed a money bill. The House of Commons' response was the passage of a 'Parliament Bill' in early 1910 which provided that the House of Lords could delay for no more than one month any bill certified by the Speaker of the House of Commons as a finance measure; further, the Bill provided that any measure approved by the House of Commons three times over a period of two years would become law no matter how the Lords voted. The Bill signalled a basic change in the British Constitution and was vigorously opposed by the Lords and by the Conservatives in the Commons.

During Parliament's recess from August to November 1910, a Conference Committee, consisting of four members from each party, sought a compromise, but failed. On the opening day of the autumn session, 18 November, Asquith announced that this crisis had forced him to ask King George V to dissolve Parliament on 28 November and call for a General Election in December.

23 Those men who could qualify for the vote in 1906 had to do one of the following: (a) occupy a property and pay the rates (taxes); (b) occupy a shop, office, land, farm, or the like valued as worth at least £10 per annum; (c) own a freehold valued as worth at least £5 per annum, or a leasehold for sixty years or more valued as worth at least £5 per annum, or a leasehold for twenty years worth £50 per annum; (d) rent lodgings with an unfurnished value worth at least £10 per annum; (e) be a graduate of certain universities.

24 For protest of last November, see above, note 21.

25 For Police Court protests, see above, note 31 to 'Genesis'.

26 For Bermondsey, see above, note 25 to 'Genesis'.

27 Herbert Gladstone became Home Secretary in 1906 and still held that office in 1909 when the forcible feeding of the hunger-striking suffragettes in prison began.

28 William Gladstone, a famous Liberal leader, was several times Prime Minister between 1868 and 1894.

29 The Representation of the People Act of 1918 enfranchised women over thirty who were either householders, or wives of householders, or occupiers of property valued at £5 per annum, and university graduates; in 1928, the age limit was made the same as men's.

30 In 1909 divorces could be obtained through a costly proceeding in centralized Divorce Courts; those unable to afford the Divorce Courts could get only a separation order from Magistrates Courts. Furthermore, women were discriminated against with regard to the sole grounds for divorce permitted – adultery. The 1909 Royal Commission made several recommendations for liberalizing divorce law, but no change came about until 1923, when women were allowed to proceed in adultery cases on the same terms as men.

31 Daisy Lord was a nineteen-year-old unmarried mother accused and convicted of murdering her new-born baby when it was but a few hours old. Coming to her defense, Charlotte Despard claimed that men who tried Daisy could understand neither her situation nor her condition. Mrs Despard also pointed out that the father of the baby was equally guilty.

32 When a newly-elected Parliament begins its first session, the monarch officially opens the session and delivers the King's (or Queen's) Speech, written by the Prime Minister, in which the legislative program of the new Parliament is outlined.

## The Consumer in Revolt

1 The Taff Vale decision refers to the judgment awarding damages against a striking union to the Taff Vale Railway Company. The railway company won its suit in the House of Lords in July 1901; thereafter unions became more ready to believe that seats in Parliament were necessary to protect their interests.

# Index

adult suffrage, 10, 93, 132, 146, 300
Agriculture, Board of, 264
Ancoats University Settlement, *see*
    Manchester University
    Settlement
Angell, Norman, *The Great
    Delusion*, 81
anti-sweating legislation, 81
Asquith, Herbert Henry, 6, 10, 100,
    112, 127, 161, 166, 169, 208
autobiographical fragments, 25–
    108; description of, 4–5, 25–6

Beatrice, Sister Mary, *see* Wilson,
    Margaret
Beef Trust, 290
Bermondsey protest, 97, 182
Billington, Beatrice, 32, 33, 36, 38,
    45, 53, 56, 58–9, 64
Billington, Helen Wilson, 1–2, 27–
    58, 69, 73–4
Billington, William, 2, 30–3, 37, 46,
    54
Billington–Greig, Fiona, 21
Billington–Greig, Frederick Lewis,
    7, 18, 21–2, 23
Billington–Greig, Teresa:
    adolescence, 38–64; on
    anarchism, 176; arrests and
    imprisonments, 6, 161, 162–3;
    articles in *The New Age*, 8, 10–11,
    12; articles in *The Vote*, 12; as
    assistant teacher, 3; attempted
    biography of Charlotte Despard,
    23; attitudes toward marriage, 81;
    attitudes toward sexual relations,
79; attitudes toward traditional
    family, 9, 18, 76; author of WSPU
    constitution, 166; autobiography,
    5, 23, 25–108; character sketches
    by J.J. Mallon and Frederick
    Pethick-Lawrence, 7;
    characterized by London
    newspapers, 6, 105; childhood,
    32–8; choice of cause to serve, 4,
    78–87; and 'conscience clause' for
    teachers, 4, 88–91; *The Consumer
    in Revolt*, 18, 19, 249–94; criticism
    of WSPU tactics, 14–17, 94–104,
    107–8; *The Militant Suffrage
    Movement passim*; in Cumberland
    drapery shop, 48–9; death of, 23;
    debate on marriage, 81; as
    debater/orator, 3; delegate to ILP
    conference, 98–9; deputation to
    Asquith's residence, 6, 10, 100;
    and dog whip, 10, 126; early
    education, 2–3, 35, 38–42; essay
    topics, 23; and Ethical Society, 4,
    80, 84–7; 'Feminism and Politics,'
    18, 19, 225–35; and feminist
    cause, 4, 78, 80–1, 162; 'The
    Feminist Revolt: An Alternate
    Policy,' 19, 240–7; first meeting
    with Emmeline Pankhurst, 89–
    91; first teaching job, 67; and
    Grille protest, 6, 174; and Guest
    Houses, 21; as Honorary
    Secretary of the Ancoats
    University Settlement
    Associates, 3, 77; as housekeeper
    for her uncle, 46–8; illness and

injury, 11–12; as ILP organizer, 4, 5, 98–9; as leader of WFL, 11–13, 154, 156, 171, 175, 176–8; leaves Catholic school teaching, 75; leaves home, 3, 56–65; and Manchester Equal Pay League, 4; Manchester study and teaching period, 3, 65–92; and Manchester University Settlement, 3, 76–7, 80–2, 83; manual dexterity of, 46; marriage to Frederick Lewis Greig, 7, 11; and Married Women's Association, 22; 'The Militant Policy of Women Suffragists,' 111–19; *The Militant Suffrage Movement*, 134–222; and moral instruction in the schools, 4, 72, 75, 80, 82, 84–9; newspaper column, 18; parental censorship of reading, 51; physical description, 3; and Police Court protests, 18, 265; proposals for militant tactics, 14–15, 97–8, 103–4, 150–1, 152–3, 188–9, 242–3, 244–6, 291–3; publisher of *The Hour and the Woman*, 11; pupil–teacher training, 41–2, 43–4; and Queen's Scholarship Examination, 3, 67–9, 73; readings in religion and philosophy, 74; relationship with mother, 33–5, 43–5, 46, 49–50, 52–3, 57–8, 73–4; religious doubts, 3–4, 42, 52–5, 71–5; resignation from WFL, 13; shopkeeper for mother, 37–8; 'Socialism and Sex Equality,' 131–4; and 'split' with WSPU, 167–70; testifies before the Royal Commission on Marriage and Divorce, 22; and vegetarianism, 49, 80; 'The Woman with the Whip,' 125–30; 'Woman's Liberty and Man's Fear,' 120–4; 'Women and Government,' 19, 236–9; and Women for Westminster, 22; and Women's Electoral Committee, 22; and WSPU, 4, 5–6, 11, 91–

107, 145, 149–52, 155–6, 161, 166, 173; as WSPU organizer in Scotland, 6, 7, 105–6, 161, 166
'black coat' brigade, 288
Black Friday, *see* Conciliation Committee and Women's Social and Political Union, breaks the truce of 1910
Black Lists, 288, 292
Blackburn, 2, 37
Boer War, 8, 80
Boggart Hole Clogh, 8, 89
Boileau, Miss, 29
Bondfield, Margaret, 93
Bow and Bromley Branch of WSPU, 104
boycott, 20, 245, 292; in sex relations, 97–8
Bradlaugh, Charles, 98, 103
Brailsford, H.N., 202, 303
Burroughes & Watts, 7, 21
Business and Professional Women's Club, 22
by-elections, 17, 155

Cabinet, 17; power of, 155–6, 158–9, 237
Campbell–Bannerman, Sir Henry, 152, 161
candidates, Liberal Party, 17; *see also* Liberal Party
capitalism, capitalists, 18, 20, 131, 252–4, 261, 272, 282; and trusts, 265–6, 292–3
Chamberlain, Austen, 159
Chapin, Alice, 300
children: father's legal control of, 128; as non-workers, 252; as consumers, 270
Christian Social Union, 284
Church of England, 298–9
Churchill, Winston, 159
Clarion Clubs/Scouts, 21, 93, 145, 299–300
Clement, Mr, 77
Clements' Inn, 105, 174, 179, 182, 189
Coates–Hansen, Mrs, 155

Cobden, Richard, 6
Cobden–Sanderson, Anne, 6–7
Cockermouth by-election, 155
Communist communities, 282
Commons, House of, 100, 112–14, 297, 237, 303–4
Conciliation Bill of 1910, 180, 303–4
Conciliation Committee for Woman Suffrage, 12, 13, 177, 202, 207–10, 212, 303–4
Conference Committee of 1910, 304
Conservative Party, 17, 158–9; *see also* 'Tory Gold'
constitutional (non-militant) suffragists, 112–13, 145, 148, 155, 159, 163, 194–5, 229
consumer: child as, 252, 268, 270; in competition with producer, 253; exploited by capitalist, 252, 263, 265–6; exploited by worker, 263–4, 266–7; ignored by Labour movement, 256; needs of, 263–4; organizations of, 278, 281, 284–5, 286–7;separate movement needed, 259–60, 292–3; tastes of, 269; women as, 269–70, 272; *see also* home-women, 'black coats,' manual laborers, sweated worker
*The Consumer in Revolt*, 18, 19–20, 22, 23, 249–94
Consumers' League, 284–5
co-operative movement: 281–2, 292, 299; societies, 20
Co-operative Union, 281
Cornish, Dr, 70
Crompton, Alice, 77, 81–2

Davitt, Michael, 216
Despard, Charlotte, 11, 23, 26, 100–1, 105, 107, 169, 173, 191, 204
divorce, 128, 234
Divorce, Royal Commission on, 204
double standard, in law, 127–8, 131; of morality, 10
Duffy, Sir Gavan, 214

Education, Acts, 89, 298–9; Boards

of, 39; Committees, 89
Ensor, R.C.K., 77
Equal Pay League, *see* Manchester Equal Pay League
equal pay, for women teachers, 23, 83; *see also* Manchester Equal Pay League, and women, wages of
Ethical Society/ Movement/ Churches, 4, 80, 84–7, 90, 96, 145

Fabians, 18, 20, 260; *see also* Socialists
Fawcett Debating Society, 81
Fawcett Library, 5, 26, 295
feminism, as a mass movement, 16–17, 18, 22, 162; defined, 8–9, 226–7; outside politics, 226–7, 230–4; restricted to vote, 228–30, 236, 246
'Feminism and Politics,' 18, 19, 225–35
'Feminist Revolt: An Alternate Policy,' 18, 19, 240–7
Fenians, 215
Fisher, Helen, 77
Fitzherbert, Maud, 105
Foote, G.W., 86
*Fortnightly Review*, 7
Free Trade Hall protest, *see* Manchester Free Trade Hall

Gandhi, M.K., 20
Gawthorpe, Mary, 6, 101, 172
general elections, and WSPU tactics, 17, 157–60; *see also* WSPU, anti-Government policy of
George, David Lloyd, 153, 159
Gladstone, Herbert, 188
Gladstone, William E., 113, 160, 194
Glasgow, 7, 21
Glasgow Painters' Union, 291
Gore–Booth, Eva, 77, 89
Gould, F.J., 8, 80, 84–6
Government, the, *see* Cabinet, Parliamentary system, Party system, and WSPU, anti-

Government policy of
Grand National Consolidated
   Trades Union, 280
Greig, Grederick Lewis, *see*
   Billington–Greig, Frederick
   Lewis
Grey, Sir Edward, 5, 111, 149
Guild Socialism, 18, 19–20

Halliwell, Fred and Frances, 77
Hammersmith, 112, 116; *see also*
   Montefiore, Dora
Hardie, Keir, 4, 78, 99, 102, 104, 105
Holloway Gaol, 6–7, 100, 161, 163,
   177, 192
Holmes, Marion, 105
Home Office, 188
home women, and consumer
   movement, 252, 278, 289–90
*The Hour and the Woman*, 11
How-Martyn, Edith, 7, 11, 104,
   105, 106, 107
hunger-striking, 191; *see also*
   Militants, as victims of violence

Independent Labour Party (ILP), 4,
   78, 93, 95, 96, 98–9, 102, 133,
   145–6
Ingersoll, Robert Green, 86
Irish Nationalists, 214
Irish Party, 214

Kenney, Annie, 5, 6, 14–15, 99–100,
   104, 105–6, 111, 150, 152, 161,
   172
King's Speech, 208
Knight, Mrs, 100

Labour: leaders, 274–5; movement,
   253, 255–6, 261, 278, 290–1;
   unrest, 1911–12, 261, 273
Labour Party, 10–11, 18, 20, 22, 78,
   93–4, 168–9, 220, 257, 259–60,
   276–8
Labour Representation Committee
   261, 275; *see also* Hardie, Keir
Labour Representation movement,
   144, 160, 169

Land League, 217
Liberal Party, 5, 10, 17, 102, 112,
   117, 126, 157, 158–60, 214
*Ligue Sociale d'Acheteurs*, 285
Local Government Boards, 264
Lodge, Charles, 68, 77–8, 92
Lonsdale, Canon, 3, 53–4
Lord, Daisy, 204
Lytton, Lord, 207

McArthur, Mary, 93
McLaren, Lady, 204
Macmillan, Margaret, 84, 96
Macmillan, Rachel, 84
Mallon, J.J. (Jimmy), 7, 77
man/men:domination of women,
   10, 115–16, 120–4, 131–2;
   hostility to women, 9–10, 120–1,
   126–7; as producers, 20, 270–1
Manchester, 3, 47, 65, 111, 145, 166,
   214
Manchester Equal Pay League, 4,
   104
Manchester Free Trade Hall protest,
   5, 111, 149–50
Manchester University Settlement,
   3, 76–7, 80–2, 83, 90, 92, 104
manual laborers, barred from
   Labour movement, 278, 288
Marriage: Billington–Greig, 7;
   control of own person in, 227,
   246; reform of, 79, 81, 123, 128,
   229
Matters, Muriel, 174
Matthews, Miss, 29
meetings, interruptions of, 5–6, 14–
   15, 111–12, 126, 152–4
militancy: 9, 17, 137, 188–90;
   arguments for, 114–16; betrayal
   of, 180–1; effects of, 14, 116–18,
   161–2, 190; as a form of rebellion,
   15, 17, 113–16, 147–8, 151, 163–4,
   170, 177; *see also* non-violent
   direct action
'The Militant Policy of Women
   Suffragists,' 7, 9, 111–19
*The Militant Suffrage Movement*: 9,
   12–18, 21, 24, 135–222;

organization of, 20
militants: as artificial victims, 243–4;
    fanaticism of, 139, 210;
    imprisonment of, 111, 149, 161,
    162–3; as victims of violence, 126,
    247; violence of, 191–3, 194–201
Mill, John Stuart, 107
Miller, Irene, 100, 161
Montefiore, Dora, 104, 161
Morris, William, 8, 258
Moseley Street Evening Institute, 68

National Union of Suffrage
    Societies, 159, 181; *see also*
    constitutional (non-militant)
    suffragists
National Women Citizens'
    Association, 22
Neilans, Alison, 300
Nelson Street, 94, 96
*New Age, The*, TBG articles in, 8,
    10–11, 12
non-conformists, 8, 89; *see also*
    Billington-Greig, Teresa, and
    moral instruction in the schools
non-productive laborers, 252, 270,
    278; *see also*, home-woman
non-violent direct action, 11, 13, 15,
    17, 19, 210–11, 240–3, 245–6,
    291–3
non-worker, as natural dependent,
    20, 252, 270; *see also* capitalism,
    capitalist
Northampton, 10, 126, 161
Notre Dame: convents of, 2, 28, 37,
    39–42, 43–5; Sisters of, 27, 35,
    39–40, 42, 70

O'Brien, Barry, 214–15
Orrell family, 32, 36–7
Orrell, Mary, 27
Owen, Robert, 8, 20, 280–1
Owens College, 77, 92

Pankhurst, Adela, 100
Pankhurst, Christabel, 5, 6, 11, 16–
    17, 89, 93, 94, 101, 105, 108, 111,
    141, 149–50, 155, 166, 168, 185,

213–18
Pankhurst, Emmeline, 4, 5, 11, 14,
    15–17, 25, 89–91, 93, 94–5, 98–9,
    102–8, 141, 145–6, 149–50, 166,
    167–9, 176, 178, 182–3, 185, 196,
    213–14, 217–18
Pankhurst, Dr Richard, 89, 94, 102,
    107, 160
Pankhurst, Sylvia, 6, 14–15, 104,
    105
Pankhursts, 11, 94, 192, 199
Parke, Miss, 70
Parliamentary system: changes in,
    155; 'Constitutional issue,' 208–9;
    Private Members' bills, 302;
    undemocratic, 237–9
Parnell, Charles Steward, 156, 214–
    18
Party system, 225, 237
Passive resistance, 8; *see also* Boggart
    Hole Clogh, non-violent direct
    action, tax-resistance
Penty, A.J., 20
Pethick-Lawrence, Emmeline, 6,
    15–16, 105, 141, 168, 169
Pethick-Lawrence, Frederick, 6, 7,
    105
Police Court: protests in, 17–18,
    104, 182, 189, 245, 301; women
    defendants in, 245
Politics, as compromise, 225, 231–2
Preston, 2, 27, 30, 43, 59
Profiteers, *see* capitalism, capitalists
Prostitution, 9, 15, 129–30
Protective legislation, 19, 230–1,
    234

Queen's Scholarship Examination,
    3, 67–9, 73

Reform Bill (1884), 160, 194, 198
Richardson, Canon, 40
Rochdale Pioneers, 281, 299
Roper, Esther, 299

Schofield, Alice, 84
schools, Roman Catholic paris, 39
Schreiner, Olive, 19

Seafarers' Union, 291
Six Point Group, 22
Smith, F.E., 159
Social Democratic Federation, 93, 96
'Socialism and Sex Equality,' 10–11, 131–4
Socialist societies, 146, 257–9, 283, 293
Socialists, 131, 132, 282, 292; *see also* Fabians
Sparborough, Mrs, 100
Sports Fellowship, 21
stewards, behavior of, 127, 153
Strangeways Gaol, 150
suffrage, *see* woman suffrage
Suffragette Fellowship, 24
'Suffragist Tactics: Past and Present,' 7
Sullivan Miss, 67–8, 70
sweated worker, 289
Syndicalists, 18, 260, 276

Taff Vale decision, 276
tax-resistance, 8, 104, 174, 182
Tax Resistance League, 18, 174
Taylor, Helen, 98
Thomson, Mrs, 61–2
'Tory Gold,' 157; *see also* Conservative Party
*Towards Women's Liberty*, 7–8, 10
Toynbee debating group, 76, 81–2
Trade Unions, 18, 20, 78, 93, 145, 257, 259–60, 275; *see also* Labour movement
Truce of 1910, 12, 16, 17
Turner, H.P., 77

vegetarianism, 49, 80
victims, as agents of reform, 19, 111, 118, 240–1, 244–5; *see also* non-violent direct action
vote: basis of men's, 133; limitations of, 19, 203–4, 230–1, 233–4, 237–9; as means to sex equality, 9, 10–11, 14, 131–2, 144, 147, 163–4, 230–1, 232; as militants only goal,

16, 165, 179–80, 205, 226, 228; necessity of, 113–14
*Vote, The*, 12, 13
*Votes for Women*, 106

Weiss, Professor, 77
WFL, *see* Women's Freedom League
White Lists, 284, 288
White Slave Acts, 18
Wilkes, John, 98
Wilson, Fanny, 63
Wilson, George, 3, 27–31, 46–8, 64, 65
Wilson, Helen, *see* Billington, Helen
Wilson, John, 2–3, 27–31, 36–7, 59–62
Wilson, John Jr, 60
Wilson, Margaret (later Sister Mary Beatrice), 27–8, 42, 44, 73
Wilson, Polly, 64, 65–7, 71
woman suffrage, 5, 93–4, 129–30, 132–3; opponents of, 93, 111–13, 115, 116–17, 124, 132–3, 160; *see also* adult suffrage, vote
Woman Suffrage Amendment, 194
Woman Suffrage Bills, (1867) 160, (1910) 208
Woman Suffrage Party, 217
'The Woman with the Whip,' 10, 125–30
Woman's Charter, 204
'Woman's Liberty and Man's Fear,' 7, 9, 120–30
women: as consumers, 19–20, 249–94; dependent role of, 9, 14, 29; in the labor force, 9, 14, 15, 16, 81, 121–2, 129, 131, 279; and the laws, 15, 113–14, 129–30, 188–9, 234, 238–9, 244–5; oppression of, 18–19, 115–16, 120–1, 127–8, 131, 234, 270, 272–3, 289; as producers, 269–71; as reformers, 238; wages of, 61, 122, 129, 245, 246; *see also* protective legislation
'Women and Government,' 19, 236–9
Women for Westminster, 22
Women's Billiards Association, 21

Women's Co-operative Guild, 281, 290
Women's Electoral Committee, 22
*Women's Franchise*, 7
Women's Freedom League, 11–12, 17–18, 22, 23, 97, 104, 107, 138, 154, 156, 158, 168–9, 171–8, 181–2, 187, 189, 193, 204, 207, 211
Women's Industrial Council, 284
Women's Liberal Federation meeting, 153
Women's Social and Political Union, 4, 6, 145, 153, 154, 168, 172, 174, 176, 179, 180–3, 185–201, 207, 214; Annual General Conference of 1907, 11, 106, 166–8; anti-Government policy of, 17, 100, 111–12, 117, 149–50, 152–3, 155–6, 214–15; breaks the truce of 1910, 12, 17, 177, 202, 208–10; claims to political independence, 17, 157, 159–60; constitution of, 11, 96, 102, 106–7, 165–6, 168; elimination of strong leaders, 16, 105–6, 172–3; establishes national headquarters in London, 104; exploitation of members, 14, 15–16, 167, 180, 191, 199, 211, 242; executive committee of 1907, 167–8; failure to create a mass movement, 16; and the General Election of 1906, 5, 14, 93, 111, 144, 149, 151; hypocrisy in, 167, 179, 231–2, 241–4, 246–7; and Labour, 93–4, 95, 102, 145–6; lack of democracy in, 11, 14, 16–17, 99, 106–8, 166–70, 176, 179, 180–4; leadership of, 15–16, 99, 106–8, 141, 165–6, 167–70, 172–3, 180–4, 188, 191, 196; and the Liberal Cabinet, 17, 111–12, 153, 158–9, 177; and the Liberal party, 14, 17, 117, 149, 157–60; motto, 16, 179–80; and the press, 16, 106, 111–12, 142, 161–3, 164, 168, 175, 185–6; public approval of, 163–5; Scottish Council of, 7, 11; and Socialist groups, 146; split of 1907, 11, 106–7, 167–70, 173, 179; structure of, 16–17, 141, 165–6; tactics of, 14–17, 96–8, 103–4, 125–6, 138, 152, 185–8, 214, 241–2; and tax resistance, 174; and upper class women, 16, 165, 180; and working class women, 16, 165
'Women's Wider World,' 18
Working Women's Society, 284
WSPU, *see* Women's Social and Political Union